Adult Math Refresher Book

"Simple Explanations and Practice for Adults"

Jacob Kohannim

All inquiries should be directed to: jacob.Kohannim2056@gmail.com

https://mathexperts.net

Welcome to

Adult Math Refresher Book

This book is designed to guide you through the exciting and rewarding journey of mastering school-level mathematics. Whether you're returning to education after some time away or continuing your studies, this book is tailored to help you succeed.

What To Expect:

Inside, you'll find a comprehensive collection of lessons, practice problems, and strategies covering the key topics you'll encounter on the Grade-5 Math Examination. We've broken down complex concepts into easy-to-understand sections, ensuring you can follow along and build your skills step-by-step.

How to Use This Book:

1. Start with the Basics: If you're feeling rusty, begin with the foundational topics. Each chapter starts with the basics and gradually progresses to more advanced concepts.

2. Practice, Practice, Practice: Math is a subject where practice makes perfect. Please take advantage of the numerous practice problems provided and try to solve them without looking at the answers first.

3. Check Your Work: Use the answer keys and explanations to check your work. Understanding your mistakes is crucial for improvement.

4. Utilize the Resources: Don't skip the tips, strategies, and review sections. They are there to help you streamline your study process and give you insights into tackling different types of problems.

Stay Motivated!

Remember, everyone learns at their own pace. It's okay to take your time and revisit challenging sections. With dedication and consistent effort, you'll find yourself improving every day. This book is more than just a study guide—it's your companion in achieving your educational goals.

Good luck, and happy studying!

Contents

Chapter # 1: Basic Algebra 12

1.1 **Fundamentals of Algebra** 12

1.1.1 **Variables and Constants** 12

1.1.2 **Algebraic Expressions** 13

1.1.3 **Simplifying Expressions** 14

Exercises 15

1.2 **Linear Equations** 17

1.2.1 Solving One-step Equations 17

1.2.2 Solving Two-step Equations 18

1.2.3 Applications in Problem Solving 18

Exercises 19

1.3 **Inequalities** 22

1.3.1 Understanding Inequalities 22

1.3.2 Graphing Inequalities 23

1.1.3 Inequality Applications 24

Exercises 24

1.4 Quadratic Equations 28

1.4.1 Factoring Quadratics 28

1.4.2 The Quadratic Formula 28

1.4.3 Completing the Square 29

Exercises 30

Chapter # 2: Geometry 34

2.1 Basic Geometric Shapes 34

2.1.1 Points, Lines, and Planes 34

2.1.2 Angles and Their Types 35

2.1.3 Circles and Arcs 35
Exercises **37**
2.2 Triangles and Polygons 39
2.2.1 Types of Triangles....................39
2.2.2 Properties of Polygons 40
2.2.3 Perimeter and Area Calculations 40
Exercises **42**
2.3 The Pythagorean Theorem....................45
2.3.1 Understanding the Theorem....................45
2.3.2 Applications in Problem Solving....................46
2.3.3 Distance Calculation....................47
Exercises **48**
2.4 Coordinate Geometry....................50
2.4.1 The Cartesian Plane 50
2.4.2 Distance and Midpoint Formulas 50
2.4.3 Slope and Equation of a Line 51
Chapter # 3: Trigonometry **54**
3.1 Introduction to Trigonometry 54
3.1.1 Understanding Angles....................54
3.1.2 Radians and Degrees....................55
3.1.3 Basic Trigonometric Ratios 55
Exercises **56**
3.2 Trigonometric Functions 59
3.2.1 Sine, Cosine, and Tangent 59
3.2.2 Graphs of Trigonometric Functions....................60
....................60
3.2.3 Applications in Real Life 60
Exercises **61**
3.3 Trigonometric Identities....................63
3.3.1 Basic Identities 63
3.3.2 Sum and Difference Formulas 64
3.3.3 Double Angle Formulas....................64
Exercises **66**
3.4 Solving Trigonometric Equations 69
3.4.1 Linear Trigonometric Equations....................69

3.4.2 Quadratic Trigonometric Equations 69
3.4.3 Applications 70
Exercises **71**
Chapter # 4: Statistics and Probability **73**
4.1 Descriptive Statistics 73
4.1.1 Measures of Central Tendency 73
4.1.2 Measures of Dispersion 74
4.1.3 Data Representation 75
Exercises **76**
4.2 Probability Basics 79
4.2.1 Concept of Probability 79
4.2.2 Addition and Multiplication Rules 79
4.2.3 Conditional Probability 80
Exercises **81**
4.3 Probability Distributions 85
4.3.1 Discrete Distributions 85
4.3.2 Continuous Distributions 86
4.3.3 Normal Distribution 87
4.4 Inferential Statistics 89
4.4.1 Sampling Methods 89
4.2.2 Confidence Intervals 90
4.4.3 Hypothesis Testing 91
Exercises **92**
Chapter # 5: Functions and Graphs **96**
5.1 Understanding Functions 96
5.1.1 Definition and Notation 96
5.1.2 Domain and Range 96
5.1.3 Types of Functions 97
Exercises **99**
5.2 Linear Functions 102
5.2.1 Graphing Linear Functions 102
5.2.2 Intersections and Slopes 103
5.2.3 Applications and Models 104
Exercises **105**
5.3 Non-linear Functions 107

5.3.1 Quadratic Functions 107
5.3.2 Exponential and Logarithmic Functions 108
5.3.3 Piecewise Functions 109
Exercises 111
5.4 Transformations of Functions 114
5.4.1 Translations 114
5.4.2 Reflections 115
5.4.3 Dilations and Compressions 116
Chapter # 6 Polynomials 117
6.1 Introduction to Polynomials 117
6.1.1 Definition and Degree 117
6.1.2 Addition and Subtraction 118
6.1.3 Polynomial Functions 118
Exercises 120
6.2 Operations with Polynomials 122
6.2.1 Multiplication of Polynomials 122
6.2.2 Division of Polynomials 122
6.2.3 Synthetic Division 123
Exercises 124
6.3 Factoring Polynomials 127
6.3.1 Greatest Common Factor (GCF) 127
6.3.2 Factoring by Grouping 128
6.3.3 Factoring Trinomials 128
Exercises 130
6.4 Roots and Zeros 132
6.4.1 Finding Roots 132
6.4.2 The Rational Root Theorem 132
6.4.3 Complex Numbers 133
Exercises 134
Chapter # 7: Exponential and Logarithmic Functions 137
7.1 Exponential Functions 137
7.1.1 Growth and Decay Models 137
7.1.2 Graphs of Exponentials 138
7.1.3 Applications 138
Exercises 139

7.2 Logarithmic Functions 142
7.2.1 Inverse of Exponential Functions 142
7.2.2 Properties of Logarithms 142
7.2.3 Logarithmic Equations 143
Exercises **144**
7.3 Solving Exponential and Logarithmic Equations 147
7.3.1 Using Properties of Logarithms 147
7.3.2 Exponential Growth and Decay Problems 148
7.3.3 Compound Interest Problems 148
7.4 Applications in Real Life 149
7.4.1 Population Growth 149
7.4.2 Radioactive Decay 150
7.4.3 Economic Applications 152
Exercises **153**
Chapter # 8: Sequences and Series **156**
8.1 Understanding Sequences 156
8.1.1 Arithmetic Sequences 156
8.1.2 Geometric Sequences 157
8.1.3 Other Types of Sequences 157
Exercises **159**
8.2 Mathematical Induction 161
8.2.1 Principle of Induction 161
8.2.2 Proving Statements 162
8.2.3 Recursive Definitions 162
Exercises **164**
8.3 Series and Summation 165
8.3.1 Finite Series 166
8.3.2 Infinite Series 166
8.3.3 Sigma Notation 166
Exercises **167**
8.4 Applications of Sequences and Series 170
8.4.1 Financial Applications 170
8.4.2 Divisibility and Number Patterns 171
8.4.3 Tiling and Geometry 171
Exercises **172**

Chapter # 9: Vectors and Matrices 175
9.1 Vector Basics 175
9.1.1 Definition and Representation 175
9.1.2 Operations on Vectors 176
9.1.3 Applications in Physics 177
Exercises 178
9.2 Dot Product and Cross Product 181
9.2.1 Definition of Dot Product 181
9.2.2 Applications of Dot Product 182
9.2.3 Definition of Cross Product 182
Exercises 184
9.3 Matrices and Determinants 187
9.3.1 Matrix Operations 187
9.3.2 Determinants 189
9.3.3 Inverse of a Matrix 189
Exercises 190
9.4 Solving Systems of Equations 193
9.4.1 Using Matrices 193
9.4.2 Cramer's Rule 194
9.4.3 Applications in Real World Problems 195
Exercises 196
Chapter # 10: Calculus Basics 199
10.1 Limits and Continuity 199
10.1.1 Understanding Limits 199
10.1.2 Continuity and Discontinuities 200
10.1.3 Evaluating Limits 200
Exercises 202
10.2 Derivatives 205
10.2.1 Concept of the Derivative 205
10.2.2 Rules of Differentiation 206
10.2.3 Applications in Motion 206
Exercises 208
10.3 Integrals 211
10.3.1 Understanding Antiderivatives 211
10.3.2 Definite and Indefinite Integrals 212

10.3.3 Applications of Integration......213
Exercises **214**
10.4 Applications of Calculus......217
10.4.1 Optimization Problems......217
10.4.2 Area and Volume Calculations 218
10.4.3 Physics and Engineering Applications 219
Exercises **220**
Chapter #10: Calculus Basics **223**
10.1 Limits and Continuity 223
10.1.1 Understanding Limits 223
10.1.2 Continuity and Discontinuities......224
10.1.3 Evaluating Limits......224
Exercises **226**
10.2 Derivatives 229
10.2.1 Concept of the Derivative......229
10.2.2 Rules of Differentiation 230
10.2.3 Applications in Motion 230
Exercises **232**
10.3 Integrals 235
10.3.1 Understanding Antiderivatives 235
10.3.2 Definite and Indefinite Integrals......236
10.3.3 Applications of Integration......237
Exercises **238**
10.4 Applications of Calculus......241
10.4.1 Optimization Problems......241
10.4.2 Area and Volume Calculations 242
10.4.3 Physics and Engineering Applications 243
Exercises **244**
Chapter # 11: Practice Tests **247**
11.1 **TEST – I** 247
11.1.1 Contents of the Book......249
11.1.2 Answer Keys 252
11.1.3 Detailed Solutions......253
11.2 **TEST – II**......255
11.2.1 Contents of the Book......257

11.2.2 Answer Keys 260
11.2.3 Detailed Solutions 261
Author's Final Note 263

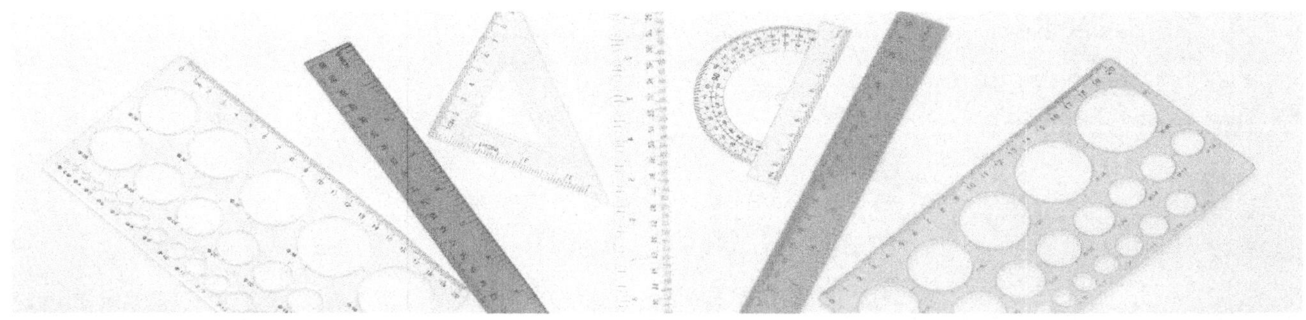

1. Basic Algebra

1.1 Fundamentals of Algebra

This section introduces you to the foundational concepts in algebra, which form the basis for more advanced mathematical studies. Algebra is not only a branch of mathematics but also an essential tool used in various fields such as sciences, engineering, and economics. We will begin with understanding variables and constants, move on to algebraic expressions, and conclude with simplifying expressions. These topics are crucial for understanding and manipulating algebraic equations and for solving a wide range of problems.

1.1.1 Variables and Constants

In algebra, variables and constants are the building blocks of algebraic expressions and equations.

Definition 1.1.1. *A variable is a symbol, often a letter, used to represent an unknown or arbitrary number in algebraic expressions or equations. For example, in the expression $2x + 3$, x is a variable.*

Definition 1.1.2. *A constant is a fixed value that does not change. Constants are often represented by numbers. For example, in $2x + 3$, the number 3 is a constant.*

Example 1.1: Consider the expression $5y - 9$. Here, y is a variable, and 5 and -9 are constants. The expression represents a relationship where the value of the entire expression changes as the value of y changes.

Variables are used to generalize mathematical problems. For example, if you wanted to express the perimeter P of a square with side length s, you could write:

$$P = 4s$$

In this equation, s is a variable representing any possible length of the side of the square, and 4 is a constant.

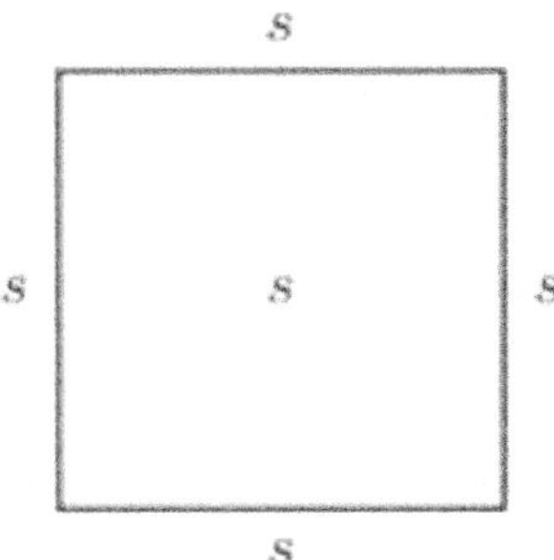

Figure 1.1: Square with side length s.

1.1.2 Algebraic Expressions

An algebraic expression is a combination of variables, constants, and operators (such as addition, subtraction, multiplication, and division).

Example 1.2: The expression $3x^2 + 2x - 5$ is an algebraic expression with three terms: $3x^2$, $2x$, and -5.

Operators in algebra include:

- Addition (+)
- Subtraction (−)
- Multiplication (× or implied by juxtaposition)
- Division (/)

Term	Description
$3x^2$	3 is a coefficient, x is a variable, and 2 is the exponent
$2x$	2 is a coefficient, x is a variable with an implied exponent of 1
-5	Constant term, no variable component

Table 1.1: Components of an Algebraic Expression

It is crucial to understand the role of coefficients and variables in expressions as they determine the behavior of the function they represent.

1.1.3 Simplifying Expressions

Simplification is the process of converting an algebraic expression into its simplest form. This often involves combining like terms and applying arithmetic operations.

Definition 1.1.3. *Like terms are terms within an expression that have the same variable raised to the same power.*

Example 1.3: Simplify the expression $4x + 3x - 2 + 6$.

$$\begin{aligned} 4x + 3x - 2 + 6 &= (4x + 3x) + (-2 + 6) \\ &= 7x + 4 \end{aligned}$$

Here, $4x$ and $3x$ are like terms because they both contain the variable x raised to the same power. -2 and 6 are constants.

Further Simplification Techniques

When simplifying complex expressions, utilize the distributive property to eliminate parentheses and combine terms where possible.

Example 1.4: Simplify $2(x + 5) - 3(x - 2)$.

$$\begin{aligned} 2(x + 5) - 3(x - 2) &= 2x + 10 - 3x + 6 \\ &= (2x - 3x) + (10 + 6) \\ &= -x + 16 \end{aligned}$$

First, apply the distributive property: $2(x + 5)$ becomes $2x + 10$ and $-3(x-2)$ becomes $-3x + 6$. Then, combine like terms.

Summary

Simplifying expressions effectively is a critical skill in algebra, facilitating solving equations and understanding functions. In this section, we've explored the foundational elements of algebra involving variables, constants, and expressions, culminating in the simplification techniques essential for tackling more complicated mathematical problems. Mastery of these basics will provide a solid groundwork for future topics in algebra and beyond.

Exercises

Exercise 1.1:

1. **Identify whether each of the following is a variable or a constant:**
   a x
   b 5
   c $y + 7$
   d π

2. **Create an algebraic expression for the following scenario: A number x is tripled and then decreased by 8.**

3. **Simplify the expression: $3(x + 4) - 2x + 7$.**

Exercise 1.2:

Given the algebraic expression $4a - 3b + 2a^2 - b^2 + 5$, identify and list all terms, their coefficients, and their respective powers.

Exercise 1.3:

Evaluate the expression $2x^2 - 3x + 1$ for $x = -3$.

Exercise 1.4:

Simplify the following expression and show each step: $2(y - 3) + 4(y + 2)$.

Answers with Explanations

Solution to 1.1:

1. (a) x is a variable, as it can change value.
   (b) 5 is a constant, as its value remains fixed.
   (c) $y + 7$ includes a variable (y) and a constant (7).
   (d) π is a constant, as it represents the fixed value of the ratio of a circle's circumference to its diameter (≈ 3.14159).

2. The algebraic expression is $3x - 8$.

3. Steps to simplify:

$$3(x + 4) - 2x + 7$$
$$= 3x + 12 - 2x + 7$$
$$= (3x - 2x) + (12 + 7)$$
$$= x + 19.$$

Solution to 1.2:

The expression $4a - 3b + 2a^2 - b^2 + 5$ consists of:

- Term: $4a$, Coefficient: 4, Power of a: 1
- Term: $-3b$, Coefficient: -3, Power of b: 1
- Term: $2a^2$, Coefficient: 2, Power of a: 2
- Term: $-b^2$, Coefficient: -1, Power of b: 2
- Term: 5, Coefficient: 5, (constant term)

Solution to 1.3:

To evaluate $2x^2 - 3x + 1$ for $x = -3$:

$$2(-3)^2 - 3(-3) + 1$$
$$= 2(9) + 9 + 1$$
$$= 18 + 9 + 1$$
$$= 28.$$

Therefore, the value of the expression is 28.

Solution to 1.4:

To simplify $2(y - 3) + 4(y + 2)$, we perform the following steps:

$$2(y - 3) + 4(y + 2)$$
$$= 2y - 6 + 4y + 8$$
$$= (2y + 4y) + (-6 + 8)$$
$$= 6y + 2.$$

The simplified expression is $6y + 2$.

1.2 Linear Equations

Linear equations form the backbone of algebra and are a stepping stone toward understanding more complex topics in mathematics. This section will delve into the techniques for solving linear equations, categorized into solving one-step equations and two-step equations, with an emphasis on applications in problem-solving.

1.2.1 Solving One-step Equations

One-step equations are foundational and involve directly applying an arithmetic operation to isolate the variable. These equations generally take the form $ax = b$ (for multiplication or division) or $x + a = b$ (for addition or subtraction).

Example 1.5: Solve the equation $x + 7 = 12$.
Solution: To solve $x+7 = 12$, subtract 7 from both sides to isolate the variable x:

$$x + 7 - 7 = 12 - 7x = 5$$

Thus, the solution is $x = 5$.

Example 1.6: Solve the equation $5x = 20$.
Solution: To solve $5x = 20$, divide both sides by 5 to isolate x:

$$\frac{5x}{5} = \frac{20}{5}x = 4$$

Therefore, the solution is $x = 4$.

1.2.2 Solving Two-step Equations

Two-step equations require performing two operations to isolate the variable. They often take the form $ax + b = c$, where the operations involve undoing addition or subtraction and then multiplication or division.

Example 1.7: Solve the equation $2x + 3 = 11$.
Solution: First, subtract 3 from both sides to remove the constant term:

$$2x + 3 - 3 = 11 - 32x = 8$$

Then, divide both sides by 2 to solve for x:

$$\frac{2x}{2} = \frac{8}{2}x = 4$$

Thus, the solution is $x = 4$.

Example 1.8: Solve the equation $4x - 5 = 7$.
Solution: First, add 5 to both sides to eliminate the subtraction:

$$4x - 5 + 5 = 7 + 54x = 12$$

Next, divide by 4 to isolate x:

$$\frac{4x}{4} = \frac{12}{4}x = 3$$

Therefore, the solution is $x = 3$.

1.2.3 Applications in Problem Solving

Linear equations extend beyond classroom exercises to real-life situations. Understanding how to set up and solve linear equations is critical in various fields, such as finance, physics, and engineering.

Example 1.9: A car rental agency charges a base fee of \$50 plus \$20 per day for renting a car. If you paid \$130 for renting a car, for how many days did you rent the car?
Solution: Let x represent the number of days the car was rented. The equation based on the situation is:

$$50 + 20x = 130$$

First, subtract 50 from both sides:

$$20x = 80$$

Then, divide by 20 to determine the number of days:

$$x = 4$$

Thus, the car was rented for 4 days.

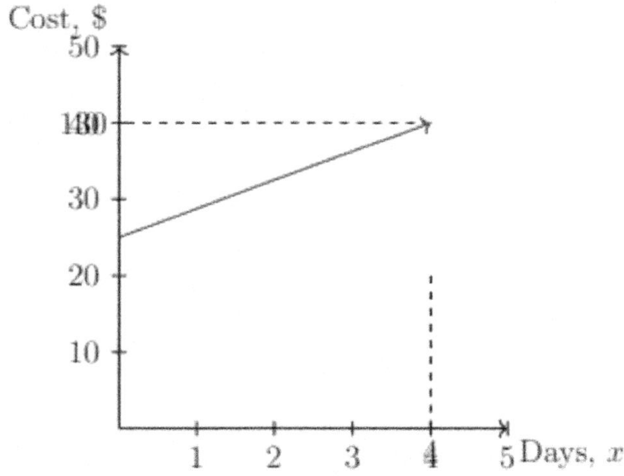

Figure 1.2: Graph depicting rental cost vs. days rented.

Conclusion

This section not only aims to arm you with the techniques for solving linear equations but also to provide insights on applying these methods to practical situations. Through examples and problems, you will see the marriage of theory and real-world applications. Adjusting your mathematical perspective to evaluate and solve problems effectively is integral to mastering linear equations.

Exercises

Exercise 1.5:

Solve the following one-step equations and verify your solutions:

a $x + 7 = 12$

b $3 = y - 4$

c $5z = 20$

d $\frac{w}{6} = 5$

Exercise 1.6:

Solve these two-step equations and provide a detailed explanation:

(a) $2x + 3 = 11$

(b) $5y - 7 = 18$

(c) $6z + 4 = 22$

(d) $\frac{w}{2} - 1 = 9$

Exercise 1.7:

Write real-world problems that can be modeled by the following linear equations and then solve for the unknown:

1. $4x + 5 = 25$
2. $7y - 3 = 42$
3. $3z + 2 = 17$

Exercise 1.8:

Given the equation $2x - 3 = 7$, solve for x and graph the equation on a number line to represent the solution.

Answers with Explanations

Solution to 1.5:

For the exercise on one-step equations:

a. $x + 7 = 12$: Subtract 7 from both sides to get x=5. Verification: 5+7=12.

b. $3 = y - 4$: Add 4 to both sides to get $y = 7$. Verification: $3 = 7 - 4$.

c. $5z = 20$: Divide both sides by 5 to get $z = 4$. Verification: $5 \times 4 = 20$.

d. $\frac{w}{6} = 5$: Multiply both sides by 6 to get $w = 30$. Verification: $\frac{30}{6} = 5$.

Solution to 1. 6:

Solving two-step equations:

(a) $2x + 3 = 11$: Subtract 3 from both sides to get $2x = 8$, then divide by 2 to get $x = 4$. Verification: $2 \times 4 + 3 = 11$.

(b) $5y - 7 = 18$: Add 7 to both sides to get $5y = 25$, then divide by 5 to get $y = 5$. Verification: $5 \times 5 - 7 = 18$.

(c) $6z + 4 = 22$: Subtract 4 from both sides to get $6z = 18$, then divide by 6 to get $z = 3$. Verification: $6 \times 3 + 4 = 22$.

(d) $\frac{w}{2} - 1 = 9$: Add 1 to both sides to get $\frac{w}{2} = 10$, then multiply by 2 to get $w = 20$. Verification: $\frac{20}{2} - 1 = 9$.

Solution to 1.7:

Real-world problems with linear equations:

1. $4x + 5 = 25$: Scenario: To buy 4 books costing x dollars each, and a bookmark costing $5, you spend 25$. Solve: Subtract 5 from both sides to get $4x = 20$, then divide by 4 to get $x = 5$. Each book costs $5.

2. $7y - 3 = 42$: Scenario: Selling 7 gadgets minus a $3 fee yields $42 total. Solve: Add 3 to both sides to get $7y = 45$, then divide by 7 to get $y = 6.43$.

3. $3z + 2 = 17$: Scenario: A store sells 3 packs of z items plus 2 additional items for $17. Solve: Subtract 2 from both sides to get $3z = 15$, then divide by 3 to get $z = 5$.

Solution to 1.8:

Solving $2x - 3 = 7$, and graphing the solution:

- Add 3 to both sides: $2x = 10$.
- Divide by 2: $x = 5$.
- On the number line, $x = 5$ is represented by a single point at 5.

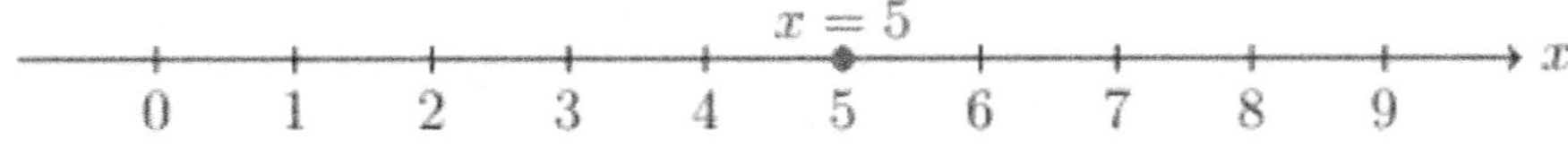

1.3 Inequalities

Inequalities are a fundamental aspect of mathematics used to express the relative size or order of two objects or expressions. In this section, we explore the concept of inequalities, the methods to graph them, and their applications in various problem-solving scenarios.

1.3.1 Understanding Inequalities

Inequalities are mathematical expressions that indicate the relationship between two values or expressions. An inequality can be represented using the following symbols:

Symbol	**Meaning**
$>$	Greater than
$<$	Less than
$\geq$	Greater than or equal to
$\leq$	Less than or equal to
$\neq$	Not equal to

Definition 1.3.1. *An inequality is a mathematical statement that compares two expressions and shows that one is greater than, less than, greater than or equal to, or less than or equal to another.*

Example 1.10: Determine whether the following is true or false: $5 > 3$.
Solution: Since 5 is greater than 3, the inequality $5 > 3$ is **true**.

Example 1.11: Determine whether $8 + 2 \neq 10$.
Solution: Since the sum of $8 + 2$ equals 10, the statement $8 + 2 \neq 10$ is **false**.

Basic properties of inequalities include:

- If $a > b$, then $a + c > b + c$ for any c.
- If $a > b$, then $a \cdot c > b \cdot c$ if $c > 0$.
- Inequalities reverse when both sides are multiplied or divided by a negative number, i.e., if $a > b$ and $c < 0$, then $a \cdot c < b \cdot c$.

Theorem 1.3.1. *Suppose a, b, c, and d are real numbers such that* $a < b$ *and* $c < d$. *Then* $a + c < b + d$.

1.3.2 Graphing Inequalities

Graphing inequalities on a number line or coordinate plane provides a visual interpretation of the solution set.

Example 1.12: Graph the inequality $x \geq 4$ on a number line.
Solution: Draw a number line, and use a closed circle to represent that 4 is included. Shade all numbers to the right of and including 4.

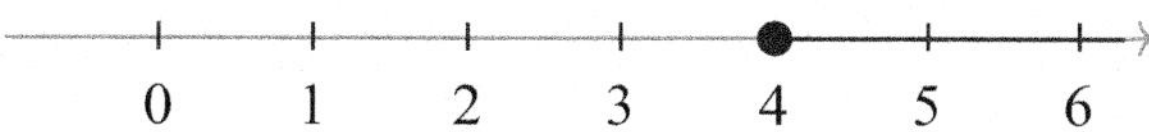

For two-dimensional inequalities, use boundaries and shading to determine the regions of solutions.

Example 1.13: Graph the inequality $y > 2x + 1$ on the Cartesian plane.
Solution: First, graph the line $y = 2x+1$ as a dashed line to indicate the boundary is not included in the solution. The region above this line is shaded because the inequality is strict ("¿"), indicating y is greater than $2x + 1$.

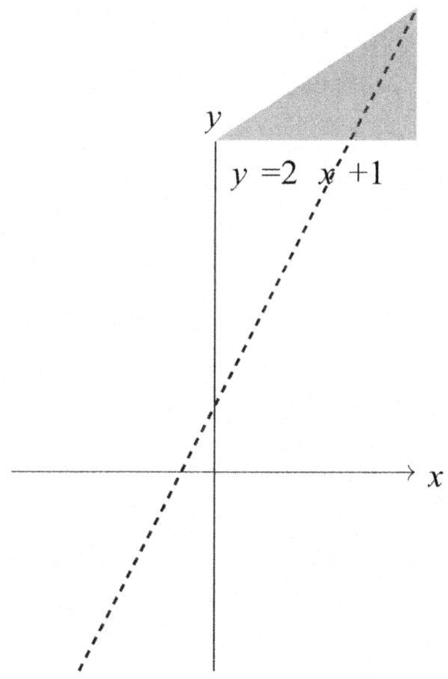

1.1.3 Inequality Applications

Inequalities play a crucial role in diverse real-world contexts, such as optimization, economics, physics, and decision-making.

Example 1.14: A company can produce up to 100 units of a product daily. Write an inequality that represents this constraint and solve for a possible production level if the minimum requirements are at least 40 units per day.
Solution: Let x represent the number of units produced daily. The inequality is $40 \leq x \leq 100$. Possible values of x include any integer from 40 to 100.

Summary

In summary, mastering inequalities involves understanding their properties, correctly graphing in one and two dimensions, and applying them to abstract and practical problems. Careful attention to symbols and boundary inclusions ensures the accuracy of solutions and their representations. Use this knowledge to confidently tackle more complex mathematical models and analyses.

Exercises

Exercise 1.9:

1. Demonstrate that the inequality $3x - 5 \leq 7$ holds for $x = 4$ and does not hold for $x = 5$. Show your calculations step-by-step.

2. Solve the inequality $5x + 3 > 2x + 9$ and represent the solution on a number line.

3. Graph the inequality $y < 2x+1$ on a cartesian plane. Highlight the solution region.

4. An apple costs x dollars and an orange costs y dollars. Given that the total cost for 3 apples and 2 oranges is less than 10 dollars, create an inequality and solve for y in terms of x. Provide a graphical representation for your findings.

Exercise 1.10:

Solve the compound inequality $2 < 3x+1 \le 8$. Represent the solution on a number line.

Exercise 1.11:

Consider the inequality $x^2 - 5x + 6 \le 0$. Solve this by finding the roots using the factoring method and test intervals to identify where the inequality holds.

Exercise 1.12:

A company allocates a budget of up to $15,000 for purchasing computers and printers. Each computer costs $800, and each printer costs $200. Formulate and solve an inequality to determine the maximum number of computers and printers that can be purchased. Provide a graph of the feasible region.

Answers with Explanations

Solution to 1.9:

1. For $x = 4$:

$$3(4) - 5 \le 7 \Rightarrow 12 - 5 \le 7 \Rightarrow 7 \le 7 \text{ (True)}$$

For $x = 5$:

$$3(5) - 5 \le 7 \Rightarrow 15 - 5 \le 7 \Rightarrow 10 \le 7 \text{ (False)}$$

2. Solve $5x + 3 > 2x + 9$:

$$5x + 3 > 2x + 9$$

$$5x - 2x > 9 - 3$$

$$3x > 6x > 2$$

Represent the solution on a number line:

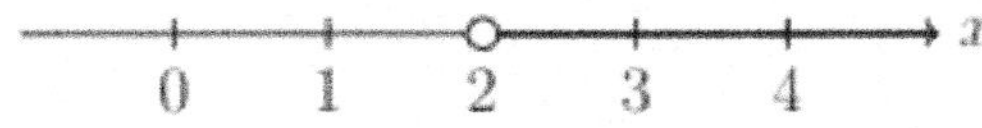

3. The inequality $y < 2x+1$ can be graphed as a dashed line because it's "less than", and shading below the line:

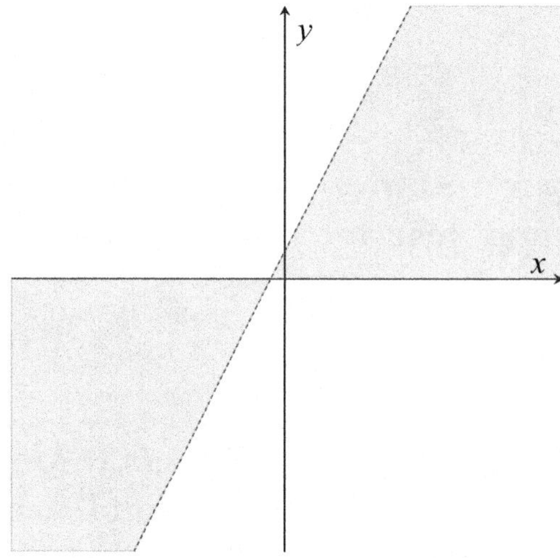

4. Given $3x + 2y < 10$ for 3 apples and 2 oranges: Solving for y in terms of x:

$$2y < 10 - 3xy < \frac{10 - 3x}{2}$$

Graphing this inequality in a cartesian plane:

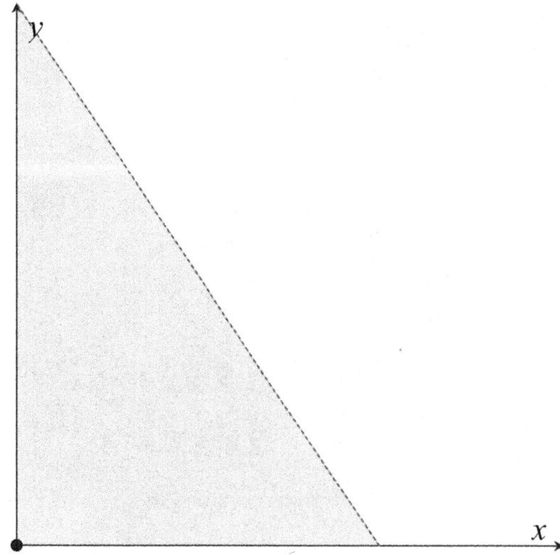

Solution to 1.10:

Solve $2 < 3x + 1 \leq 8$:

$$2 < 3x + 1 \Rightarrow 2 - 1 < 3x \Rightarrow 1 < 3x \Rightarrow x > \frac{1}{3}$$

$$3x + 1 \leq 8 \Rightarrow 3x \leq 7 \Rightarrow x \leq \frac{7}{3}$$

Combine the solutions:

$$\frac{1}{3} < x \leq \frac{7}{3}$$

And, the graphical representation:

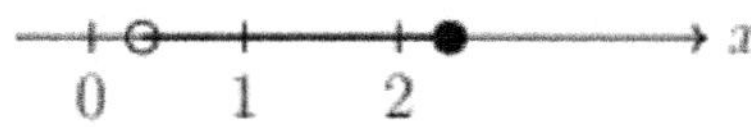

Solution to 1.11:

Consider the inequality $x^2 - 5x + 6 \leq 0$:

$$(x - 2)(x - 3) \leq 0$$

The roots are $x = 2$ and $x = 3$. Testing intervals:

- Test $x < 2$: Let $x = 0$, then $(0 - 2)(0 - 3) = 6$ (False)
- Test $2 \leq x \leq 3$: Let $x = 2.5$, then $(2.5 - 2)(2.5 - 3) = -0.25$ (True)
- Test $x > 3$: Let $x = 4$, then $(4 - 2)(4 - 3) = 2$ (False)

Thus, the solution is $2 \leq x \leq 3$.

Solution to 1.12:

Budget inequality: $800x + 200y \leq 15000$. Simplify:

$$4x + y \leq 75$$

Graphing the feasible region:

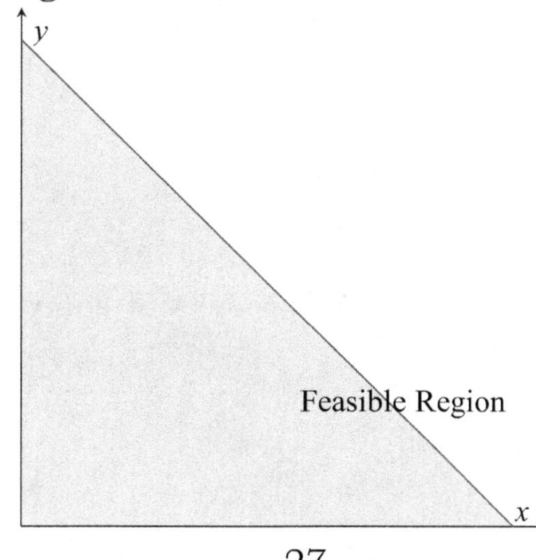

1.4 Quadratic Equations

Quadratic equations are a cornerstone in algebra. They take the general form $ax^2 + bx + c = 0$, where a, b, and c are constants and $a \neq 0$. This section delves into various techniques for solving quadratic equations, including factoring, the quadratic formula, and completing the square. Each method offers unique insights and applicability, making it essential to understand all three.

1.4.1 Factoring Quadratics

Factoring is often the quickest method for solving quadratic equations when the quadratic trinomial can be expressed as a product of two binomials. To factor a quadratic equation:

1. Identify the equation: $ax^2 + bx + c = 0$.

2. Search for two numbers that multiply to ac and add to b.

Example 1.16: Solve the equation $x^2 + 5x + 6 = 0$.
Solution: The equation can be expressed as the product of two binomials:

$$x^2 + 5x + 6 = (x + 2)(x + 3) = 0$$

Setting each factor to zero gives:

$$x + 2 = 0 \quad \Rightarrow \quad x = -2$$
$$x + 3 = 0 \quad \Rightarrow \quad x = -3$$

Thus, the solutions are $x = -2, -3$.

1.4.2 The Quadratic Formula

When a quadratic can't be easily factored, the quadratic formula offers a failsafe method. The formula is:

$$x = \frac{-b \pm \sqrt{b^2 - 4ac}}{2a}$$

This formula is derived from the process of completing the square as we'll see in the next subsection.

Example 1.17: Solve the equation $2x^2 + 4x - 6 = 0$ using the quadratic formula.
Solution: Identify $a = 2$, $b = 4$, and $c = -6$. Apply the quadratic formula:

$$x = \frac{-4 \pm \sqrt{4^2 - 4 \cdot 2 \cdot (-6)}}{2 \cdot 2}$$

Calculate the discriminant:

$$4^2 - 4 \cdot 2 \cdot (-6) = 64$$

Substitute back into the formula:

$$x = \frac{-4 \pm \sqrt{64}}{4} = \frac{-4 \pm 8}{4}$$

Solutions are:

$$x = \frac{4}{4} = 1 \; and \; x = \frac{-12}{4} = -3$$

Thus, the roots are $x = 1, -3$.

1.4.3 Completing the Square

Completing the square transforms a quadratic equation into a perfect square trinomial. This process is useful for solving equations and understanding the derivation of the quadratic formula.

To complete the square:

1. Ensure $a = 1$. If not, factor out a from the x^2 and x terms.
2. Rewrite the equation, separating the constant term from the x terms.
3. Add and subtract $(b/2)^2$ to form a perfect square trinomial.

Example 1.18: Solve $x^2 + 6x + 5 = 0$ by completing the square.
Solution: 1. Rewrite the equation:

$$x^2 + 6x = -5$$

2. Add $(6/2)^2 = 9$ to both sides:

$$x^2 + 6x + 9 = 4$$

3. Express as a square:

$$(x + 3)^2 = 4$$

4. Solve for x:

$$x + 3 = \pm 2$$

Thus,

$$x = -1 \text{ or } \quad x = -5$$

Hence, the solutions are $x = -1, -5$.

Examples and Exercises

To further solidify these methods, let's consider some exercises. Attempt these problems by deploying the techniques discussed above.

Exercise 1.13: Solve the quadratic equation $x^2 - 3x - 4 = 0$ using all three methods: factoring, the quadratic formula, and completing the square.

Exercise 1.14: Verify the solutions for the equation $3x^2 + 12x + 11 = 0$ by graphing the quadratic function and identifying the x-intercepts.

Solution: Challenge yourself by applying the quadratic formula and confirm the roots x using a graphing utility. Note any potential discrepancy due to rounding errors.

Summary

By understanding and practicing these methods, solving any quadratic equation becomes an achievable task. The choice of method often depends on the specific equation and the context in which it appears.

Exercises

Exercise 1.15:

Consider the quadratic equation $ax^2 + bx + c = 0$. Derive the quadratic formula step by step starting from the general form of the quadratic equation. Highlight each transformation and algebraic manipulation clearly.

1. Start by moving c to the right side of the equation.
2. Divide the entire equation by a to make the coefficient of x^2 equal to 1.
3. Complete the square by adding and subtracting $\frac{b}{2a})^2$ on the left side.
4. Factor the perfect square trinomial.
5. Solve for x by taking the square root of both sides and isolate x.

Exercise 1.16:

Given the quadratic function $f(x) = 2x^2 - 4x + 1$, find the roots using the quadratic formula. Verify your solutions by substituting them back into the original equation.

1. Identify the coefficients a, b, and c.

2. Substitute these values into the quadratic formula.

3. Simplify inside the square root and compute the discriminant.

4. Calculate the two possible solutions for x.

5. Check each solution by substituting back into the equation.

Exercise 1.17:

A projectile is launched from a height of 20 meters and its height in meters after t seconds is given by $h(t) = -5t^2 + 15t + 20$. Determine the time when the projectile will hit the ground using the quadratic formula.

1. Set the height equation equal to zero to find when $h(t) = 0$.

2. Identify the coefficients and substitute them into the quadratic formula.

3. Simplify to obtain the discriminant and find the roots.

4. Ignore the negative root since time cannot be negative, and state the time of impact.

Exercise 1.18:

Suppose the area of a rectangular garden is described by the quadratic equation $3x^2 + 7x - 6 = 0$. Solve this equation to find the possible values of x and interpret the results in the context of garden dimensions.

1. Write down the quadratic formula and identify a, b, and c.

2. Substitute these values into the formula and simplify.

3. Discuss the meaning of each solution in terms of positive dimensions for the garden.

4. Conclude with a feasible range of x based on real-world garden constraints.

Answers with Explanations

Solution to 1.15:

To derive the quadratic formula:

1. Start from $ax^2 + bx + c = 0$ and move c: $ax^2 + bx = -c$.
2. Divide by a: $x^2 + \frac{b}{a}x = -\frac{c}{a}$.
3. Complete the square: $x^2 + \frac{b}{a}x + \left(\frac{b}{2a}\right)^2$.
4. Rewrite as a perfect square: $\left(x + \frac{b}{2a}\right)^2 = \frac{b^2}{4a^2} - \frac{c}{a}$.
5. Solve: $x = \frac{-b \pm \sqrt{b^2 - 4ac}}{2a}$.

Solution to 1.16:

For the function $f(x) = 2x^2 - 4x + 1$:

1. $a = 2$, $b = -4$, and $c = 1$.
2. Using the quadratic formula, $x = \frac{-(-4) \pm \sqrt{(-4)^2 - 4.2.1}}{2.2}$.
3. Calculate $x = \frac{4 \pm \sqrt{16-8}}{4}$.
4. Roots are $x = \frac{4 \pm \sqrt{8}}{4} = x = \frac{4 \pm 2\sqrt{2}}{4} = x = 1 \pm \frac{\sqrt{2}}{2}$.
5. Verify by substitution: true for both solutions.

Solution to 1.17:

For the projectile $h(t) = -5t^2 + 15t + 20$:

1. Set $h(t) = 0$: $-5t^2 + 15t + 20 = 0$.

2. Coefficients are $a = -5$, $b = 15$, $c = 20$.

3. Using $t = \frac{-b\pm\sqrt{b^2-4ac}}{2a}$, calculate $t = \frac{-15\pm\sqrt{225+400}}{-10}$.

4. Simplify: $t = \frac{-15\pm\sqrt{25}}{-10}$.

5. Roots $t = -1$ or $t = 4$. Time of impact $t = 4$ seconds.

Solution to 1.18:

Solving $3x^2 + 7x - 6 = 0$:

1. Using $x = \frac{-b\pm\sqrt{b^2-4ac}}{2a}$, we find $a = 3$, $b = 7$, $c = -6$.

2. Calculate $x = \frac{-7\pm\sqrt{49+72}}{6}$.

3. Resulting in $x = \frac{-7\pm\sqrt{121}}{6}$.

4. Roots are $x = \frac{-7\pm 11}{6}$, thus $x = \frac{4}{6}$ and $x = -3$.

5. Positive solution: $x = \frac{2}{3}\ m$.

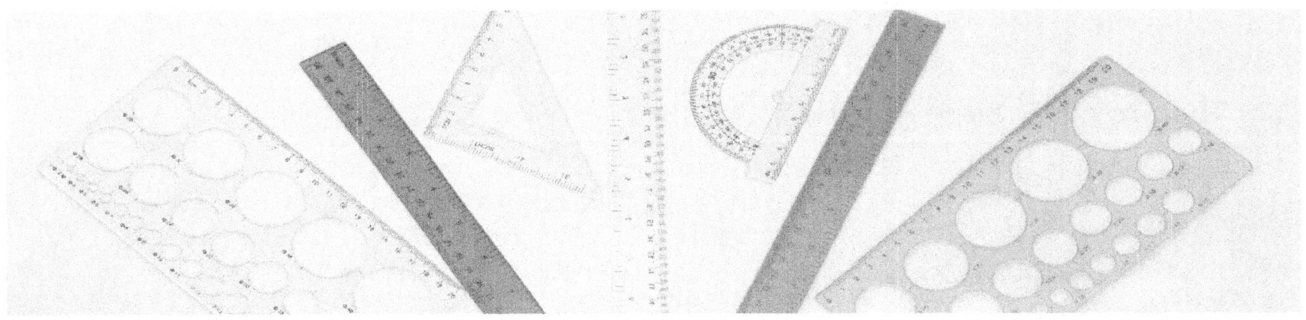

2. Geometry

2.1 Basic Geometric Shapes

Understanding basic geometric shapes is crucial as they form the foundation for more complex geometrical concepts. This section explores points, lines, planes, angles, and circles, laying out the fundamental properties and relationships that will support further studies in geometry. We will use examples, illustrations, and tables to enhance our understanding.

2.1.1 Points, Lines, and Planes

Definition 2.1.1. *A point is a fundamental concept in geometry that indicates a location in space. It has no dimensions (length, width, height) and is usually represented by a dot and labeled with a capital letter.*

Definition 2.1.2. *A line is a straight one-dimensional figure having no thickness and extending infinitely in both directions.*

Definition 2.1.3. *A plane is a flat two-dimensional surface that extends infinitely far. It can be defined by three non-collinear points.*

Example 2.1: Consider points A, B, and C. If these points are non-collinear, they define a plane. The line passing through points A and B can be extended infinitely and is part of this plane.

Illustration of these concepts can be seen in Figure 2.1.

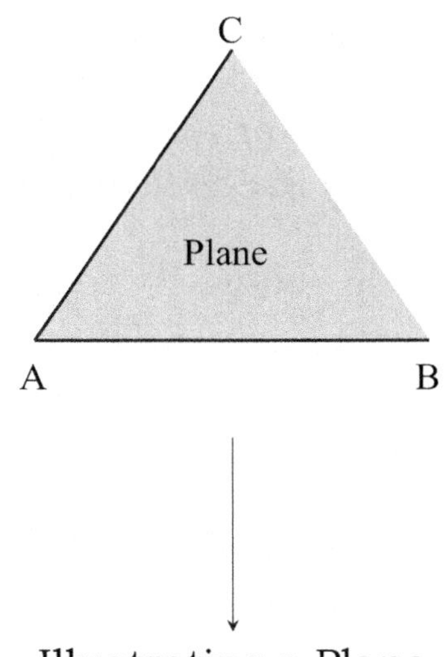

Illustrating a Plane

Figure 2.1: Illustration of Points, Lines, and Planes

2.1.2 Angles and Their Types

Angles are a measure of rotation between two rays with a common endpoint, known as the vertex.

Definition 2.1.4. *An angle is formed by two rays, called the sides of the angle, sharing a common endpoint, known as the vertex.*

Definition 2.1.5. *Types of Angles:*

- Acute Angle: An angle less than 90°.
- Right Angle: An angle exactly equal to 90°.
- Obtuse Angle: An angle greater than 90° and less than 180°.
- Straight Angle: An angle equal to 180°.

Example 2.2: Consider an angle of 45°. Since it is less than 90°, it is classified as an acute angle. On a Cartesian plane, such an angle might be found in the first quadrant where both x and y values are positive.

2.1.3 Circles and Arcs

A circle is a simple closed shape where all points are equidistant from a central point.

Definition 2.1.6. *A circle is a set of all points in a plane that are at a given distance from a given point, the center of the circle.*

Definition 2.1.7. *An arc is a portion of the circumference of a circle. If the endpoints of the arc are a diameter of the circle, the arc is a semicircle.*

Example 2.3: Given a circle with a radius of 5 cm, determine the length of an arc that subtends an angle of 60° at the center. Use the formula for the arc length $L = r \times \theta$, where θ is in radians.

Solution: First, convert 60° into radians:

$$60^\circ = \frac{\pi}{3} \text{ radians}$$

Using the arc length formula:

$$L = 5 \times \frac{\pi}{3} = \frac{5\pi}{3} \approx 5.24 \text{ cm}$$

Thus, the arc length is approximately 5.24 cm.

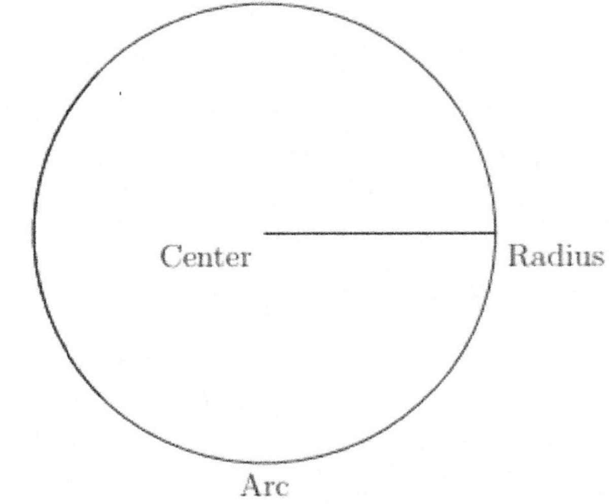

Figure 2.2: Illustration of a Circle and an Arc

Conclusion

In conclusion, understanding basic geometric shapes such as points, lines, planes, angles, and circles is essential for progressing through more advanced geometrical topics. These fundamental concepts support their use in real-world applications and advanced mathematics.

Exercises

Exercise 2.1:

Label the following points, lines, and planes in a diagram:

1. Draw a plane labeled a and a line m passing through it.
2. Identify and label point A on line m.
3. Draw another line n intersecting m at point B.
4. Place point C on a such that it is not on-line m or line n.

Clearly identify all elements and label them on your diagram.

Exercise 2.2:

For the following angles, classify them as acute, obtuse, right, or straight:

1. An angle measuring 45°
2. An angle measuring 110°
3. An angle measuring 180°
4. An angle measuring 90°

Draw each angle using a protractor and label them accordingly.

Exercise 2.3:

Given a circle with center *O* and a radius of 5 cm:

1. Draw the circle and label it appropriately.
2. Identify and label a chord AB inside the circle such that $AB = 6$ cm.
3. Draw the diameter CD of the circle.
4. Calculate the circumference and area of the circle using $\pi \approx 3.14$.

Exercise 2.4:

Construct a table listing the types of angles based on their measures and provide a brief description for each type:

- Acute angle
- Right angle
- Obtuse angle
- Straight angle

Use at least three columns in your table: Angle Type, Degree Measure Range, and Description.

Answers with Explanations

Solution to 2.1:
Diagram for Points, Lines, and Planes:

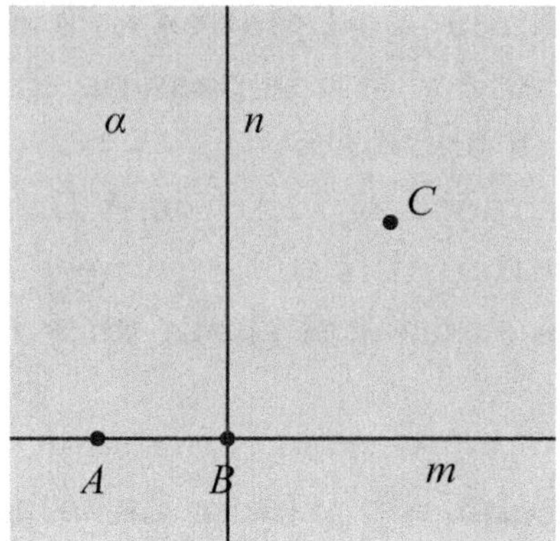

Solution to 2.2:

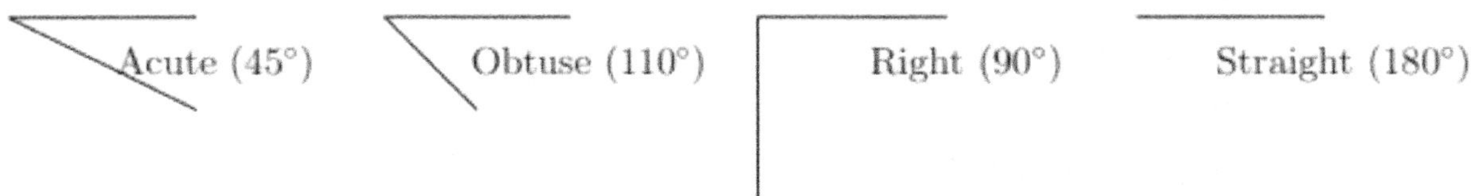

Classification:

1. 45° is an Acute Angle.
2. 110° is an Obtuse Angle.
3. 180° is a Straight Angle.
4. 90° is a Right Angle.

Solution to 2.3:
Circle with Center *O*:

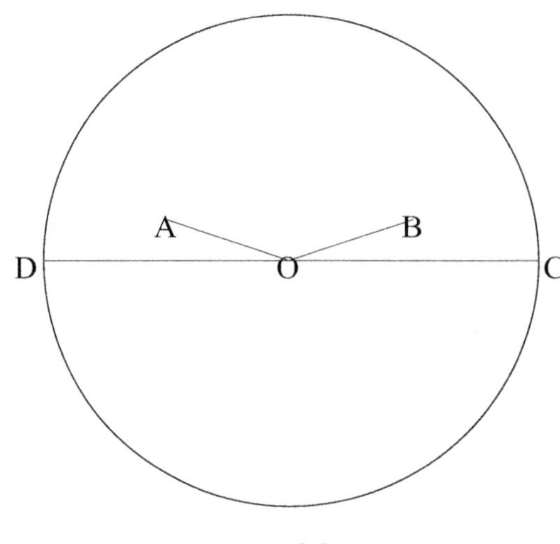

Calculations:
Circumference = $2\pi \times 5 = 10\pi \approx 31.4$ cm. Area = $\pi \times 5^2 = 25\pi \approx 78.5$ cm^2.

Solution to 2.4:
Table of Angle Types:

Angle Type	Degree Measure Range	Description
Acute Angle	$0^\circ < \theta < 90^\circ$	An angle that is more than 0° but less than 90°.
Right Angle	$\theta = 90^\circ$	An angle that is exactly 90°, commonly seen in perpendicular lines.
Obtuse Angle	$90^\circ < \theta < 180^\circ$	An angle that is greater than 90° but less than 180°.
Straight Angle	$\theta = 180^\circ$	An angle that forms a straight line, measuring exactly 180°.

2.2 Triangles and Polygons

In this section, we will delve into the fundamental concepts surrounding triangles and polygons. We will explore the different types of triangles, the properties of polygons, and calculations related to perimeter and area. Understanding these concepts is crucial for solving a wide range of geometric problems and applications.

2.2.1 Types of Triangles

Triangles are the simplest form of polygons, consisting of three edges and three vertices. They are classified based on their side lengths and angle measures.

Definition 2.2.1. *A triangle is a polygon with three sides and three angles.*

- **Equilateral Triangle**: All sides are of equal length, and all internal angles are 60°.
- **Isosceles Triangle**: At least two sides are of equal length, and the angles opposite these sides are equal.
- **Scalene Triangle**: All sides and all angles are different.
- **Right Triangle**: One of the angles is 90°. The side opposite this angle is called the hypotenuse.

Example 2.4: Consider a triangle with the side lengths of 5 cm, 5 cm, and 8 cm. Determine the type of triangle.
Solution: The triangle has two equal sides. Therefore, it is an isosceles triangle.

2.2.2 Properties of Polygons

A polygon is a plane figure that is described by a finite number of straight-line segments connected to form a closed polygonal chain.

Definition 2.2.2. *A polygon is a two-dimensional geometric figure with at least three straight sides and angles, typically five or more.*

- **Regular Polygon**: All sides and angles are equal.
- **Convex Polygon**: All interior angles are less than 180°.
- **Concave Polygon**: At least one interior angle is more than 180°.

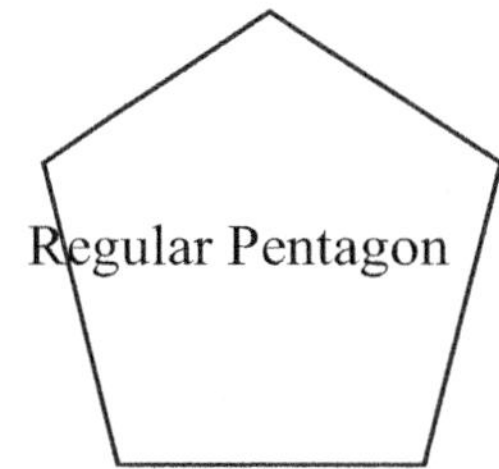

Figure 2.3: Example of a Regular Pentagon

Example 2.5: If a polygon has five angles and all angles are equal, and each measures 108°, what type of polygon is it?
Solution: It is a regular pentagon because all sides and angles are equal, and it has five sides.

2.2.3 Perimeter and Area Calculations

Calculating the perimeter and area of polygons is essential for measuring their size and extent.

Perimeter of Polygons

The perimeter of a polygon is the sum of the lengths of its sides.

Definition 2.2.3. *The perimeter of a polygon is the total distance around the edges of the polygon.*

$$\text{Perimeter of a regular polygon} = n \times s$$

where n is the number of sides and s is the length of each side.

Example 2.6: Calculate the perimeter of a hexagon with each side measuring 6 cm.

Solution: Perimeter = $6 \times 6 = 36$cm.

Area of Polygons

The area of a polygon is related to its shape and size of its surface.

Definition 2.2.4. *The area of a polygon is the measure of the space enclosed by its sides.*

For regular polygons, the area can be calculated using:

$$\text{Area} = \frac{1}{4} n s^2 \cot\left(\frac{\pi}{n}\right)$$

where n is the number of sides and s is the side length.

Example 2.7: Calculate the area of a regular octagon with a side length of 4 cm.

$$\text{Area} = \frac{1}{4} \times 8 \times 4^2 \times \cot\left(\frac{\pi}{8}\right)$$
$$\approx 77.25\,\text{cm}^2$$

Polygon Type	Form of Perimeter	Form of Area
Triangle	$a+b+c$	$\frac{bh}{2}$
Quadrilateral	$a+b+c+d$	Varies (e.g., $b \times h$ for rectangle)
Regular Pentagon	$5s$	$\frac{1}{4}n \times s^2 \times \cot(\pi/n)$

Table 2.1: Perimeter and Area for Common Polygons

Conclusion

This comprehensive insight into triangles and polygons is fundamental to advancing your understanding of geometry and equips you for more complex problem-solving scenarios.

Exercises

Exercise 2.5:

1. **Define the following types of triangles and provide an example of each using labeled diagrams:**
   (a) Equilateral Triangle

   (b) Isosceles Triangle

   (c) Scalene Triangle

   (d) Right Triangle

   Use *TikZ* to illustrate each type of triangle.

2. **Prove that the sum of the angles in any triangle is 180°. Discuss for different types of triangles, citing properties that remain constant regardless of triangle type.**

3. **For a given triangle with side lengths a = 3cm, b = 4cm, and c = 5cm, calculate the perimeter and verify using the formula:**

   $$\text{Perimeter} = a + b + c$$

   Next, verify if this triangle is a right triangle.

4. **Analyze the properties of a regular pentagon. Calculate its perimeter when each side is 10cm and use *TikZ* to draw the pentagon.**

Exercise 2. 6:

Create a table that lists the types of triangles based on sides and angles, their characteristics, and examples. Provide a brief analysis of how understanding triangle properties is beneficial in real-world applications.

Exercise 2.7:

A polygon has vertices at coordinates (1, 2), (4, 2), (4, 5), and (1, 5).

1. Identify the type of polygon and calculate its perimeter and area.

2. Provide a sketch using *TikZ* and label all vertices.

Exercise 2.8:

Given a rectangle and an equilateral triangle sharing a common side, calculate the combined area if the rectangle measures 8cm × 4cm and each side of the triangle is 4cm. Include a *TikZ* drawing to represent the given shapes.

Answers with Explanations

Solution to 2.5:

1. We define types of triangles, use *TikZ* to illustrate them, and describe:

(a) Equilateral Triangle: All sides equal; all angles are 60°. Diagram: 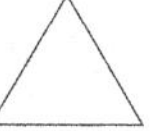

(b) Isosceles Triangle: Two sides equal, two angles equal. Diagram: 

(c) Scalene Triangle: All sides and angles are different. Diagram: 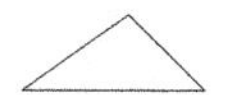

(d) Right Triangle: One angle is 90°. Diagram: 

2. Sum of angles proof: Use a large triangle cut into two right triangles; angle sum verified as 180°.

3. For $a = 3\text{cm}$, $b = 4\text{cm}$, $c = 5\text{cm}$:

$$\text{Perimeter} = 3 + 4 + 5 = 12\text{cm}$$

   Verification as right triangle:

$$3^2 + 4^2 = 9 + 16 = 25 = 5^2$$

   Thus, it's a right triangle.

4. Regular pentagon properties, perimeter:

$$\text{Perimeter} = 5 \times 10 = 50\text{cm}$$

   Diagram using *TikZ*: 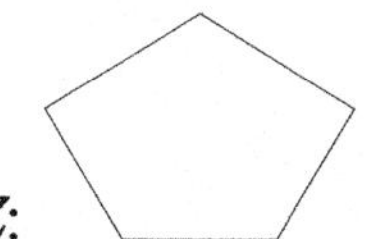

Solution to 2.6:
Table of triangle types:

Types of Triangle	Sides	Angles	Examples
Equilateral	All sides equal	All 60°	Equilateral
Isosceles	Two sides equal	Two angles equal	Isosceles
Scalene	All sides different	All angles different	Scalene

Real-world usage: Triangles fundamental in structural engineering, art, and design for stability and aesthetic properties.

Solution to 2.7:
Given polygon:

- Type: Rectangle
- Perimeter:

$$2 \times (3 + 3) = 12\,\text{units}$$

- Area:

$$3 \times 3 = 9\,\text{square units}$$

- Sketch with *TikZ*:

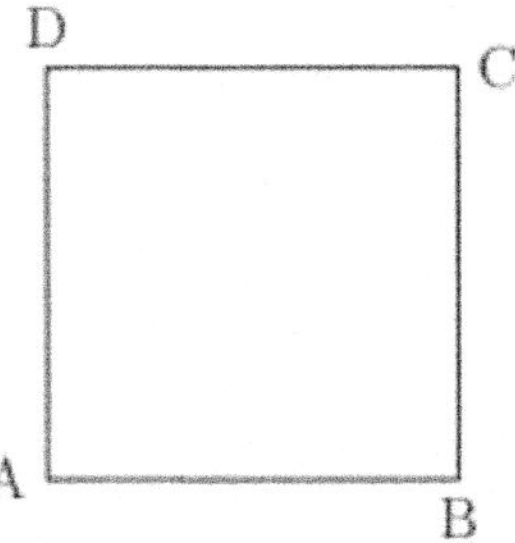

Solution to 2.8:
For rectangle and triangle:

- Rectangle area:

$$8 \times 4 = 32\,\text{cm}^2$$

- Equilateral triangle area:

$$\frac{\sqrt{3}}{4} \times (4)^2 = 4\sqrt{3}\,\text{cm}^2$$

- Combined area:

$$32 + 4\sqrt{3}\,\text{cm}^2$$

- Diagram using *TikZ*:

2.3 The Pythagorean Theorem

The Pythagorean Theorem is one of the most fundamental results in mathematics, forming the foundation for many aspects of geometry, trigonometry, and even algebra. This section will explore the theorem's history, its proof, applications, and how it is used in solving real-world problems.

2.3.1 Understanding the Theorem

The Pythagorean Theorem, named after the ancient Greek mathematician Pythagoras, states that in a right-angled triangle, the square of the length of the hypotenuse (the side opposite the right angle) is equal to the sum of the squares of the other two sides.

Theorem 2.3.1 (Pythagorean Theorem). *In a right triangle with legs a and b, and hypotenuse c, the relationship is given by:*

$$a^2 + b^2 = c^2$$

Proof: Consider a right-angled triangle with side lengths a, b, and hypotenuse c. Construct a square with side length $(a + b)$, which can be decomposed into the original triangle repeated four times within the square, alongside a smaller square with side length c in the center.

The area of the larger square is $(a + b)^2$. It can be expressed as the sum of the area of the four triangles and the smaller square:

$$(a+b)^2 = 4\left(\frac{1}{2}ab\right) + c^2$$

Simplifying, we find:

$$a^2 + 2ab + b^2 = 2ab + c^2$$

Subtracting $2ab$ from both sides, we confirm the relationship:

$$a^2 + b^2 = c^2$$

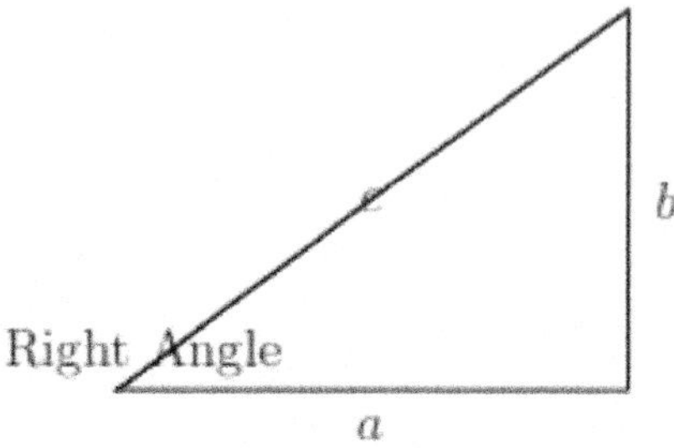

Figure 2.4: A right triangle with legs a and b, and hypotenuse c.

2.3.2 Applications in Problem Solving

The Pythagorean Theorem has numerous applications in various fields. It is extensively used in mathematics, physics, architecture, engineering, and computer graphics. We will explore some problems demonstrating the use of the Pythagorean Theorem.

Example 2.8: Suppose you have a ladder that is leaning against a wall. The base of the ladder is 3 meters away from the wall, and the ladder reaches 4 meters high on the wall. What is the length of the ladder?

Solution: Let the distance from the ground to the point where the ladder touches the wall be $b = 4$ meters, the distance from the wall to the base of the ladder be $a = 3$ meters, and the length of the ladder be c meters. According to the Pythagorean Theorem:

$$a^2 + b^2 = c^2$$

Substituting in the given values:

$$3^2 + 4^2 = c^2$$

$$9 + 16 = c^2$$

$$25 = c^2$$

Solving for c, we find:

$$c = \sqrt{25} = 5$$

Therefore, the length of the ladder is 5 meters.

2.3.3 Distance Calculation

The Pythagorean Theorem can also be used to calculate distances, particularly in coordinate geometry. This section outlines the method for determining the distance between two points in the Cartesian plane.

Given two points $P(x_1, y_1)$ and $Q(x_2, y_2)$, the distance d between them is given by:

$$d = \sqrt{(x_2 - x_1)^2 + (y_2 - y_1)^2}$$

This formula is derived directly from the Pythagorean Theorem by considering a right triangle formed by the points and the differences in their x and y coordinates as the legs.

Example 2.9: Find the distance between the points $P(2, 3)$ and $Q(5, 7)$.
Solution: Using the distance formula:

$$d = \sqrt{(5 - 2)^2 + (7 - 3)^2}$$

$$d = \sqrt{3^2 + 4^2}$$

$$d = \sqrt{9 + 16}$$

$$d = \sqrt{25} = 5$$

Therefore, the distance between points P and Q is 5 units.

Conclusion

The Pythagorean Theorem remains a cornerstone of mathematical problem-solving and understanding. Its utility extends beyond simple geometric interpretations, providing tools for advanced mathematical concepts and real-world applications.

Exercises

Exercise 2.9:

1. **Prove the Pythagorean Theorem using an area-based approach with a square and four identical right triangles inside it. Provide a detailed diagram.**

2. **Apply the Pythagorean Theorem to find the length of the hypotenuse of a right triangle where the two legs measure 9 cm and 12 cm.**

3. **Using the Pythagorean Theorem, determine the distance between the points $A(1, 2)$ and $B(6, 10)$ on the Cartesian plane.**

4. **A ladder is leaning against a wall. The base of the ladder is 3 meters away from the wall, and the ladder reaches a height of 4 meters on the wall. Calculate the length of the ladder.**

5. **Verify the Pythagorean Theorem for a triangle with sides of length 5, 12, and 13.**

Exercise 2.10:

Demonstrate how the Pythagorean Theorem can be used to find the diagonal length of a rectangle with sides 8 units and 15 units.

Exercise 2.11:

A square has a diagonal length of 10 cm. Calculate the length of each side of the square using the Pythagorean Theorem.

Exercise 2.12:

A painter has a 10-foot ladder. What is the maximum height he can reach if he places the base of the ladder 6 feet away from the wall?

Answers with Explanations

Solution to 2.9:

1. The Pythagorean Theorem can be proven by rearranging four identical right triangles within a square. Consider a square with side length c, the hypotenuse, and inside it, arrange four right triangles with legs a and b. The empty area forms a smaller square with side $(c - b)$.

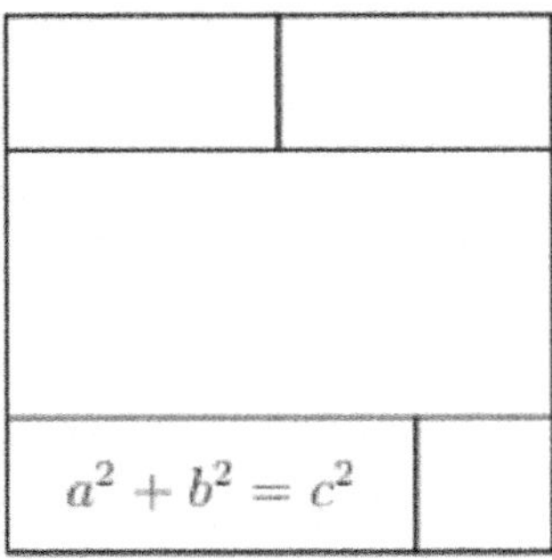

2. Using the formula $c = \sqrt{a^2 + b^2}$, we find the hypotenuse: $c = \sqrt{9^2 + 12^2} = \sqrt{225} = 15$ cm.
3. The distance between the points $A(1, 2)$ and $B(6, 10)$ is $d = \sqrt{(6-1)^2 + (10-2)^2} = \sqrt{25 + 64} = \sqrt{89}$.
4. The ladder length L satisfies $L = \sqrt{3^2 + 4^2} = \sqrt{25} = 5$ meters.
5. For the triangle with sides 5, 12, and 13, we check $5^2 + 12^2 = 25 + 144 = 169 = 13^2$.

Solution to 2.10:

In a rectangle with sides 8 and 15, the diagonal d is calculated as:

$$d = \sqrt{8^2 + 15^2} = \sqrt{64 + 225} = \sqrt{289} = 17\ units$$

Solution to 2.11:

In a square, the sides s can be determined from the diagonal d:

$$s = \frac{d}{\sqrt{2}} = \frac{10}{\sqrt{2}} = 5\sqrt{2}\ cm$$

Solution to 2.12:

Using the Pythagorean Theorem, the maximum height reached by the ladder is:

$$h = \sqrt{10^2 - 6^2} = \sqrt{100 - 36} = \sqrt{64} = 8\ feet$$

2.4 Coordinate Geometry

Coordinate Geometry, also known as analytic geometry, involves studying geometry using a coordinate system. This section will cover the fundamental aspects of coordinate geometry, including the Cartesian Plane, Distance and Midpoint Formulas, and Slope and Equation of a Line. This knowledge provides essential tools for understanding geometric properties algebraically, solving problems, and exploring further applications in fields such as physics and engineering.

2.4.1 The Cartesian Plane

The Cartesian Plane, introduced by René Descartes, is a two-dimensional coordinate system where each point is represented by a pair of numerical coordinates. These coordinates specify the point's position in the plane in relation to two perpendicular directed lines, called axes. The horizontal axis is the x-axis and the vertical axis is the y-axis. The point where these axes intersect is the origin, denoted by (0, 0).

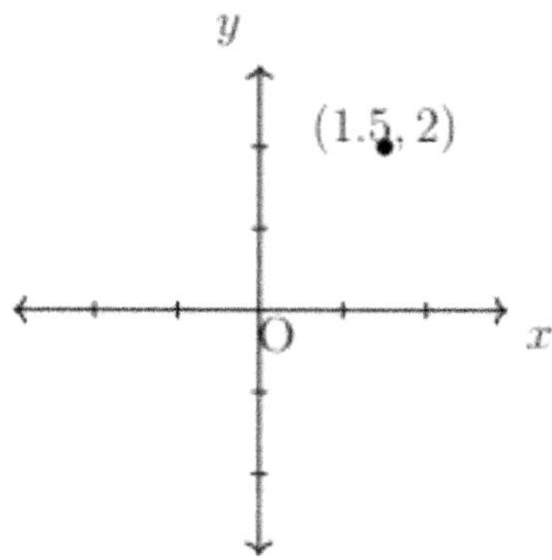

Figure 2.5: The Cartesian Plane

Definition 2.4.1. *A point P in the Cartesian Plane is represented by an ordered pair (x, y), where x is the abscissa (or x-coordinate) and y is the ordinate (or y-coordinate).*

2.4.2 Distance and Midpoint Formulas

Distance Formula

The distance between two points $A(x_1, y_1)$ and $B(x_2, y_2)$ in the Cartesian Plane is derived from the Pythagorean theorem and is given by:

$$d = \sqrt{(x_2 - x_1)^2 + (y_2 - y_1)^2}$$

Example 2.10: Find the distance between the points $A(2, 3)$ and $B(5, 7)$.
Solution: Applying the distance formula:

$$\begin{aligned} d &= \sqrt{(5-2)^2 + (7-3)^2} \\ &= \sqrt{3^2 + 4^2} \\ &= \sqrt{9 + 16} \\ &= \sqrt{25} \\ &= 5 \end{aligned}$$

Thus, the distance between A and B is 5 units.

Midpoint Formula

The midpoint M of a line segment connecting two points $A(x_1, y_1)$ and $B(x_2, y_2)$ is the point that divides the segment into two equal parts, given by:

$$M = \left(\frac{x_1 + x_2}{2}, \frac{y_1 + y_2}{2}\right)$$

Example 2.11: Find the midpoint of the segment connecting $A(-1,4)$ and $B(3,-2)$.
Solution: Applying the midpoint formula:

$$\begin{aligned} M &= \left(\frac{-1+3}{2}, \frac{4-2}{2}\right) \\ &= \left(\frac{2}{2}, \frac{2}{2}\right) \\ &= (1, 1) \end{aligned}$$

Therefore, the midpoint is (1,1).

2.4.3 Slope and Equation of a Line

Slope of a Line

The slope of a line measures the steepness and direction of the line. For a line passing through two points $A(x_1,y_1)$ and $B(x_2,y_2)$, the slope m is:

$$m = \frac{y_2 - y_1}{x_2 - x_1}$$

Example 2.12: Calculate the slope of the line passing through points $A(2, 3)$ and $B(6, 11)$.
Solution: Using the slope formula:

$$\begin{aligned} m &= \frac{11 - 3}{6 - 2} \\ &= \frac{8}{4} \\ &= 2 \end{aligned}$$

Hence, the slope of the line is 2.

Equation of a Line

The equation of a line in the slope-intercept form is given by $y = mx+b$, where m is the slope and b is the y-intercept.

Another common form is the point-slope form: $y - y_1 = m(x - x_1)$.

Example 2.13: Find the equation of the line with slope 3 that passes through the point (1, 2).
Solution: Using the point-slope form:

$$y - 2 = 3(x - 1)$$

$$y - 2 = 3x - 3$$

$$y = 3x - 1$$

The equation of the line is $y = 3x - 1$.

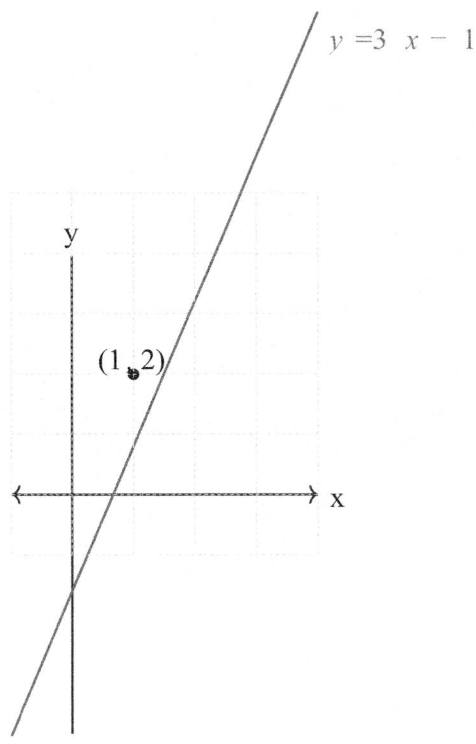

Figure 2.6: Graph of $y = 3x - 1$

Conclusion

With these foundational tools in coordinate geometry, you can adeptly analyze and solve a multitude of geometric problems ranging from simple line equations to more complex applications involving conic sections and transformations.

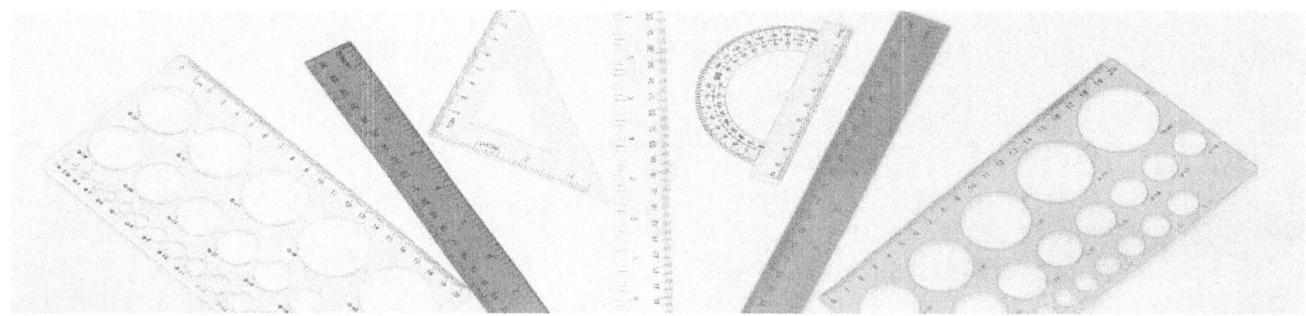

3. Trigonometry

3.1 Introduction to Trigonometry

Trigonometry is a branch of mathematics that studies the relationships between the angles and sides of triangles, particularly right triangles. It is a critical component in various fields such as physics, engineering, astronomy, and even art. This section will focus on introducing some foundational concepts in trigonometry: understanding angles, the conversion between radians and degrees, and basic trigonometric ratios.

3.1.1 Understanding Angles

Angles are a fundamental aspect of trigonometry. An angle is formed when two rays share a common endpoint, known as the vertex. The measured amount of rotation between the two rays about the vertex determines the angle's size.

Definition 3.1.1. *An angle can be described in several ways: in degrees, radians, or sometimes in terms of revolutions. For instance, a full revolution around a circle corresponds to* 360° *or* 2π *radians.*

Types of Angles

- **Acute Angle**: An angle less than 90°.
- **Right Angle**: An angle exactly 90°.
- **Obtuse Angle**: An angle greater than 90° but less than 180°.
- **Straight Angle**: An angle exactly 180°.

Example of Angles

Example 3.1: Consider a right triangle where one of its angles is 30°. The complementary angle must, therefore, be $90^\circ - 30^\circ = 60^\circ$.

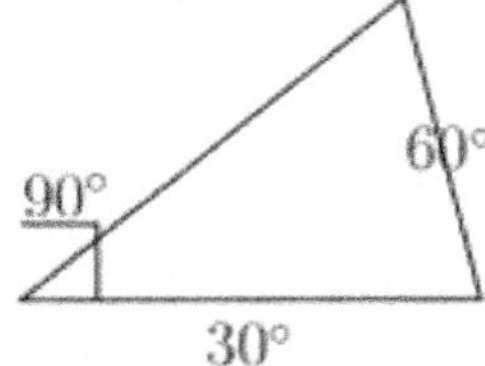

Figure 3.1: A Right Triangle with Angles 30°, 60°, and 90°

3.1.2 Radians and Degrees

Degrees and radians are two units of measuring angles, and understanding both is crucial in solving trigonometric problems.

Definition 3.1.2. *One radian is the measure of an angle at the center of a circle that intercepts an arc equal in length to the circle's radius.*

Lemma 3.1.1. *The conversion between degrees and radians is given by:*

$$1 \text{ radian} = \frac{180^\circ}{\pi} \quad \text{or conversely} \quad 1^\circ = \frac{\pi}{180} \text{ radian}$$

Example 3.2: To convert 45° to radians, use the fact that:

$$45^\circ \times \frac{\pi \text{ radians}}{180^\circ} = \frac{\pi}{4} \text{ radians}$$

3.1.3 Basic Trigonometric Ratios

Trigonometry mainly deals with the ratios derived from the angles and sides of a right triangle.

Definition 3.1.3. *The primary trigonometric ratios are defined as follows for an angle θ in a right triangle:*

- *Sine ($\sin\theta$): It is the ratio of the length of the opposite side to the hypotenuse.*
- *Cosine ($\cos\theta$): It is the ratio of the length of the adjacent side to the hypotenuse.*
- *Tangent ($\tan\theta$): It is the ratio of the length of the opposite side to the adjacent side.*

Example 3.3: Consider a right triangle with sides 3, 4, and 5, where the hypotenuse is 5, and one non-right angle θ. The trigonometric ratios would be:

$$\sin\theta = \frac{3}{5}, \qquad \cos\theta = \frac{4}{5}, \qquad \tan\theta = \frac{3}{4}$$

Trigonometric Ratio	Ratio of Sides	Example Value
Sine (sin)	Opposite / Hypotenuse	3/5
Cosine (cos)	Adjacent / Hypotenuse	4/5
Tangent (tan)	Opposite / Adjacent	3/4

Table 3.1: Basic Trigonometric Ratios for a Right Triangle

Conclusion

This deep dive into the foundational aspects of trigonometry should provide a strong base for understanding more advanced topics in this rich field of mathematics.

Exercises

Exercise 3.1:

1. Define the following angles in both degrees and radians:

(a) 90°

(b) 180°

(c) 270°

(d) 360°

Exercise 3.2:

Convert the following angle measures from degrees to radians:

1. 45°
2. 120°
3. 225°
4. 315°

Show all your calculations.

Exercise 3.3:

Describe the relationship between degrees and radians. Explain the importance of this relationship in trigonometry with examples of its applications.

Exercise 3.4:

Given an angle of $\frac{\pi}{4}$ radians, calculate its sine, cosine, and tangent values. Ensure to use trigonometric ratios and provide a detailed explanation of each step.

Exercise 3.5:

Compare and contrast the unit circle definition of sine and cosine with right triangle definitions, using a specific angle (e.g., 30° or $\frac{\pi}{6}$ radians) to illustrate your explanation.

Answers with Explanations

Solution to 3.1:

Using the formula for conversion between degrees and radians, *radians* = *degrees* × $\frac{\pi}{180}$:

(a) $90° = 90 \times \frac{\pi}{180} = \frac{\pi}{2}$ radians

(b) $180° = 180 \times \frac{\pi}{180} = \pi$ radians

(c) $270° = 270 \times \frac{\pi}{180} = \frac{3\pi}{2}$ radians

(d) $360° = 360 \times \frac{\pi}{180} = 2\pi$ radians

Solution to 3.2:

For conversion of degrees to radians:

1. $45° = 45 \times \frac{\pi}{180} = \frac{\pi}{4}$ radians
2. $120° = 120 \times \frac{\pi}{180} = \frac{2\pi}{3}$ radians
3. $225° = 225 \times \frac{\pi}{180} = \frac{5\pi}{4}$ radians
4. $315° = 315 \times \frac{\pi}{180} = \frac{7\pi}{4}$ radians

Each calculation multiplies the degree measure by $\frac{\pi}{180}$.

Solution to 3.3:

Degrees and radians are two units for measuring angles. One complete revolution is equal to 360° or 2π radians. Thus, 1 degree equals $\frac{\pi}{180}$ radians, and 1 radian equals $\frac{180}{\pi}$ degrees.

Importance in trigonometry includes: - Facilitating the use of trigonometric functions in calculus. - Common in physics for angular measurements.

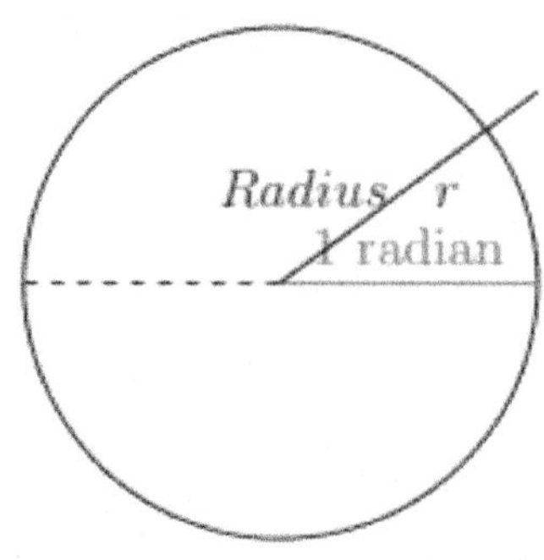

Solution to 3.4:

For $\frac{\pi}{4}$ radians, a 45-degree angle: -

$$\sin\left(\frac{\pi}{4}\right) = \frac{\sqrt{2}}{2} - \cos\left(\frac{\pi}{4}\right) = \frac{\sqrt{2}}{2} - \tan\left(\frac{\pi}{4}\right) = 1$$

Illustration is derived from the unit circle and properties of $45^{\circ} - 45^{\circ} - 90^{\circ}$ triangles.

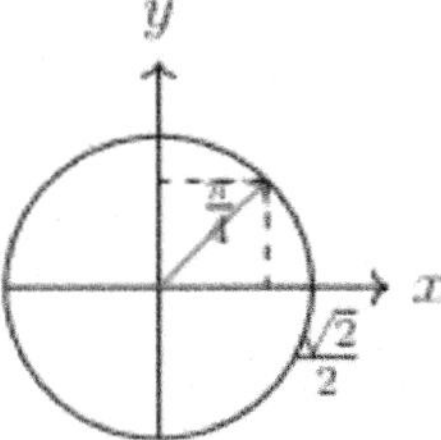

Solution to 3.5:

The unit circle approach represents angles as measures within a circle, yielding defined values for sine and cosine based on coordinates:

For 30° or $\frac{\pi}{6}$: - In a right triangle, $\sin 30^{\circ} = \frac{1}{2}, \cos 30^{\circ} = \frac{\sqrt{3}}{2}$. - The unit circle provides identical results.

This uniformity confirms trigonometric function consistency irrespective of definition method.

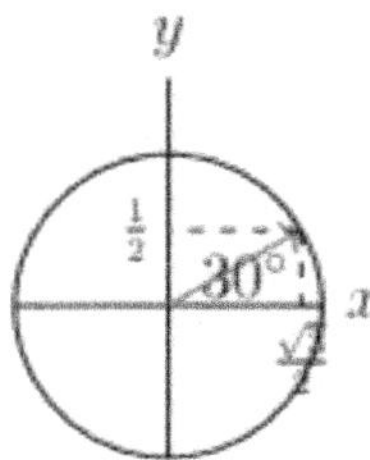

3.2 Trigonometric Functions

Trigonometric functions are fundamental in various fields of mathematics and science. This section will provide an in-depth exploration of the basic trigonometric functions—sine, cosine, and tangent—their graphical representations, and some practical applications in real life.

3.2.1 Sine, Cosine, and Tangent

Trigonometric functions relate the angles of a triangle to the lengths of its sides. The primary trigonometric functions are sine (sin), cosine (cos), and tangent (tan).

Definition 3.2.1. *For a right triangle with angle θ, the sine, cosine, and tangent functions are defined as follows:*

$$\sin\theta = \frac{\textit{opposite side}}{\textit{hypotenuse}}, \quad \cos\theta = \frac{\textit{adjacent side}}{\textit{hypotenuse}}, \quad \tan\theta = \frac{\textit{opposite side}}{\textit{adjacent side}}.$$

Example 3.4: Consider a right triangle where the hypotenuse is 10 units, the side opposite angle θ is 6 units, and the adjacent side is 8 units. Calculate $\sin\theta$, $\cos\theta$, and $\tan\theta$.

$$\sin\theta = \frac{6}{10} = 0.6, \quad \cos\theta = \frac{8}{10} = 0.8, \quad \tan\theta = \frac{6}{8} = 0.75.$$

3.2.2 Graphs of Trigonometric Functions

The trigonometric functions can be graphed on the Cartesian plane, providing a visual representation of how they behave.

The sine and cosine functions have a period of 2π, and their range is $[-1, 1]$. The tangent function, not shown here, has a period of π and breaks to infinity at odd multiples of $\pi/2$.

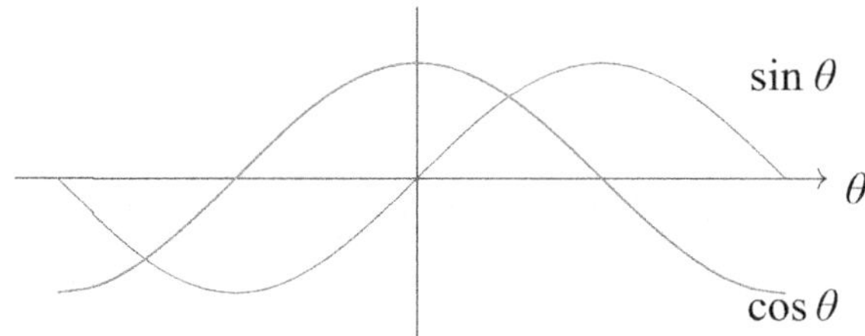

Figure 3.2: Graphs of the $\sin\theta$ (blue) and $\cos\theta$ (red) functions.

Example 3.5: Graph the function $y = \sin x$ over the interval $[-2\pi, 2\pi]$ and identify its amplitude, period, and any phase shifts.
Solution: The amplitude of $y = \sin x$ is 1, its period is 2π, and there is no phase shift. The function oscillates between -1 and 1 with these characteristics.

3.2.3 Applications in Real Life

Trigonometric functions play a critical role in various real-life applications such as sound and light waves, tides, and oscillations.

Example 3.6: Consider a scenario where a Ferris wheel with a diameter of 20 meters rotates once every 1 minute. If a rider starts from the lowest point, model the height of the rider above the ground as a function of time.
Solution: The height $h(t)$ can be modeled as:

$$h(t) = 10(1 - \cos\left(\frac{2\pi}{60}t\right)) + 5$$
,

where t is time in seconds. The wheel's center is 10 meters off the ground, and the maximum height will be 20 meters.

Summary

In conclusion, trigonometric functions not only serve as a tool for understanding angles and triangles but also provide a foundation for describing periodic phenomena in diverse scientific and engineering disciplines. Their study, especially through graphs, enhances comprehensibility and practical application.

Exercises

Exercise 3.6:

1. **For a right triangle, if the angle θ is 30°, calculate the sine, cosine, and tangent of θ. Use appropriate trigonometric ratios.**

2. **Verify whether the identity $\sin^2 \theta + \cos^2 \theta = 1$ holds true for $\theta = 45°$.**

3. **Plot the graphs of $\sin x$, $\cos x$, and $\tan x$ over the interval $[0, 2\pi]$. Analyze their periodicity and amplitude.**

Exercise 3.7:

Consider the real-world application of a pendulum. If a pendulum swings at an angle θ, where $\theta(t) = \theta_0 \cos(\omega t)$ with $\theta_0 = 0.1$, and $\omega = 1.5$, determine the maximum angle and the period of the pendulum's swing.

Exercise 3.8:

Investigate the following problem: A ladder leaning against a wall makes an angle *a* with the ground. If the ladder's length is 10 feet and tan*a* = 1.2, find the height at which the ladder touches the wall.

Exercise 3.9:

1. **Calculate the angular displacement in radians for a tire of 0.5 meters radius that covers a distance of 4 meters along the ground.**

2. **Discuss the relationship between linear speed and angular speed for a point on the tire's edge.**

Answers with Explanations

Solution to 3.6:

1. For a 30° angle in a right triangle, $\sin 30^\circ = \frac{1}{2}, \cos 30^\circ = \frac{\sqrt{3}}{2}, \tan 30^\circ = \frac{1}{\sqrt{3}}$.

2. Using the identity $\sin^2\theta + \cos^2\theta = 1$, for $\theta = 45^\circ$, $\sin 45^\circ = \frac{\sqrt{2}}{2}$, and $\cos 45^\circ = \frac{\sqrt{2}}{2}$. Hence, $\left(\frac{\sqrt{2}}{2}\right)^2 + \left(\frac{\sqrt{2}}{2}\right)^2 = 1$.

3. Plots for $\sin x$, $\cos x$, and $\tan x$ can be created using `tikz` as shown below:

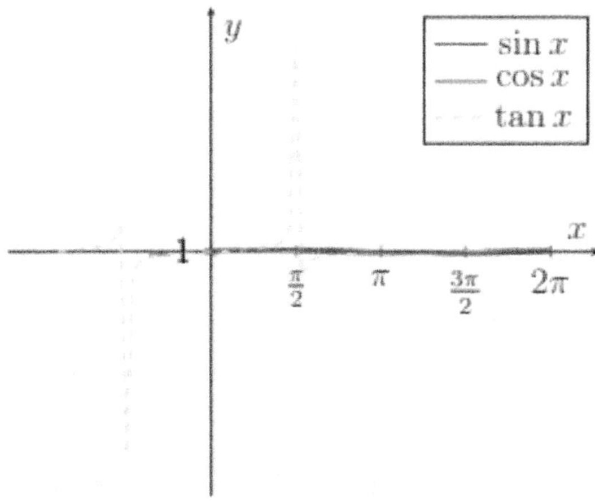

The graphs reveal that $\sin x$ and $\cos x$ are periodic with a period 2π, while $\tan x$ has a period of π.

Solution to 3.7:

$$\theta(t) = 0.1\cos(1.5t)$$

θ_0 is the maximum displacement and the period T is given by $T = \frac{2\pi}{\omega} = \frac{2\pi}{1.5} \approx 4.19$ seconds.

Solution to 3.8:
For the ladder,

$$\tan\alpha = \frac{\text{height}}{\text{base}}, \quad \text{Base} = \sqrt{10^2 - \text{height}^2}$$

Solving $\tan a = 1.2$, height $= 1.2 \times$ base. Substitute in the Pythagorean theorem to solve:

$$height = \frac{12}{5} \approx 2.4\, m$$

Solution to 3.9:

1. The angular displacement θ in radians is given by:
$$\theta = \frac{distance}{radius} = \frac{4}{0.5} = 8\, radius$$
2. Linear speed $v = r\omega$, where r is the radius and ω is the angular speed. Linear speed is proportional to angular speed and the proportionality factor is the radius.

3.3 Trigonometric Identities

Trigonometric identities are fundamental equations involving trigonometric functions. These identities are used extensively in simplifying expressions, solving trigonometric equations, and proving other mathematical concepts. This section will delve into three primary types of trigonometric identities: Basic Identities, Sum and Difference Formulas, and Double Angle Formulas. This exploration will be complemented by detailed examples and visual illustrations to enhance understanding.

3.3.1 Basic Identities

The foundation of trigonometric identities rests on a few fundamental equations that relate the basic trigonometric functions to one another. These identities hold true for any angle θ.

Definition 3 .3.1 *The most important basic trigonometric identities are:*

$$\begin{aligned} &\textit{Pythagorean Identity:} && \sin^2\theta + \cos^2\theta = 1, \\ &\textit{Quotient Identities:} && \tan\theta = \frac{\sin\theta}{\cos\theta}, \quad \cot\theta = \frac{\cos\theta}{\sin\theta}, \\ &\textit{Reciprocal Identities:} && \csc\theta = \frac{1}{\sin\theta}, \quad \sec\theta = \frac{1}{\cos\theta}, \quad \cot\theta = \frac{1}{\tan\theta}. \end{aligned}$$

Example 3.7: Let us verify the Pythagorean identity for $\theta = 45^\circ$.
Solution: We know that: $\sin 45^\circ = \cos 45^\circ = \frac{\sqrt{2}}{2}$.
Substitute these into the Pythagorean identity:

$$\left(\frac{\sqrt{2}}{2}\right)^2 + \left(\frac{\sqrt{2}}{2}\right)^2 = \frac{2}{4} + \frac{2}{4} = 1.$$

Thus, the identity is verified.

3.3.2 Sum and Difference Formulas

The sum and difference formulas are powerful tools for computing the trigonometric function values of sum or difference of angles, α and β.

Proposition 3.3.1. *The sum and difference formulas are:*

$$\begin{aligned}\sin(\alpha \pm \beta) &= \sin\alpha\cos\beta \pm \cos\alpha\sin\beta,\\ \cos(\alpha \pm \beta) &= \cos\alpha\cos\beta \mp \sin\alpha\sin\beta,\\ \tan(\alpha \pm \beta) &= \frac{\tan\alpha \pm \tan\beta}{1 \mp \tan\alpha\tan\beta}.\end{aligned}$$

Example 3.8: Calculate $\sin(75^\circ)$.
Solution: Using the sum formula, express 75° as $45^\circ + 30^\circ$:

$$\sin(75^\circ) = \sin(45^\circ + 30^\circ) = \sin 45^\circ \cos 30^\circ + \cos 45^\circ \sin 30^\circ.$$

Substitute in the known values:

$$= \left(\frac{\sqrt{2}}{2}\right)\left(\frac{\sqrt{3}}{2}\right) + \left(\frac{\sqrt{2}}{2}\right)\left(\frac{1}{2}\right) = \frac{\sqrt{6}}{4} + \frac{\sqrt{2}}{4} = \frac{\sqrt{6}+\sqrt{2}}{4}.$$

3.3.3 Double Angle Formulas

The double angle formulas are derived from the sum formulas and relate the trigonometric functions of twice an angle to the functions of the original angle.

Theorem 3.3.2. *The double angle formulas are:*

$$\begin{aligned}\sin(2\theta) &= 2\sin\theta\cos\theta,\\ \cos(2\theta) &= \cos^2\theta - \sin^2\theta = 2\cos^2\theta - 1 = 1 - 2\sin^2\theta,\\ \tan(2\theta) &= \frac{2\tan\theta}{1 - \tan^2\theta}.\end{aligned}$$

Example 3.9: Using the double angle formula, find $\cos(60^\circ)$ using $\cos(2 \times 30^\circ)$.
Solution:

$$\cos(60^\circ) = \cos(2 \times 30^\circ) = 2\cos^2 30^\circ - 1.$$

Substitute the known values:

$$= 2\left(\frac{\sqrt{3}}{2}\right)^2 - 1 = 2 \cdot \frac{3}{4} - 1 = \frac{3}{2} - 1 = \frac{1}{2}.$$

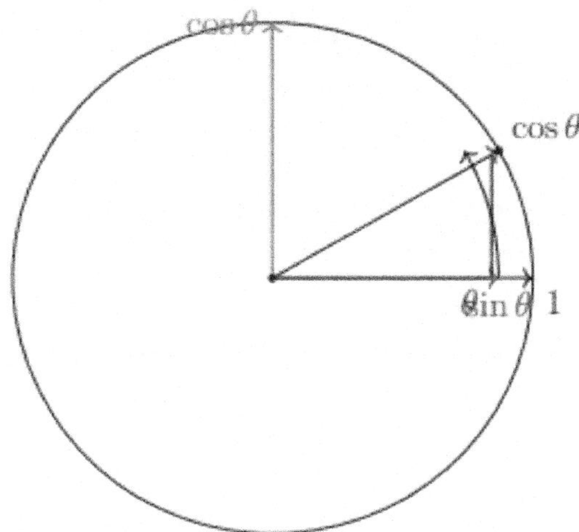

Figure 3.3: Geometric representation of the Pythagorean Identity.

Summary

Understanding these principles of balancing and manipulating equations forms a foundation that will enable you to tackle more complex algebraic problems. Practice these techniques to enhance your confidence and efficiency in solving equations.

Exercises

Exercise 3.10:

1. **Verify the identity: $\sin^2 \theta + \cos^2 \theta = 1$ for $\theta = 30°, 45°$ and $60°$. Express your answers in exact values.**

2. **Prove the Sum and Difference Formulas for Cosine:**

$$\cos(\alpha \pm \beta) = \cos\alpha\cos\beta \mp \sin\alpha\sin\beta$$

by considering the unit circle and position of the angles.

3. **Compute $\sin(75°)$ using the Sum Formula for sine, given that $75°$ can be expressed as $45° + 30°$.**

4. **Use the Double Angle Formula to find $\cos(2\theta)$ given that $\sin\theta = \frac{3}{5}$ and θ is in the first quadrant.**

Exercise 3.11:

Simplify the expression $\cos^4 x - \sin^4 x$ using trigonometric identities.

Exercise 3.12:

Derive the formula for $\tan(\alpha + \beta)$ from the sine and cosine sum formulae.

Exercise 3.13:

If $\tan\theta = \frac{3}{4}$ and θ is an acute angle, calculate $\sin 2\theta$ and $\cos 2\theta$ using the Double Angle Formulas.

Answers with Explanations

Solution to 3.10:

1. To verify $\sin^2\theta + \cos^2\theta = 1$ for $\theta = 30°, 45°,$ and $60°$:
   - For $\theta = 30°$: $\sin 30° = \frac{1}{2}, \cos 30° = \frac{\sqrt{3}}{2}$,
   $$\sin^2 30° + \cos^2 30° = \left(\frac{1}{2}\right)^2 + \left(\frac{\sqrt{3}}{2}\right)^2 = \frac{1}{4} + \frac{3}{4} = 1.$$
   - For $\theta = 45°$: $\sin 45° = \cos 45° = \frac{\sqrt{2}}{2}$,
   $$\sin^2 45° + \cos^2 45° = \left(\frac{\sqrt{2}}{2}\right)^2 + \left(\frac{\sqrt{2}}{2}\right)^2 = \frac{2}{4} + \frac{2}{4} = 1.$$
   - For $\theta = 60°$: $\sin 60° = \frac{\sqrt{3}}{2}, \cos 60° = \frac{1}{2}$,
   $$\sin^2 60° + \cos^2 60° = \left(\frac{\sqrt{3}}{2}\right)^2 + \left(\frac{1}{2}\right)^2 = \frac{3}{4} + \frac{1}{4} = 1.$$

2. To prove $\cos(\alpha \pm \beta) = \cos\alpha\cos\beta \mp \sin\alpha\sin\beta$, visualize angles α and β on the unit circle.

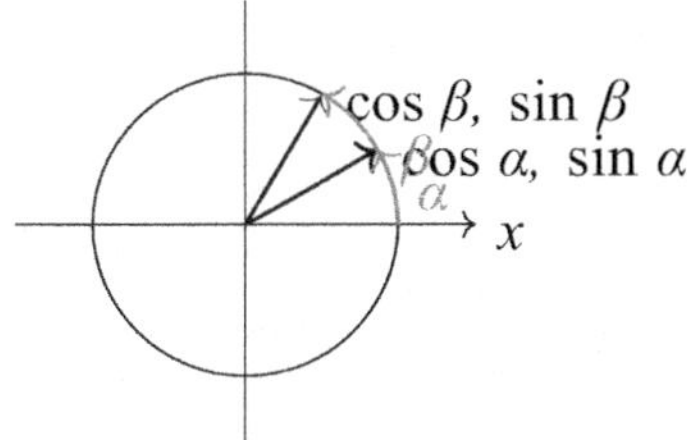

The coordinates of the points represent cos and sin. Using the angle addition formulas,

$$\cos(\alpha \pm \beta) = \cos\alpha\cos\beta \mp \sin\alpha\sin\beta$$

follows from considering the rotation and properties of the inner products formed by these unit vectors.

3. To compute $\sin(75^\circ)$:

$$\sin(75^\circ) = \sin(45^\circ + 30^\circ)$$

Using the sum formula for sine:

$$\sin(45^\circ + 30^\circ) = \sin 45^\circ \cos 30^\circ + \cos 45^\circ \sin 30^\circ$$

With known values: $\sin 45° = \frac{\sqrt{2}}{2}, \cos 30° = \frac{\sqrt{3}}{2}, \cos 45° = \frac{\sqrt{2}}{2}, \sin 30° = \frac{1}{2}$,

$$= \frac{\sqrt{2}}{2} \cdot \frac{\sqrt{3}}{2} + \frac{\sqrt{2}}{2} \cdot \frac{1}{2} = \frac{\sqrt{6}}{4} + \frac{\sqrt{2}}{4} = \frac{\sqrt{6} + \sqrt{2}}{4}$$

4. Given $\boldsymbol{sin\ \theta} = \frac{3}{5}$ and θ in the first quadrant, by Pythagorean identity, $cos\ \theta = \frac{4}{5}$

Double Angle Formulas:

$$\sin 2\theta = 2\sin\theta\cos\theta = 2\cdot\frac{3}{5}\cdot\frac{4}{5} = \frac{24}{25}$$

$$\cos 2\theta = \cos^2\theta - \sin^2\theta = \left(\frac{4}{5}\right)^2 - \left(\frac{3}{5}\right)^2 = \frac{16}{25} - \frac{9}{25} = \frac{7}{25}$$

Solution to 3.11:

To simplify $\cos^4 x - \sin^4 x$, use the identity:

$$a^2 - b^2 = (a - b)(a + b)$$

Therefore, $\cos^4 x - \sin^4 x = (\cos^2 x - \sin^2 x)(\cos^2 x + \sin^2 x)$

$$= (\cos^2 x - \sin^2 x) \cdot 1 = \cos^2 x - \sin^2 x$$

Simplifying further using cosine double angle identity, you find

$$\cos 2x = \cos^2 x - \sin^2 x$$

Resulting in: $\cos^4 x - \sin^4 x = \cos 2x$

Solution to 3.12:

To derive $\tan(\alpha + \beta)$ from sine and cosine formulas: Start with

$$\tan(\alpha + \beta) = \frac{\sin(\alpha + \beta)}{\cos(\alpha + \beta)}$$

Using sum formulas:

$$= \frac{\sin\alpha\cos\beta + \cos\alpha\sin\beta}{\cos\alpha\cos\beta - \sin\alpha\sin\beta}$$

Divide numerator and denominator by $\cos\alpha\cos\beta$:

$$= \frac{\left(\frac{\sin\alpha}{\cos\alpha}\right) + \left(\frac{\sin\beta}{\cos\beta}\right)}{1 - \left(\frac{\sin\alpha}{\cos\alpha}\right)\left(\frac{\sin\beta}{\cos\beta}\right)}$$

Substitute $\tan\alpha = \frac{\sin\alpha}{\cos\alpha}$ and $\tan\beta = \frac{\sin\beta}{\cos\beta}$:

$$= \frac{\tan\alpha + \tan\beta}{1 - \tan\alpha\tan\beta}$$

Solution to 3.13:

Given $an\ \theta = \frac{3}{4}$ and θ acute, we use:

$$\sin\theta = \frac{3}{5}, \cos\theta = \frac{4}{5} \text{ (since } \tan\theta = \frac{\sin\theta}{\cos\theta})$$

Double Angle Formulas:

$$\sin 2\theta = 2 \cdot \sin\theta \cdot \cos\theta = 2 \times \frac{3}{5} \times \frac{4}{5} = \frac{24}{25}$$

$$\cos 2\theta = \cos^2\theta - \sin^2\theta = \left(\frac{4}{5}\right)^2 - \left(\frac{3}{5}\right)^2 = \frac{16}{25} - \frac{9}{25} = \frac{7}{25}$$

3.4 Solving Trigonometric Equations

Solving trigonometric equations involves techniques that are pivotal for understanding advanced mathematics. This section will explore various methods to solve both linear and quadratic trigonometric equations and discuss their applications. Mastery of these concepts is crucial for tackling problems in physics, engineering, and other scientific fields.

3.4.1 Linear Trigonometric Equations

Linear trigonometric equations are those which involve trigonometric functions of a single angle, typically in the form $\sin x = a$, $\cos x = b$, or $\tan x = c$.

Example 3.10: Consider the equation $\sin x = \frac{1}{2}$. To solve for x, we first recall the basic angles where sine has a value of $\frac{1}{2}$:

$$x = \frac{\pi}{6} + 2k\pi \quad \text{and} \quad x = \frac{5\pi}{6} + 2k\pi, \quad k \in \mathbb{Z},$$

since the sine function is periodic with period 2π.

3.4.2 Quadratic Trigonometric Equations

Quadratic trigonometric equations are equations that can be expressed in the form $a\sin^2 x + b\sin x + c = 0$ or similar forms for cosine and tangent. These are analogous to quadratic equations in algebra.

Example 3.11: Solve the equation $2\cos^2 x - \cos x - 1 = 0$.
Solution: First, let $u = \cos x$, transforming the equation to a quadratic in u:

$$2u^2 - u - 1 = 0.$$

We solve this using the quadratic formula:

$$u = \frac{-b \pm \sqrt{b^2 - 4ac}}{2a}$$

Here, $a = 2$, $b = -1$, $c = -1$. Calculating the determinant:

$$b^2 - 4ac = 1 + 8 = 9.$$

Thus, the solutions for u are:

$$u = \frac{1 \pm 3}{4}.$$

$$u_1 = 1, \quad u_2 = -\frac{1}{2}.$$

Returning to x, for $u_1 = 1$, $\cos x = 1$, giving $x = 2k\pi$, $k \in \mathbb{Z}$.
For $u_2 = -\frac{1}{2}$, $\cos x = -\frac{1}{2}$, so:

$$x = \frac{2\pi}{3} + 2k\pi \quad \text{and} \quad x = \frac{4\pi}{3} + 2k\pi, \quad k \in \mathbb{Z}.$$

3.4.3 Applications

Trigonometric equations have numerous applications in real-world scenarios, from calculating angles and distances to modeling periodic phenomena.

Example 3.12: A pendulum swings following the equation $\theta(t) = \theta_0 \cos(\omega t + \phi)$. At a given time t, the angle is measured to be zero. Find the time intervals when this occurs. To find t, solve $\cos(\omega t + \phi) = 0$. The cosine function equals zero at:

$$\omega t + \phi = \frac{\pi}{2} + k\pi, \quad k \in \mathbb{Z}.$$

Solving for t:

$$t = \frac{\frac{\pi}{2} + k\pi - \phi}{\omega}$$

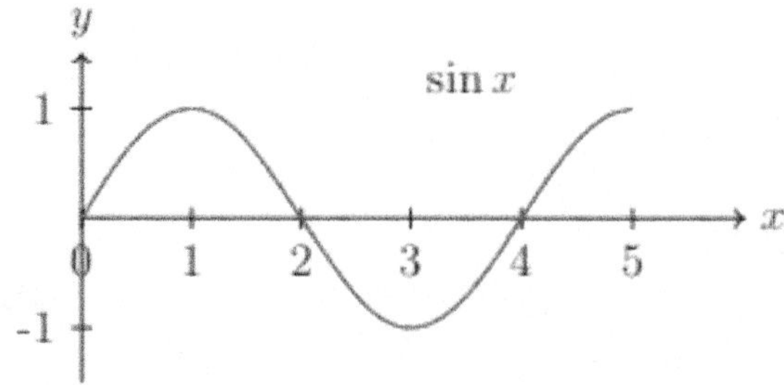

Figure 3.4: Graph of $y = \sin x$

Equation Type	General Solution	Example
$\sin x = a$	$x = \sin^{-1}(a)+2k\pi$	$\sin x = \frac{1}{2}$
$\cos x = b$	$x = \cos^{-1}(b)+2k\pi$	$\cos x = -\frac{1}{2}$
$\tan x = c$	$x = \tan^{-1}(c) + k\pi$	$\tan x = 1$

Table 3.2: General Solutions for Basic Trigonometric Equations

Summary

Through these examples and applications, one can gain a comprehensive understanding of how to solve trigonometric equations and apply these solutions in various practical situations.

Exercises

Exercise 3.14:

Solve the following linear trigonometric equations for $0 \leq x < 2\pi$:

(a) $\sin x = \frac{1}{2}$

(b) $\cos x = -\sqrt{3}/2$

(c) $2\tan x - 1 = 0$

Exercise 3.15:

Solve the following quadratic trigonometric equations for $0 \leq x < 2\pi$:

(a) $\cos^2 x - \frac{3}{2}\cos x + \frac{1}{2} = 0$

(b) $2\sin^2 x - 3\sin x + 1 = 0$

(c) $4\sin^2 x - \cos x - 2 = 0$

Exercise 3.16:

A wheel makes one complete rotation every 24 seconds. Express the height, $h(t)$, of a point P on the edge of the wheel as a function of time t, assuming P starts at the highest point. Calculate the height after 6 seconds.

Exercise 3.17:

1. **Determine the general solution for the trigonometric equation tan x = √3.**

2. **Discuss in detail how the periodic nature of trigonometric functions affects the solutions.**

Exercise 3.18:

Prove the identity sin² x − cos² x = 0 using trigonometric equations and interpret the solution geometrically on the unit circle.

Answers with Explanations

Solution to 3.14:

For the equation $\sin x = \frac{1}{2}$, the solutions are $x = \frac{\pi}{6}, \frac{5\pi}{6}$. Use the unit circle where these values correspond to the points $(\frac{\sqrt{3}}{2}, \frac{1}{2})$ and $(-\frac{\sqrt{3}}{2}, \frac{1}{2})$. For $\cos x = -\sqrt{3}/2$, the solutions are $x = \frac{5\pi}{6}, \frac{7\pi}{6}$. For $2\tan x - 1 = 0$, solve $\tan x = \frac{1}{2}$. It has solutions $\arctan \frac{1}{2}$ and $\arctan \frac{1}{2} + \pi$, as tan is periodic with period π.

Solution to 3.15:

For $\cos^2 x - \frac{3}{2}\cos x + \frac{1}{2} = 0$, let $u = \cos x$, the equation transforms to $u^2 - \frac{3}{2}u + \frac{1}{2} = 0$. Solving for u, $u = 1$ or $\frac{1}{2}$. Hence, $\cos x = 1$ gives $x = 0$, and $\cos x = \frac{1}{2}$ gives $x = \pm\frac{\pi}{3}$. Similarly solve for other cases.

Solution to 3.16:

Given $h(t) = R\cos(\frac{2\pi}{24}t)$, where R is the radius (let's assume $R = 10$), at $t = 6$, $h(6) = 10\cos(\frac{\pi}{2}) = 0$. Use a sinusoidal function with cos starting at the highest point with maximum amplitude R.

Solution to 3.17:

General solution for $\tan x = \sqrt{3}$ is $x = \frac{\pi}{3} + n\pi$, $n \in \mathbb{Z}$ due to the periodicity of the tan function. Verify that the solutions lie at $\frac{\pi}{3}$ intervals when plotted.

Solution to 3.18:

Using the identity, $\sin^2 x - \cos^2 x = \sin^2 x - (1 - \sin^2 x) = 2\sin^2 x - 1 = 0$, results in $\sin^2 x = \frac{1}{2}$. So $\sin x = \pm\frac{\sqrt{2}}{2}$, leading to $x = \frac{\pi}{4}, \frac{3\pi}{4}$. Each solution corresponds to 45-degree intervals forming angles on the unit circle.

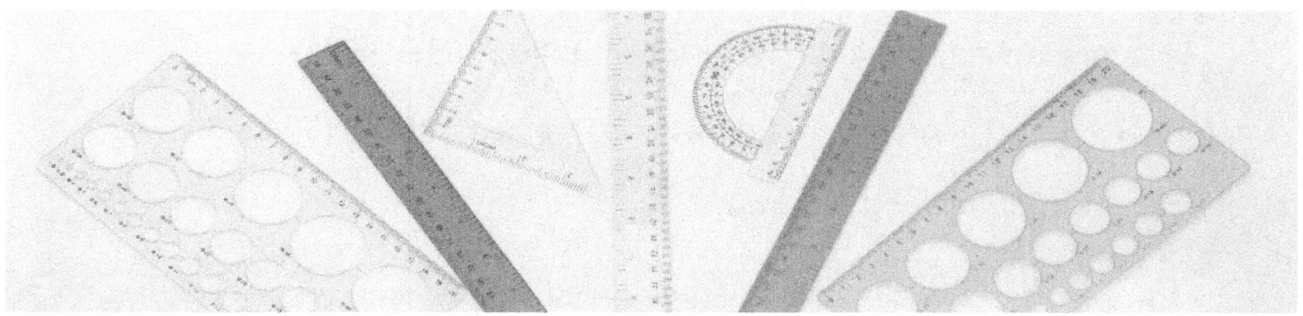

4. Statistics and Probability

4.1 Descriptive Statistics

Descriptive statistics involves the summarization and organization of data in a way that makes it easy to understand and interpret. This section provides a comprehensive overview of the foundational concepts, with a focus on measures of central tendency, measures of dispersion, and data representation.

4.1.1 Measures of Central Tendency

Measures of central tendency describe the center of a data set. They include:

Mean

The mean is the arithmetic average of a data set.

Definition 4.1.1. *Given a data set* $\{x_1, x_2, \ldots, x_n\}$*, the mean* $\bar{x}$ *is calculated as:*

$$\overline{x} = \frac{1}{n}\sum_{i=1}^{n} x_i$$

where n is the number of data points.

Example 4.1: Calculate the mean of the data set {5,10,15,20,25}.

$$\begin{aligned}\overline{x} &= \frac{1}{5}(5 + 10 + 15 + 20 + 25)\\ &= \frac{1}{5} \times 75\\ &= 15\end{aligned}$$

Median

The median is the middle value when a data set is ordered.

Definition 4.1.2. *For an ordered data set of n observations, the median is:*

- *The middle number if n is odd.*
- *The average of the two middle numbers if n is even.*

Example 4.1: Find the median of the data set {5,10,15,20,25}.
Solution: Since there are 5 numbers, the median is the third value:

$$\text{Median} = 15$$

Mode

The mode is the value that appears most frequently in a data set.

Definition 4.1.3. *In a set of values, the mode is the value that occurs with the greatest frequency.*

Example 4.1: Determine the mode of the data set {1,2,2,3,4}.
Solution: The mode is 2 since it appears most frequently.

4.1.2 Measures of Dispersion

Measures of dispersion indicate how spread out the data values are around the central tendency. They include:

Range
Definition 4.1.4. *The range is the difference between the maximum and minimum values in the data set:*

$$Range = x_{max} - x_{min}$$

Example 4.1: For the data set {2,4,6,8,10}, the range is:

$$\text{Range} = 10 - 2 = 8$$

Variance and Standard Deviation

Definition 4.1.5. *Variance is the average of the squared differences from the mean. The standard deviation is the square root of the variance.*

$$\sigma^2 = \frac{1}{n}\sum_{i=1}^{n}(x_i - \overline{x})^2$$

$$\sigma = \sqrt{\sigma^2}$$

Example 4.1: Calculate the variance and standard deviation for the data set {5,7,7,8,10}.

$$\begin{aligned}\overline{x} &= \frac{1}{5}(5+7+7+8+10) = 7.4 \\ \sigma^2 &= \frac{1}{5}((5-7.4)^2 + (7-7.4)^2 + (7-7.4)^2 + (8-7.4)^2 + (10-7.4)^2) \\ &= \frac{1}{5}(5.76 + 0.16 + 0.16 + 0.36 + 6.76) \\ &= \frac{13.2}{5} = 2.64 \\ \sigma &= \sqrt{2.64} \approx 1.62\end{aligned}$$

4.1.3 Data Representation

Data representation methods include graphs and charts that make data easier to interpret. Common forms include:

Histograms

Definition 4.1.6. *A histogram is a type of bar graph that represents the frequency distribution of a data set.*

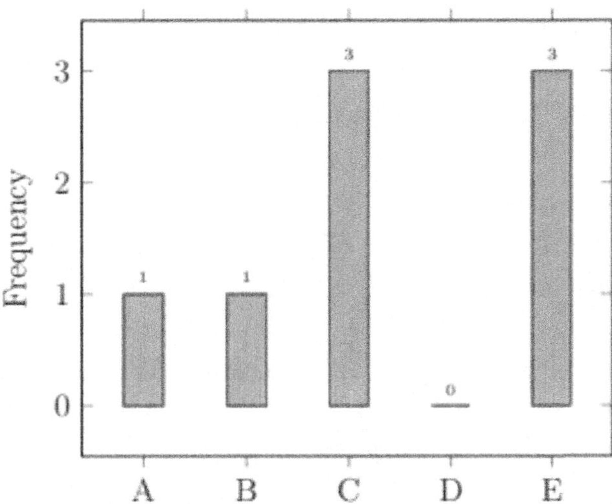

Figure 4.1: Histogram representing frequency of grades A to E.

Box Plots

Definition 4.1.7. *A box plot (or box-and-whisker plot) displays the five-number summary of a data set: minimum, first quartile (Q1), median, third quartile (Q3), and maximum.*

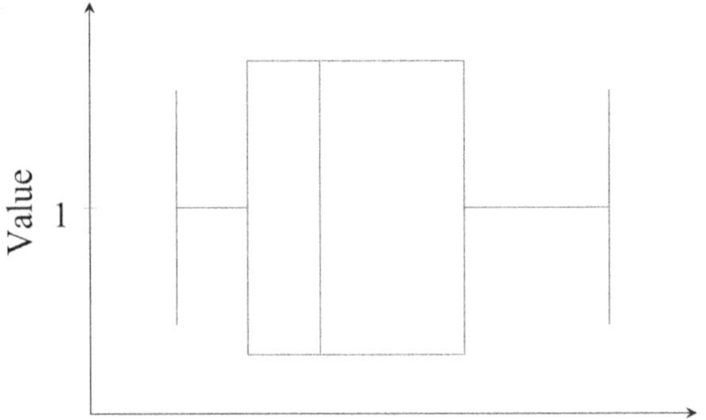

Figure 4.2: Box plot showing the spread of the data.

Summary

Each measure and method offers insights into different aspects of a data set, helping to summarize large amounts of information succinctly and effectively.

Exercises

Exercise 4.1:

1. **Consider a data set consisting of the ages (in years) of a group of people: 18, 22, 22, 20, 24, 30, 29, 33, 31, 27. Calculate the mean, median, and mode of this data set.**

2. **The following data represents the test scores of a class of 10 students: 78, 85, 82, 90, 88, 76, 95, 89, 84, 91. Determine the range, variance, and standard deviation.**

3. **A survey of daily step counts (in thousands) for a group of people gives the following data: 5, 8, 10, 6, 7, 9, 12, 4, 11, 10. Represent this data using a histogram and a box plot.**

4. **Analyzing data visualizations: Examine the following pie chart representing the distribution of favorite ice cream flavors among 100 people. Evaluate which flavor is most and least popular, and justify your answer with appropriate statistics.**

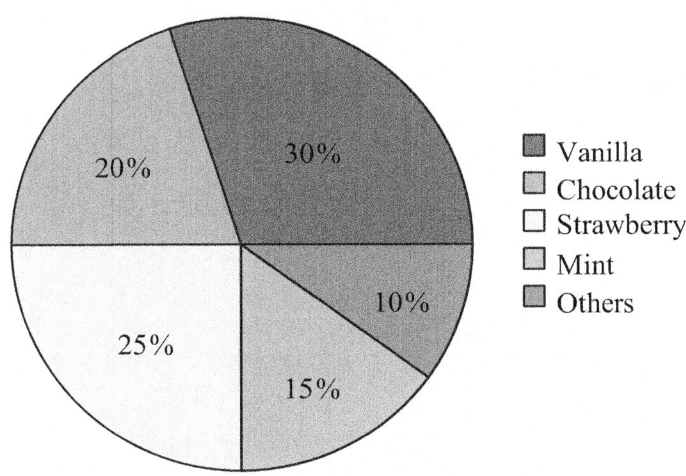

Exercise 4.2:

A data set of yearly sales (in thousands) for a small business over 6 years is given: \$150, \$180, \$160, \$200, \$190, \$210. Create a line graph of this data. Identify any trends or patterns, and discuss potential causes behind these patterns.

Exercise 4.3:

A class is analyzing the shoe sizes of students and finds these sizes: 6, 7, 7, 8, 9, 9, 9, 10, 11, 12, 10. Create a frequency distribution table for this data with appropriate class intervals, and draw the corresponding frequency polygon.

Answers with Explanations

Solution to 4.1:

1. For the ages data set (18, 22, 22, 20, 24, 30, 29, 33, 31, 27):
   (a) **Mean**: Calculate by summing all values and dividing by the number of values: $\frac{18+22+22+\cdots+27}{10} = 25.6$ years.

   (b) **Median**: Arrange in ascending order (18, 20, 22, 22, 24, 27, 29, 30, 31, 33) — median is the average of the 5th and 6th values: $\frac{24+27}{2} = 25.5$ years.

   (c) **Mode**: The most frequent value is 22.

2. For the test scores (78, 85, 82, 90, 88, 76, 95, 89, 84, 91):
   a. **Range**: Difference between the highest and lowest scores: 95 − 76 = 19.

   b. **Variance**: Use the formula $\sigma^2 = \frac{\sum(x_i - \overline{x})^2}{n}$ where x is the mean: variance is 38.89.

   c. **Standard Deviation**: $\sigma = \sqrt{38.89} \approx 6.24$.

3. For step counts (5, 8, 10, 6, 7, 9, 12, 4, 11, 10):

   a. **Histogram**: Construct bins and calculate frequency for 3-13 with, e.g., 2-k increment.

   b. **Box Plot**: Represents median, quartiles, and outliers using the IQR approach.

4. For the survey pie chart:

   a. **Most Popular Flavor:** Vanilla (30)

   b. **Least Popular Flavor:** Others (10)

   c. **Interpretation**: Using percentages shows preferences easily.

Solution to 4.2:

For sales ($150, $180, $160, $200, $190, $210):

Pattern shows increasing sales, possibly due to market expansion or product improvements.

Solution to 4.3:

For shoe sizes (6, 7, 7, 8, 9, 9, 9, 10, 11, 12, 10):

- **Frequency Table**: Group with intervals e.g., 6 − 7, 8 − 9, etc.

- **Frequency Polygon**: Plot midpoints of intervals.

4.2 Probability Basics

4.2.1 Concept of Probability

Probability is a fundamental concept in mathematics that deals with the likelihood or chance of different outcomes occurring in an event. It is used extensively across various fields such as statistics, finance, gaming, science, and everyday decision-making.

Definition 4.2.1. *The probability of an event is a measure of the likelihood that the event will occur. It is quantified as a number between 0 and 1, where 0 indicates the impossibility of the event and 1 indicates certainty.*

Mathematically, the probability $P(E)$ of an event E is given by:

$$P(E) = \frac{\text{Number of favorable outcomes}}{\text{Total number of possible outcomes}}$$

Example 4.5: Consider a standard six-sided die. What is the probability of rolling a number greater than 4?
Solution: The favorable outcomes are 5 and 6. Therefore, there are 2 favorable outcomes. The total possible outcomes when rolling the die are 6. Thus, the probability is:

$$P(\textit{rolling a number greater than 4}) = \frac{2}{6} = \frac{1}{3}$$

1	2	6
3	4	5

Figure 4.3: A standard six-sided die and its outcomes.

4.2.2 Addition and Multiplication Rules

Addition Rule

The addition rule is used to find the probability that either of two events will occur. For mutually exclusive events A and B, the rule is:

$$P(A \cup B) = P(A) + P(B)$$

For non-mutually exclusive events, the rule becomes:

$$P(A \cup B) = P(A) + P(B) - P(A \cap B)$$

Example 4.6: Suppose we draw a card from a standard deck of 52 cards. What is the probability of drawing a king or a heart?
Solution: There are 4 kings and 13 hearts in the deck. However, one of the hearts is also a king. So, applying the addition rule for non-mutually exclusive events:

$$P(\text{King or Heart}) = P(\text{King}) + P(\text{Heart}) - P(\text{King and Heart}) = \frac{4}{52} + \frac{13}{52} - \frac{1}{52} = \frac{16}{52} = \frac{4}{13}$$

Multiplication Rule

The multiplication rule is used to find the probability that both of two independent events will occur. For two independent events A and B, the rule is:

$$P(A \cap B) = P(A) \times P(B)$$

Example 4.7: What is the probability of rolling a 6 on a die and flipping a heads on a coin?

Solution: The probability of rolling a 6 is $\frac{1}{6}$ and the probability of flipping a heads is $\frac{1}{2}$. Using the multiplication rule:

$$P(\text{6 and Heads}) = \frac{1}{6} \times \frac{1}{2} = \frac{1}{12}$$

4.2.3 Conditional Probability

Conditional probability is the probability of an event occurring given that another event has already occurred. The conditional probability of event A given event B is denoted by $P(A \mid B)$.

Definition 4.2.2. *The conditional probability of A given B is defined as:*

$$P(A \mid B) = \frac{P(A \cap B)}{P(B)}$$

Example 4.8: Suppose a bag contains 3 red and 2 blue marbles. If one marble is drawn and is blue, what is the probability that the next marble drawn is red?
Solution: There are initially 3 red and 2 blue marbles. The first event is drawing a blue marble, leaving us with 3 red and 1 blue. The probability of drawing a red next is:

$$P(\text{Red} \mid \text{Blue already drawn}) = \frac{3}{4}$$

Events	Probability	Description
Rolling a die	$\frac{1}{6}$	Probability of any face
Drawing a king or heart	$\frac{4}{13}$	Non-mutually exclusive
Heads then tails	$\frac{1}{4}$	Product of individual outcomes

Table 4.1: Probability Rules and Examples

Conclusion

Through these examples and definitions, we have explored the foundational principles of probability, which form the basis for more complex statistical concepts and real-world applications.

Exercises

Exercise 4.5:

1. **Define probability and explain its significance in real-life applications.**

2. **A single six-sided die is rolled. What is the probability of rolling a number greater than 4?**

3. **In a deck of 52 cards, what is the probability of drawing a heart or drawing a king?**

4. **Two events, A and B, are independent. P(A) = 0.3 and P(B) = 0.5. What is the probability of both events occurring (P(A and B))?**

5. **Three coins are tossed simultaneously. What is the probability of obtaining at least one head?**

6. **In a class of 30 students, 18 like mathematics and 12 like science. If 5 students like both subjects, what is the probability of randomly selecting a student who likes either mathematics or science?**

Exercise 4.6:

1. **Formulate the Addition Rule of Probability and give an example that illustrates the rule.**

2. **A jar contains 4 red, 5 blue, and 6 green marbles. If a marble is drawn at random, what is the probability that it is either red or blue?**

3. **Events C and D are overlapping events where P(C) = 0.4, P(D) = 0.5, and P(C and D) = 0.1. Calculate the probability P(C or D).**

4. **A standard pack of cards is shuffled, and one card is drawn at random. What is the probability that the card is either a spade or a face card?**

Exercise 4.7:

1. **Describe the concept of Conditional Probability and illustrate with an example.**

2. **In a company, 60% of the employees are male, and 70% of the employees have a college degree. If 40% of the employees are male and have a college degree, find the probability that a randomly selected employee is male given that the employee has a college degree.**

3. **Suppose you have two bags. Bag A contains 3 red and 2 blue balls, while Bag B contains 1 red and 4 blue balls. A ball is drawn at random from one of the bags, and it is blue. What is the probability that the ball was drawn from Bag B?**

4. **Consider an experiment where a die is rolled and then a coin is flipped. Compute the probability that the die shows a number greater than 4 given that the coin lands on heads.**

Exercise 4.8:

1. **Develop and prove the formula for finding the probability of the union of two events using the addition rule.**

2. **Given the events X and Y are mutually exclusive with P(X) = 0.25 and P(Y) = 0.35, find P(X or Y).**

3. **Analyze a situation where the multiplication rule of probability would be applicable and demonstrate its use through a real-world example.**

4. **Draw Venn diagrams as necessary to explain the concepts of probability involving intersection, union, and complement.**

Answers with Explanations

Solution to 4.5:

1. Probability is the measure of how likely an event is to occur. It is used in diverse fields such as gambling, statistics, and in many day-to-day areas such as risk assessment and decision-making.

2. The sample space for a six-sided die is {1, 2, 3, 4, 5, 6}. The favorable outcomes for rolling a number greater than 4 are {5, 6}. Probability $\frac{2}{6} = \frac{1}{3}$.

3. Total hearts: 13; Total kings: 4. Total heart kings: 1. Probability = $\frac{13+4-1}{52} = \frac{16}{52} = \frac{4}{13}$.

4. Since events A and B are independent, P(A and B) = P(A) × P(B) = 0.3 × 0.5 = 0.15.

5. Total combinations for three coins: $2^3 = 8$. Combinations with at least 1 head = 7. Probability = $\frac{7}{8}$.

6. Using inclusion-exclusion principle: P(M ∪ S) = P(M) + P(S) – P (M and S) = $\frac{18+12-5}{30}$ = 0.833.

Solution to 4.6:

1. The Addition Rule: P(C or D) = P(C) + P(D) - P(C and D). For example...

2. P(Red or Blue) $= \frac{4}{15} + \frac{5}{15} = \frac{9}{15} = \frac{3}{5}$.

3. P(C or D) = P(C) + P(D) - P(C and D) = 0.4 + 0.5 - 0.1 = 0.8.

4. P(Spade or Face Card) $= \frac{13}{52} + \frac{12}{52} - \frac{3}{52} = \frac{22}{52} = \frac{11}{26}$.

Solution to 4.7:

1. Conditional Probability: $P(A|B) = \frac{P(A \cap B)}{P(B)}$.

2. Applying Bayes' theorem: P(Male — Degree) $= \frac{0.4}{0.7} \approx 0.571$.

3. Use Bayes' theorem: P(Bag B — Blue) = ...

4. Consider the sample space with pairs...

5. Out of 6 possibilities, 2 (5, 6) are numbers ¿ 4. Since they must coincide with heads:

   P(¿4 — Heads) =...

Solution to 4.8:

1. Addition Rule Formula: Demonstrate using a complete analysis.

2. P(X or Y) = P(X) + P(Y) = 0.25 + 0.35 = 0.6 (since they are mutually exclusive).

3. Consider the situation "two dice rolled"... P(4 on one die and 5 on second).

4.3 Probability Distributions

In this section, we delve into the foundational concept of probability distributions, which are at the heart of statistical analysis and interpretational frameworks of data. Understanding these distributions is essential to interpret the probabilistic nature of different phenomena, ranging from simple experiments like tossing a coin to complex scenarios such as predicting stock market trends.

4.3.1 Discrete Distributions

Discrete probability distributions describe scenarios where the set of possible outcomes is discrete, or countable. Such distributions include the well-known Binomial, Poisson, and Geometric distributions. We will explore these in detail, providing examples and applications to help solidify the concepts.

Binomial Distribution

The Binomial distribution models the number of successes in n independent Bernoulli trials, each with a probability of success p. It is denoted as Binomial(n, p) with the probability mass function:

$$P(X = k) = \binom{n}{k} p^k (1-p)^{n-k}$$

where $\binom{n}{k}$ is the binomial coefficient.

Example 4.9: Suppose you have a fair coin and you flip it 10 times. Each flip of the coin is an independent Bernoulli trial with $p = 0.5$. The probability of getting exactly 4 heads is:

$$P(X = 4) = \binom{10}{4} (0.5)^4 (1-0.5)^{10-4} = \binom{10}{4} (0.5)^{10}$$

Calculating this gives:

$$P(X = 4) = \frac{10 \times 9 \times 8 \times 7}{4 \times 3 \times 2 \times 1} \times \frac{1}{1024} = 210 \times 0.0009765625$$

$$P(X = 4) \approx 0.205$$

Poisson Distribution

The Poisson distribution is used to model the number of events occurring within a fixed interval of time or space. It is parameterized by λ, which represents the average number of events in the interval. The probability mass function is:

$$P(X = k) = \frac{\lambda^k e^{-\lambda}}{k!}$$

Example 4.9: Consider a call center receiving an average of 3 calls per hour. The probability that exactly 5 calls are received in an hour can be computed using:

$$P(X = 5) = \frac{3^5 e^{-3}}{5!} = \frac{243e^{-3}}{120}$$

$$P(X = 5) \approx 0.1008$$

4.3.2 Continuous Distributions

Continuous probability distributions apply to scenarios where the set of possible outcomes is a continuum. Important examples include the Uniform, Exponential, and Normal distributions.

Uniform Distribution

A continuous uniform distribution is characterized by a constant probability density function (pdf) between two values a and b. It is given by:

$$f(x) = \begin{cases} \frac{1}{b-a}, & a \leq x \leq b \\ 0, & \text{otherwise} \end{cases}$$

Example 4.10: If a random variable X is uniformly distributed over the interval [0, 10], the probability density function is:

$$f(x) = \frac{1}{10 - 0} = 0.1$$

Thus, the probability of X lying between 2 and 5 is:

$$P(2 \leq X \leq 5) = \int_2^5 0.1\, dx = 0.1 \times (5 - 2) = 0.3$$

Normal Distribution

The Normal (or Gaussian) distribution is one of the most significant continuous distributions in statistics, characterized by its bell-shaped curve. It is defined by its mean μ and standard deviation σ, with the probability density function:

$$f(x) = \frac{1}{\sqrt{2\pi\sigma^2}} e^{-\frac{(x-\mu)^2}{2\sigma^2}}$$

Example 4.10: Assume the test scores of a large class follow a Normal distribution with a mean of 70 and a standard deviation of 10. The probability that a randomly selected student scored between 60 and 80 is evaluated using the standard normal table, by converting to the standard normal variable Z:

$$P(60 \leq X \leq 80) = P\left(\frac{60-70}{10} \leq Z \leq \frac{80-70}{10}\right)$$

$$= P(-1 \leq Z \leq 1)$$

Using standard normal distribution tables, we find:

$$P(-1 \leq Z \leq 1) \approx 0.6826$$

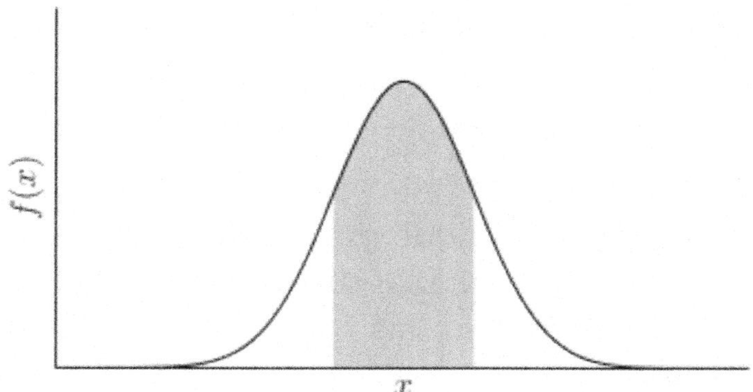

Figure 4.4: Normal distribution with the area shaded between $Z = -1$ and $Z = 1$.

4.3.3 Normal Distribution

The Normal distribution deserves special focus due to its pivotal role in the central limit theorem and its widespread applications.

Proposition 4.3.1. *The sum of a large number of independent and identically distributed random variables tends to follow a Normal distribution, regardless of the original distribution of the variables.*

This insight underscores the Central Limit Theorem and highlights why normality is inherent in many real-world processes.

To provide a clearer understanding, consider the table below summarizing key characteristics of major distributions discussed:

Distribution	**Parameters**	**Characteristics**
Binomial	n, p	Number of successes in n trials.
Poisson	λ	Number of events in a fixed interval.
Uniform (Continuous)	a, b	Equal probability within $[a,b]$.
Normal	μ, σ	Bell-shaped, symmetric about mean.

Table 4.2: Summary of Key Probability Distributions

Summary

Each distribution serves a unique purpose in modeling various types of data and events. The comprehension of these probability distributions not only aids in statistical analysis but also enriches understanding across diverse scientific disciplines.

4.4 Inferential Statistics

Inferential Statistics is the branch of statistics that allows us to make predictions or inferences about a population based on a sample of data drawn from that population. It provides the tools for hypothesis testing and estimating population parameters. This section will delve into the fundamental concepts of inferential statistics, including sampling methods, confidence intervals, and hypothesis testing, with a focus on providing clarity through detailed examples and explanations.

4.4.1 Sampling Methods

Sampling methods are crucial in inferential statistics because the conclusions about the entire population are drawn based on a sample. The choice of sampling method impacts the reliability and validity of the inference. Here, we discuss some common sampling methods.

Definition 4.4.1. *A sampling method is a systematic way of selecting a sample from a population. Different methods exist based on the nature and requirements of the study.*

Types of Sampling Methods

- **Simple Random Sampling**: Every member of the population has an equal chance of being selected. This can be achieved using lottery methods or random number generators.

- **Stratified Sampling**: The population is divided into distinct subgroups or strata, and random samples are taken from each stratum to ensure representation from each subgroup.

- **Systematic Sampling**: Members are selected at regular intervals from a sorted list. For instance, every 10th name on a list can be picked for the sample.

- **Cluster Sampling**: The population is divided into clusters, usually geographically, and entire clusters are randomly chosen.

- **Convenience Sampling**: Samples are chosen based on ease of access and availability, often used in preliminary research.

Example 4.12: Consider a university wants to study the average GPA of its students. They decide to use stratified sampling. The population is divided into strata based on year (freshman, sophomore, junior, senior). They choose 10 students randomly from each year to form the sample.

4.2.2 Confidence Intervals

Confidence intervals are used to estimate population parameters and express the degree of uncertainty or certainty in a sampling estimate.

Definition 4.4.2. *A confidence interval is a range of values derived from a sample statistic that is likely to contain the population parameter with a certain level of confidence (e.g., 95%).*

Calculating Confidence Intervals

The formula for a confidence interval is typically expressed as:

$$\bar{x} \pm z^* \left(\frac{\sigma}{\sqrt{n}}\right)$$

where $\bar{x}$ is the sample mean, z^* is the critical value from the standard normal distribution, σ is the population standard deviation, and n is the sample size.

Example 4.14: A researcher found that a sample of 50 students had a mean test score of 75 with a standard deviation of 8. Construct a 95% confidence interval for the true mean score.
Solution: First, find the critical value (z^*) for a 95% confidence level: $z^* = 1.96$.

$$\text{Margin of Error} = 1.96 \times \left(\frac{8}{\sqrt{50}}\right) \approx 2.2155$$

The confidence interval is:

$$75 \pm 2.2155 = (72.7845, 77.2155)$$

Thus, we are 95% confident that the true mean score is between 72.78 and 77.22.

Figure 4.5: Confidence Interval in a Normal Distribution

4.4.3 Hypothesis Testing

Hypothesis testing is a statistical method that uses sample data to evaluate a hypothesis about a population parameter.

Definition 4.4.3. *A* hypothesis test *is a procedure for testing a claim or hypothesis about a parameter in a population, using data measured in a sample.*

Steps in Hypothesis Testing

1. State the Null and Alternative Hypotheses: - The **null hypothesis** (H_0) is a statement of no effect or no difference, and it is what we assume to be true until proven otherwise. - The **alternative hypothesis** (H_a) is what we want to prove.

2. Choose the Significance Level (α): - Common choices are 0.05, 0.01, and 0.10.

3. Calculate the Test Statistic: - Compare the sample data to the population under the null hypothesis.

4. Make a Decision: - Based on the test statistic and the significance level, rejector fail to reject the null hypothesis.

Example 4.15: A company claims their light bulbs last an average of 1000 hours. A sample of 40 bulbs has a mean lifetime of 990 hours with a standard deviation of 30 hours. Test the claim at a 5% significance level.
Solution:
1. Hypotheses: - $H_0 : \mu = 1000$ - $H_a : \mu < 1000$

2. Significance Level: $\alpha = 0.05$

3. Calculate Test Statistic:

$$z = \frac{\bar{x} - \mu}{\frac{\sigma}{\sqrt{n}}} = \frac{990 - 1000}{\frac{30}{\sqrt{40}}} = -2.1082$$

4. Decision: - The critical value for $\alpha = 0.05$ in a left-tailed test is -1.645. Since $-2.1082 < -1.645$, we reject H_0.

Thus, there is sufficient evidence to conclude that the average life of the bulbs is less than 1000 hours.

Element	Description
Null Hypothesis (H_0)	Assumed true until evidence suggests otherwise. Usually a statement of no effect.
Alternative Hypothesis (H_a)	Contradicts H_0, representing what we seek evidence for.
Significance Level (α)	Probability of rejecting H_0 when it is true (Type I error).
Test Statistic	Value computed from sample data used to decide whether to reject H_0.
P-value	Probability of observing a more extreme result under the null hypothesis.
Critical Value	Threshold value for deciding whether to reject H_0.

Table 4.3: Key Elements of Hypothesis Testing

Through careful application of sampling methods, confidence intervals, and hypothesis testing, inferential statistics facilitate the drawing of meaningful conclusions from data, thus proving indispensable for decision-making in various fields.

Exercises

Exercise 4.5:

Consider a population where the mean annual income is known to be 50,000. A sample size of 30 is randomly selected with a sample mean of 52,000 and a standard deviation of 5,000. Assume that the annual income is normally distributed. Construct a 95

Exercise 4.6:

A medical researcher claims that the proportion of people who have a certain disease is less than 0.1. In a sample of 1000 people, 80 are found to have the disease. Conduct a hypothesis test to test the researcher's claim at a significance level of 0.05.

Exercise 4.7:

Distinguish between Type I and Type II errors in hypothesis testing. Provide examples of each error in the context of a quality control testing process in a manufacturing company.

Exercise 4.8:

Using the data below, perform an independent t-test to determine if there is a significant difference in the means of two groups. Group A: [5, 7, 8, 6, 9], Group B: [6, 9, 11, 8, 10]. Use a significance level of 0.05.

Group	Mean	Standard Deviation
A	7	1.58
B	8.8	1.48

Answers with Explanations

Solution to 4.5:

To construct the 95,

$$\bar{x} \pm t^* \frac{s}{\sqrt{n}}$$

where $\bar{x}$ = 52,000, s = 5,000, n = 30, and t^* is the t-value from the t-distribution for a 95.

Substituting these values, the confidence interval is:

$$52,000 \pm 2.045 \left(\frac{5,000}{\sqrt{30}} \right) \approx 52,000 \pm 1,867$$

Thus, the interval is [50, 133, 53, 867].

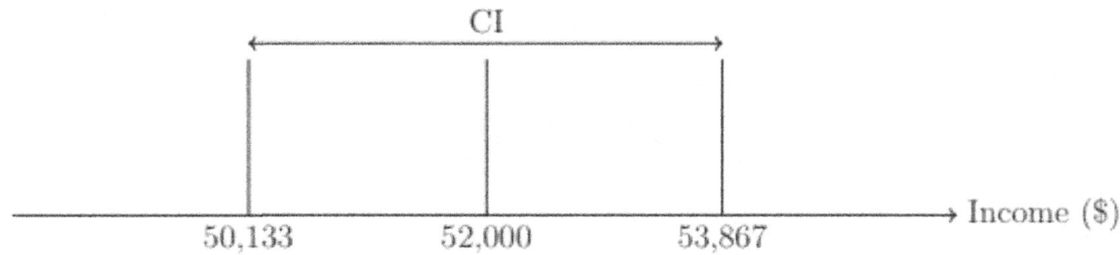

Solution to 4.6:

To test the researcher's claim, we set up the hypothesis:

$$H_0 : p = 0.1$$
$$H_a : p < 0.1$$

Using the sample proportion $\hat{p} = \frac{80}{1000} = 0.08$, we calculate the test statistic:

$$z = \frac{\hat{p} - p_0}{\sqrt{\frac{p_0(1-p_0)}{n}}} = \frac{0.08 - 0.1}{\sqrt{\frac{0.1\times0.9}{1000}}} \approx -2.11$$

Comparing $z = -2.11$ to the critical value of $z = -1.645$ at $a = 0.05$, we reject H_0. Therefore, there is sufficient evidence to support the claim that the proportion is less than 0.1.

Solution to 4.7:

A Type I error occurs when we reject the null hypothesis when it is in fact true. For example, in a quality control setting, this error happens when a product that actually meets quality standards is rejected, leading to unnecessary waste.

Conversely, a Type II error occurs when we fail to reject the null hypothesis when it is false. For instance, a faulty product passing the quality check represents this error, potentially leading to customer dissatisfaction and brand damage.

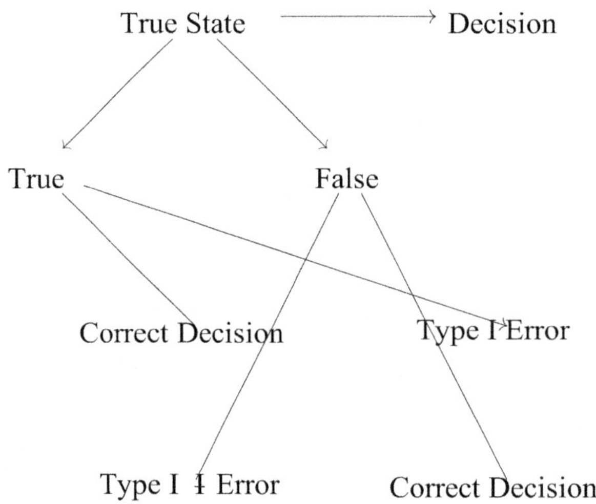

Solution to 4.8:

For the t-test, we first calculate the test statistic:

$$t = \frac{\bar{x}_1 - \bar{x}_2}{\sqrt{\frac{s_1^2}{n_1} + \frac{s_2^2}{n_2}}}$$

where $\bar{x}_1 = 7, \bar{x}_2 = 8.8, s_1 = 1.58, s_2 = 1.48, n_1 = n_2 = 5$.

The calculated t-value is:

$$t = \frac{7 - 8.8}{\sqrt{\frac{1.58^2}{5} + \frac{1.48^2}{5}}} \approx -2.196$$

With 8 degrees of freedom, using a t-table, $t_{critical} = 2.306$. Since $|t| < t_{critical}$, we fail to reject the null hypothesis. There is no significant difference between the group means at $a = 0.05$.

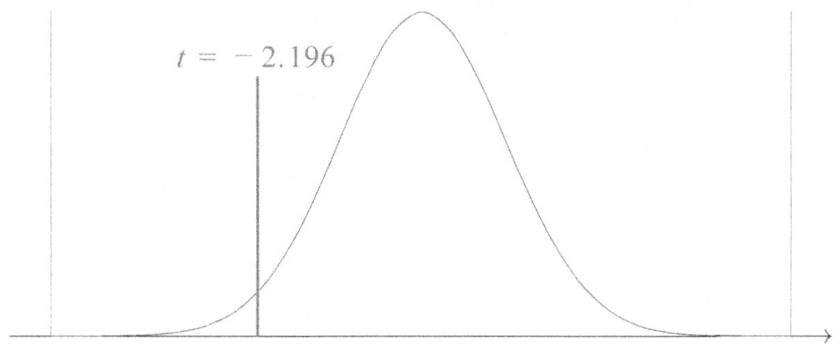

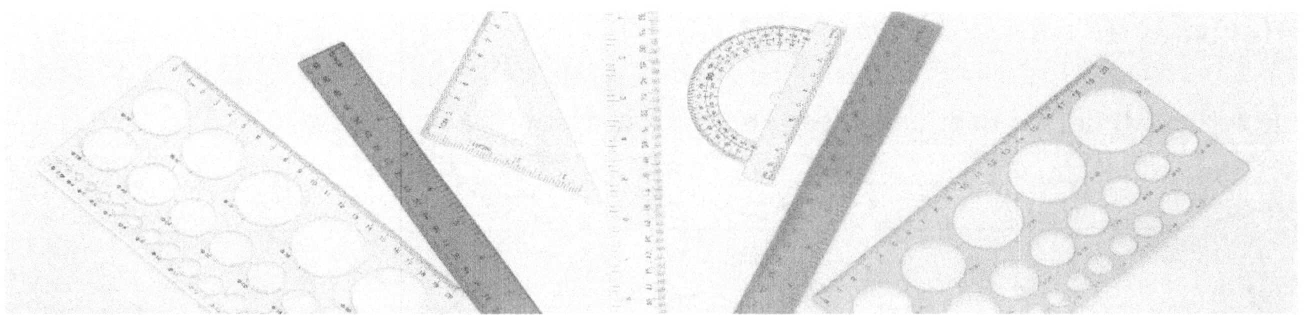

5. Functions and Graphs

5.1 Understanding Functions

Functions are fundamental concepts in mathematics, serving as building blocks for expressing relationships between quantities. They describe how one quantity depends on another and are omnipresent in both theoretical studies and real-world applications. In this section, we will delve into the definition and notation of functions, explore the concepts of domain and range, and examine various types of functions.

5.1.1 Definition and Notation

Definition 5.1.1 *A function f from a set X to a set Y is a relation that assigns exactly one element of Y to each element of X. The set X is called the domain of the function, and the set Y is called the codomain.*

The notation $f : X \to Y$ is used to denote that f is a function with domain X and codomain Y. For an element $x \in X$, $f(x)$ denotes the element of Y that f assigns to x. This value is known as the *image* of x under f.

Example 5.1: Consider the function $f : \mathrm{R} \to \mathrm{R}$ defined by $f(x) = x^2$. This function assigns to each real number x its square. If $x = 3$, then $f(3) = 9$. Similarly, if $x = -2$, then $f(-2) = 4$.

5.1.2 Domain and Range

Definition 5.1.2 *The domain of a function $f : X \to Y$ is the set X, whereas the range of f is the set of all images $f(x)$ for $x \in X$.*

The domain of a function defines the permissible inputs, whereas the range provides a description of the outputs that the function can produce.

Example 5.2: Let's consider the function $f(x) = \sqrt{x}$. The domain of this function is $\{x \in R : x \geq 0\}$ since the square root of a negative number is not a real number. The range of the function is $\{y \in R : y \geq 0\}$ since any non-negative number has a non-negative square root.

In graphical representations, the domain and range can often be visualized as the projection of the graph of a function onto the horizontal and vertical axes, respectively.

5.1.3 Types of Functions

Functions can be categorized into different types based on their properties and characteristics:

- **Linear Functions:** Defined by $f(x) = ax+b$, where a and b are constants. Linear functions have constant slopes and produce straight lines.

Example 5.3: Consider $f(x) = 2x + 3$. Here, $a = 2$ is the slope and $b = 3$ is the y-intercept. The graph is a straight line that passes through the point (0,3) with a slope of 2.

- **Quadratic Functions:** Generally expressed as $f(x) = ax^2+bx+c$. These functions form parabolas.

Example 5.4: The function $f(x) = x^2 - 4x + 5$ is quadratic. Its graph is a parabola with vertex form. Completing the square or using the vertex formula shows the vertex as (2,1).

$$\begin{aligned} f(x) &= x^2 - 4x + 5 \\ &= (x - 2)^2 + 1 \end{aligned}$$

- **Exponential Functions:** Described by $f(x) = a \cdot b^x$, where b is a positive real number different from 1. These functions exhibit exponential growth or decay.

Example 5.5: For $f(x) = 3 \cdot 2^x$, this represents exponential growth with base 2. The function rapidly increases as x increases.

- **Logarithmic Functions:** These are the inverses of exponential functions, given by $f(x) = \log_b x$.

> **Example 5.6:** Consider $f(x) = \log_2(x)$. This function measures the power to which the base 2 must be raised to yield x, displaying slow growth as x increases.

- **Trigonometric Functions:** Such as $\sin(x)$, $\cos(x)$, and $\tan(x)$, these functions are crucial for modeling periodic phenomena.

> **Example 5.7:** The function $f(x) = \sin(x)$ produces a wave-like graph ideal for describing oscillations.

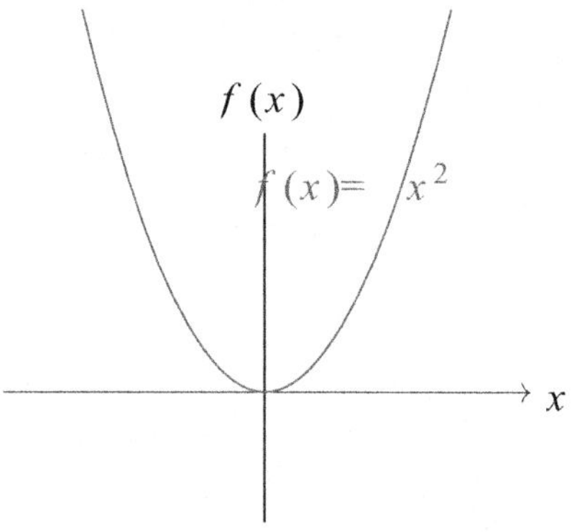

Figure 5.1: Graph of the quadratic function $f(x) = x^2$.

Conclusion

This section highlighted essential foundations of functions ranging from definitions to diverse examples and visual illustrations. Understanding these concepts provides a comprehensive backdrop for exploring more sophisticated mathematical analyses and applications across varied fields.

Exercises

Exercise 5.1:

1. **Define a function. Include details about function notation and how a function is different from a general relation.**

2. **Consider the function $f(x) = x^2 + 3x + 5$. Identify the domain and range of this function.**

3. **Graph the function $f(x) = 2x + 1$ and specify its domain and range.**

4. **Provide examples of three different types of functions, and describe their characteristics.**

5. **Determine whether the relation represented by the set of ordered pairs $\{(1, 2),(2, 3),(3, 4),(4, 4)\}$ is a function. Justify your answer.**

Exercise 5.2:

Consider the function $g(x) = \frac{1}{x-2}$. Identify and explain any restrictions on the domain. Discuss how these restrictions affect the graph of the function.

Exercise 5.3:

Describe and compare the graphs of the following functions: $h(x) = \sqrt{x}$ and $k(x) = \sqrt[3]{x}$. Provide a rough sketch and comment on the domain and range of each function.

Exercise 5.4:

Find the inverse of the function $f(x) = 3x - 7$. Then, determine the domain and range of both the function and its inverse.

Answers with Explanations

Solution to 5.1:

1. A function is a relation between a set of inputs and a set of permissible outputs, where each input is related to exactly one output. Function notation is typically represented as $f(x)$, where f denotes the function and x is an element from the domain.

2. The function $f(x) = x^2 + 3x + 5$ is a polynomial function with a domain of all real numbers R. The range is $[5,\infty)$ because the quadratic term x^2 ensures the output is always ≥ 5.

3. The graph of $f(x) = 2x + 1$ is a straight line with a slope of 2 and a y-intercept of 1. The domain and range are both all real numbers R.

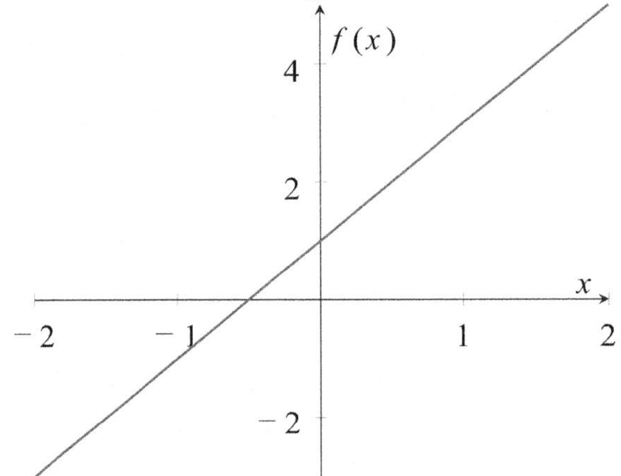

4. Examples of different types of functions include:

   a. Linear Function: $f(x) = 3x + 2$, characterized by a constant rate of change.

   b. Quadratic Function: $g(x) = x^2 - 4x + 4$, characterized by a parabolic graph.

   c. Exponential Function: $h(x) = 2^x$, characterized by rapid growth or decay.

5. The relation $\{(1, 2),(2, 3),(3, 4),(4, 4)\}$ is a function because each input maps to a unique output.

Solution to 5.2:

The function $g(x) = \frac{1}{x-2}$ has a domain of all real numbers except $x = 2$, because the denominator cannot be zero. This restriction creates a vertical asymptote at $x = 2$ where the function is undefined. The range is all real numbers since the function can produce both asymptotically large positive and negative values.

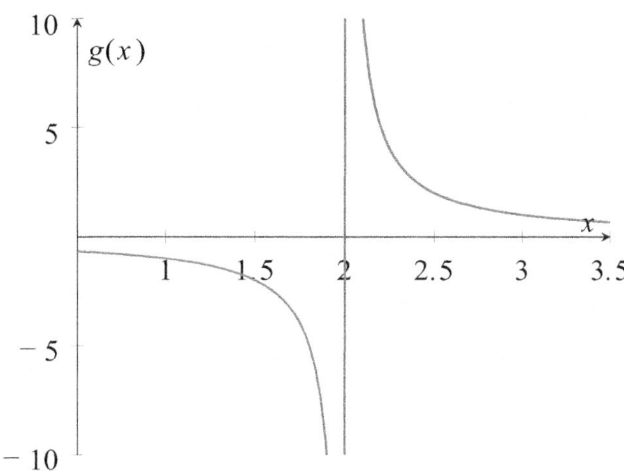

Solution to 5.3:

The function $h(x) = \sqrt{x}$ is defined for $x \geq 0$ and its graph is a half parabola opening to the right. Its range is $[0,\infty)$.

The function $k(x) = \sqrt[3]{x}$ is defined for all real numbers and its graph includes both positive and negative values. The range is all real numbers R.

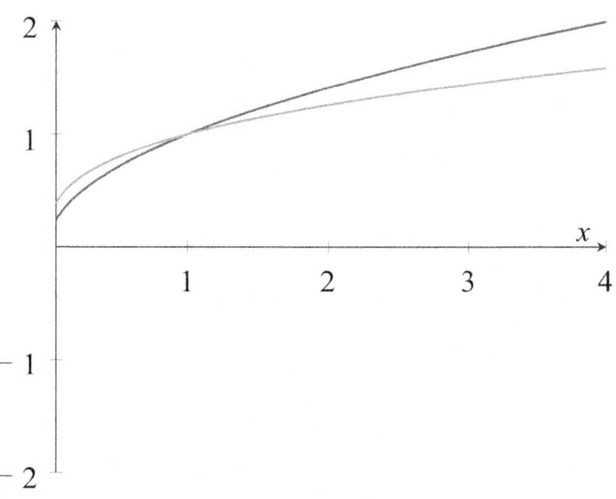

Solution to 5.4:

To find the inverse of $f(x) = 3x - 7$, swap x and y to get $x = 3y - 7$, and solve for y.

$$y = \frac{x+7}{3}$$

The inverse function is $f^{-1}(x) = \frac{x+7}{3}$.

The domain of $f(x) = 3x-7$ is all real numbers R and its range is also all real numbers. Similarly, the domain and range of the inverse function are both all real numbers R.

5.2 Linear Functions

Linear functions are pivotal in understanding the world of mathematics, providing a foundation for algebraic concepts and real-world applications. Their simplicity, represented by a straight line when graphed, makes them accessible and integral to students at the high school level and beyond.

5.2.1 Graphing Linear Functions

Graphing linear functions involves plotting points on a coordinate plane, resulting in a straight line. Linear functions are usually expressed in the form $y = mx + b$, where m is the slope, and b is the y-intercept.

Definition 5.2.1 *A linear function is any function that can be expressed in the form $f(x) = mx + b$, where m and b are real numbers. The graph of a linear function is a straight line.*

Example 5.8: Graph the linear function $f(x) = 2x + 3$.
Solution: To graph $f(x) = 2x + 3$, follow these steps:
1. Identify the y-intercept $b = 3$. This is the point where the line crosses the y-axis.
2. Use the slope $m = 2$ to find another point. Since the slope is 2, rise 2 units and run 1 unit to the right from the y-intercept. This gives the point (1,5).
3. Draw a line through the points (0,3) and (1,5).
The resulting graph is a line passing through these points.

The resulting graph is a line passing through these points.

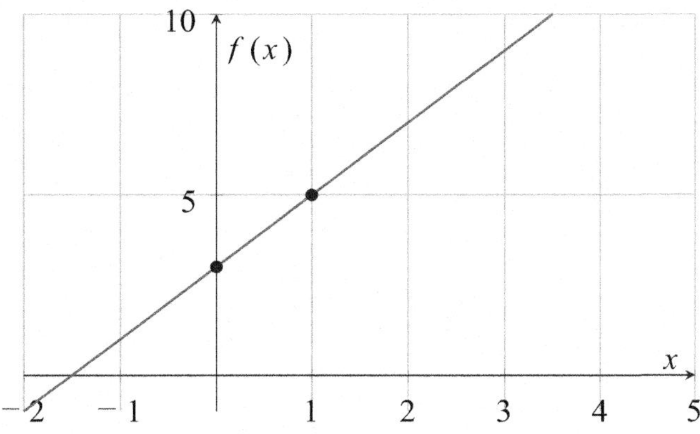

5.2.2 Intersections and Slopes

The intersection points of linear functions provide valuable information about their solutions.

Definition 5.2.2. *The slope of a linear function $y = mx + b$ is the ratio $\frac{\Delta y}{\Delta x}$, where Δy is the change in y and Δx is the change in x. It indicates the steepness and direction of the line.*

Example 5.9: Find the intersection point of the lines $y = 2x + 3$ and $y = -x + 1$. Set the equations equal to find the intersection:

$$2x + 3 = -x + 1$$

Add x to both sides:

$$3x + 3 = 1$$

Subtract 3 from both sides:

$$3x = -2$$

Divide by 3:

$$x = -\frac{2}{3}$$

Substitute $x = -\frac{2}{3}$ back into the first equation to find y:

$$y = 2\left(-\frac{2}{3}\right) + 3 = -\frac{4}{3} + 3 = \frac{9}{3} - \frac{4}{3} = \frac{5}{3}$$

Thus, the intersection point is $\left(-\frac{2}{3}, \frac{5}{3}\right)$.

Graphically:

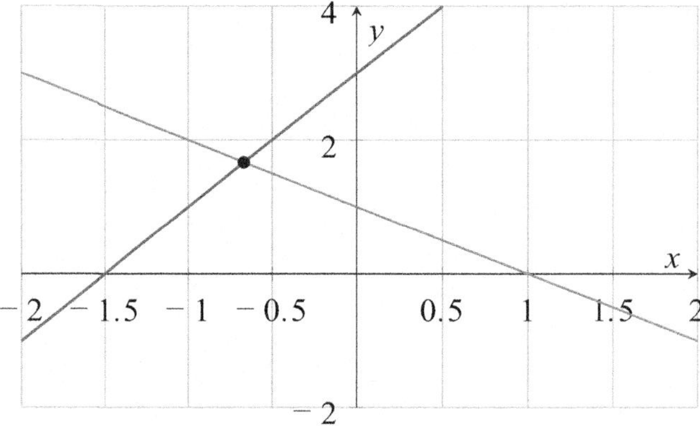

5.2.3 Applications and Models

Linear functions model direct relationships between variables and have numerous applications across various fields such as economics, physics, and social sciences.

Example 5.10: Suppose a company has fixed costs of 500 and produces items at a cost of 8 per item. Express the total cost C as a linear function of the number of items x produced. The total cost can be expressed as:

$$C(x) = 8x + 500$$

If the company produces 100 items, the total cost is:

$$C(100) = 8(100) + 500 = 800 + 500 = 1300$$

Thus, producing 100 items will cost the company \$1300.

Conclusion

Linear functions are therefore essential tools in both mathematical theory and practical application, providing a stepping stone to more complex concepts and real-life problem solving.

Exercises

Exercise 5.5:

Consider the linear function $f(x) = 3x + 2$.

1. Graph the function on the Cartesian plane.
2. Calculate the slope of the line.
3. Determine the y-intercept and explain its significance on the graph.
4. Find the x-intercept and explain how it can be derived from the function.

Exercise 5.6:

Given two points $A(1,2)$ and $B(3,6)$, find the equation of the line passing through these points.

1. Calculate the slope of the line using the given points.
2. Use the point-slope form to write the equation of the line.
3. Convert the equation to slope-intercept form $y = mx + b$.

Exercise 5.7:

The cost to produce x items is given by the linear function $C(x) = 5x + 20$.

1. Interpret the slope and y-intercept in the context of this problem.
2. Calculate the cost to produce 100 items.
3. Determine the number of items produced when the cost is $70.

Exercise 5.8:

Analyze the intersection of the following two lines: $y = 2x + 1$ and $y = -x + 4$.

1. Find the point of intersection algebraically.
2. Discuss the significance of the point of intersection.
3. Graph both lines and verify the solution visually.

Answers with Explanations

Solution to 5.5:

1. To graph $f(x) = 3x+2$, plot the y-intercept at (0, 2) and use the slope, which is 3, meaning each increase of 1 in x corresponds to an increase of 3 in y.

2. The slope of the line is 3, indicating the line rises 3 units for every 1 unit it moves to the right.

3. The y-intercept is 2. It represents the point where the line crosses the y-axis when $x = 0$.

4. Setting $f(x) = 0$ gives $0 = 3x+2$, hence $x = \frac{-2}{3}$. The x-intercept is $-\frac{2}{3}$, where the line crosses the x-axis.

Solution to 5.6:

1. The slope m is calculated as $m = \frac{6-2}{3-1} = 2$.

2. Using point-slope form $y-y_1 = m(x-x_1)$ with $A(1, 2)$, it becomes $y - 2 = 2(x-1)$.

3. Expanding gives $y - 2 = 2x - 2$, or $y = 2x$.

Solution to 5.7:

1. The slope 5 represents the cost increase per item produced. The y-intercept 20 is the fixed cost regardless of production.

2. Plugging 100 into the function gives $C(100) = 5(100) + 20 = 520$.

3. Solving $70 = 5x + 20$ for x gives $x = 10$ items.

Solution to 5.8:

1. Solve $2x + 1 = -x + 4$. Rearrange to $3x = 3$, hence $x = 1$. Substitute into one equation to find $y = 3$. Intersection is (1,3).

2. The intersection point represents the solution where both linear equations are true simultaneously.

3. Graphing confirms the intersection at (1, 3) using a tikz figure:

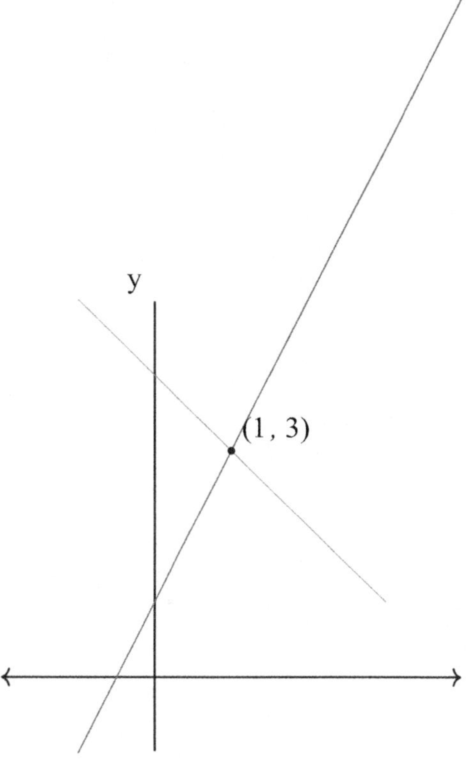

5.3 Non-linear Functions

In this section, we delve into the realm of non-linear functions. These functions, in contrast to linear functions, exhibit curves in their graphs and are defined by mathematical expressions that involve variables raised to powers other than one. Our focus will be on three major types of non-linear functions: Quadratic Functions, Exponential and Logarithmic Functions, and Piecewise Functions.

5.3.1 Quadratic Functions

A quadratic function is a second-degree polynomial function of the form:

$$f(x) = ax^2 + bx + c$$

where a, b, and c are constants and $a \neq 0$. The graph of a quadratic function is a parabola. If $a > 0$, the parabola opens upwards, while if $a < 0$, it opens downwards.

Example 5.11: Consider the function $f(x) = 2x^2 - 4x + 1$. Let's find its vertex, axis of symmetry, and intercepts.
Vertex:

$$x = -\frac{b}{2a} = -\frac{-4}{2 \times 2} = 1$$
$$f(1) = 2(1)^2 - 4(1) + 1 = -1$$

Vertex is at (1,−1)
Axis of Symmetry:

$$x = 1$$

Y-intercept:

$$f(0) = 2(0)^2 - 4(0) + 1 = 1$$

Roots (X-intercepts):

$$x^2 - 4x + 1 = 0$$
$$x = \frac{-b \pm \sqrt{b^2 - 4ac}}{2a} = \frac{4 \pm \sqrt{(-4)^2 - 4 \cdot 2 \cdot 1}}{2 \cdot 2}$$
$$x = \frac{4 \pm \sqrt{8}}{4} = \frac{4 \pm 2\sqrt{2}}{4}$$
$$x = 1 \pm \frac{\sqrt{2}}{2}$$

Below is the graph of this quadratic function:

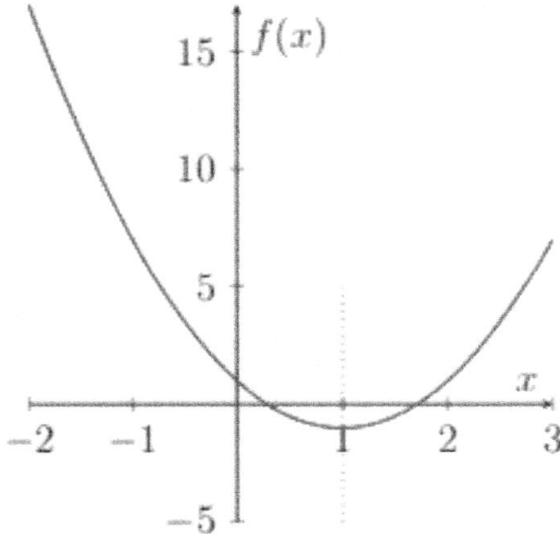

Figure 5.2: Graph of the quadratic function $f(x) = 2x^2 - 4x + 1$.

5.3.2 Exponential and Logarithmic Functions

Exponential functions have the form $f(x) = a \cdot b^x$, where a is a non-zero constant, b is the base of the exponential, and $b > 0$. These functions describe many real-world situations like population growth, radioactive decay, and compound interest.

Example 5.12: Consider the function $f(x) = 3 \cdot 2^x$. Find the y-intercept and the value of the function when $x = 3$.
Y-intercept:

$$f(0) = 3 \cdot 2^0 = 3$$
$$f(3) = 3 \cdot 2^3 = 3 \cdot 8 = 24$$

Logarithmic functions are inverses of exponential functions and have the form $f(x) = a \cdot \log_b(x)$, where b is the base of the logarithm. The exponential equation $b^y = x$ is equivalent to the logarithmic equation $y = \log_b(x)$.

Example 5.13: Convert the logarithmic expression $\log_2(8)$ to its exponential form.

$$\log_2(8) = x \Rightarrow 2^x = 8$$
$$x = 3 \text{ since } 2^3 = 8$$

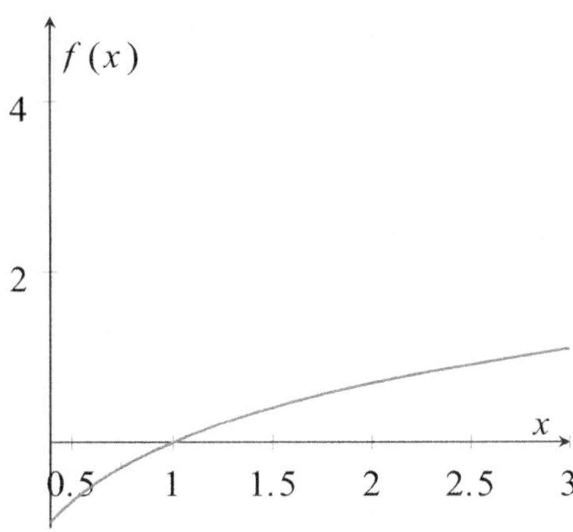

Figure 5.3: Graph of the logarithmic function $f(x) = \ln(x)$.

5.3.3 Piecewise Functions

Piecewise functions are defined by different expressions depending on the value of the independent variable. These functions are often used to describe situations where a rule or relationship changes as the input changes.

Example 5.14: Consider the function:

$$f(x) = \begin{cases} x^2 & \text{if } x \leq 1 \\ 2x + 1 & \text{if } x > 1 \end{cases}$$

Evaluate $f(x)$ for $x = -1$, $x = 1$, and $x = 2$.

Solution:

$$f(-1) = (-1)^2 = 1$$
$$f(1) = (1)^2 = 1$$
$$f(2) = 2(2) + 1 = 5$$

Below is the piecewise function graph:

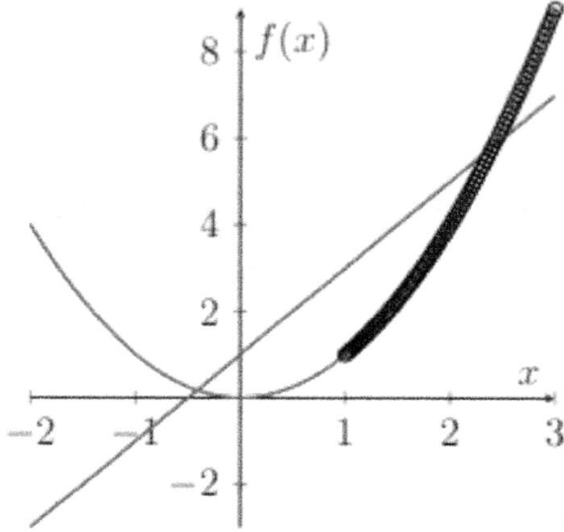

Figure 5.4: Graph of the piecewise function $f(x)$.

Conclusion

With these examples and illustrations, you should now have a robust understanding of various non-linear functions and their applications.

Exercises

Exercise 5.9:

Consider the quadratic function $f(x) = ax^2 + bx + c$.

1. Given that $f(x) = 2x^2 - 4x + 3$, find the vertex of the parabola.

2. Determine whether the parabola opens upwards or downwards and explain why.

3. Calculate the axis of symmetry.

4. Find the x-intercepts, if any, of the parabola.

Exercise 5.10:

Graph the exponential function $g(x) = 3e^{0.5x}$ considering the following:

1. Determine the y-intercept of the function.

2. Calculate the value of $g(x)$ when $x = 0,1,2,3$.

3. Sketch the graph of $g(x)$ over the interval $x \in [-2,2]$.

4. Discuss the behavior of the function as $x \to -\infty$ and $x \to \infty$.

Exercise 5.11:

Solve and graph the piecewise function defined by:

$$h(x) = \begin{cases} 2x + 3 & \text{if } x < 0 \\ x^2 & \text{if } 0 \leq x \leq 3 \\ 4 - x & \text{if } x > 3 \end{cases}$$

1. Find the point(s) where $h(x)$ is not continuous.

2. Calculate $h(x)$ for $x = -2,0,1,4$.

3. Sketch the graph of the piecewise function and indicate breaks in the graph.

Exercise 5.12:

Analyze the logarithmic function $j(x) = \log_2(x - 1)$.

1. Determine the domain of $j(x)$.

2. Solve for x such that $j(x) = 3$.

3. Graph the function $j(x)$ and find the plot's vertical asymptote.

4. Explain how transformations affect the graph of $j(x)$.

Answers with Explanations

Solution to 5.9:

For the quadratic function $f(x) = 2x^2 - 4x + 3$:

1. The vertex is given by the formula $x = -\frac{b}{2a}$. Thus, $x = \frac{4}{4} =$. Substituting back, $f(1) = 2(1)^2 - 4(1) + 3 = 1$. So, the vertex is (1,1).

2. Since $a = 2 > 0$, the parabola opens upwards.

3. The axis of symmetry is $x = 1$.

4. Using the quadratic formula $x = \frac{-b\pm\sqrt{b^2-4ac}}{2a}$, the x-intercepts are found by solving $2x^2 - 4x + 3 = 0$.

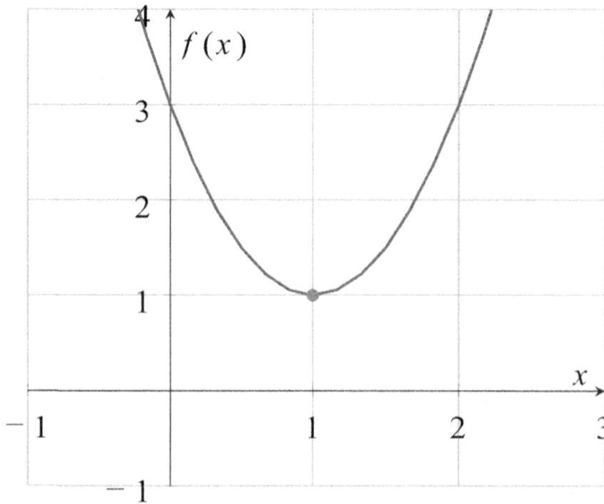

Solution to 5.10:

For the function $g(x) = 3e^{0.5x}$:

1. The y-intercept is $g(0) = 3e^0 = 3$.

2. The values are: $g(1) = 3e^{0.5}, g(2) = 3e^1, g(3) = 3e^{1.5}$.

3. Sketch the graph using these points and describing the exponential growth.

4. As $x \to -\infty$, $g(x) \to 0$; as $x \to \infty$, $g(x) \to \infty$.

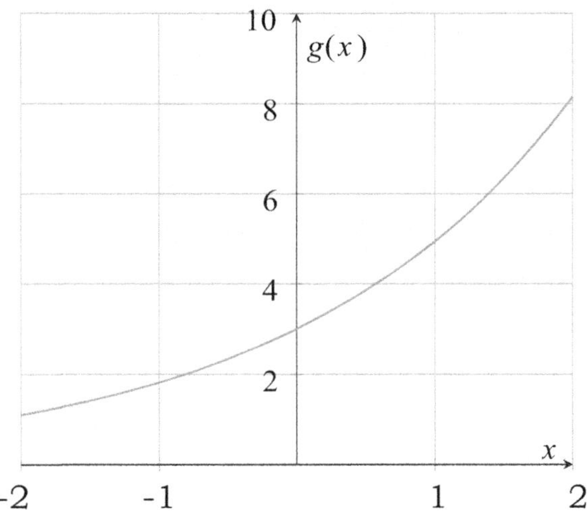

Solution to 5.11:

For the piecewise function $h(x)$:

1. The points of discontinuity occur at $x = 0$ and $x = 3$.

2. Calculations: $h(-2) = -1, h(0) = 0, h(1) = 1, h(4) = 0$.

3. The graph:

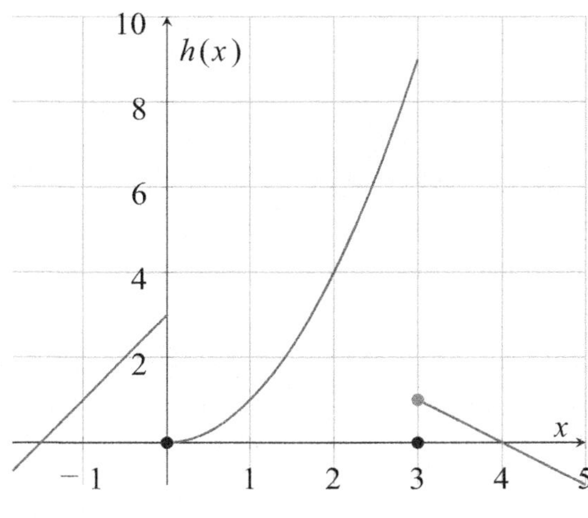

Solution to 5.12:

For the logarithmic function $j(x) = \log_2(x - 1)$:

1. Domain is $x > 1$.
2. Solving $\log_2(x - 1) = 3$ gives $(x - 1) = 8$, so $x = 9$.
3. Graph the function and note the vertical asymptote at $x = 1$.
4. Transformations affect shifts in the graph as follows.

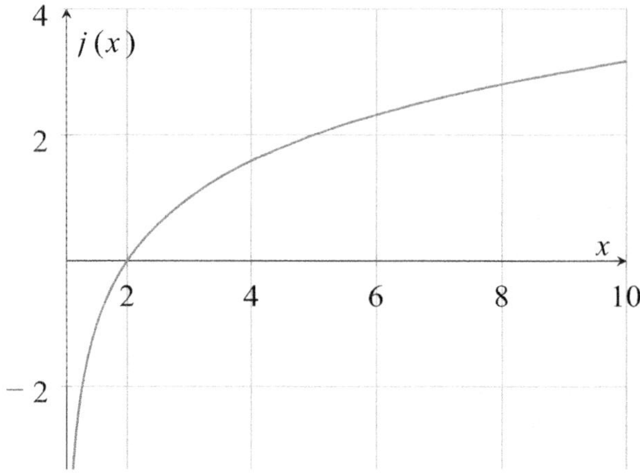

5.4 Transformations of Functions

In this section, we explore the various transformations that can be applied to functions to change their graphs in different ways. Understanding these transformations is crucial for interpreting and graphing functions correctly in complex mathematical models. We will delve into translations, reflections, dilations, and compressions, illustrating each with detailed examples and figures.

5.4.1 Translations

Translations involve shifting the graph of a function horizontally, vertically, or in both directions. This process does not affect the shape or orientation of the graph; it only moves the position.

Definition 5.4.1. *A translation of a function f(x) by a units horizontally and b units vertically produces a new function g(x) such that:*

$$g(x) = f(x - a) + b$$

where a is a horizontal shift and b is a vertical shift.

Example 5.15: Consider the function $f(x) = x^2$. Let's translate this function 3 units to the right and 2 units up.
The new function is:

$$g(x) = (x - 3)^2 + 2$$

The vertex of the function shifts from (0,0) to (3,2).

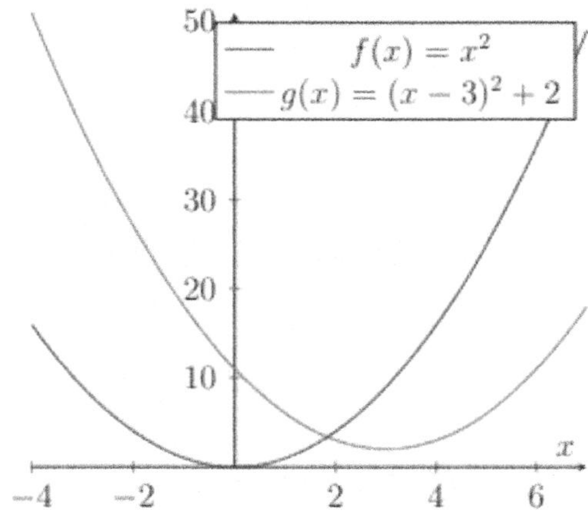

Figure 5.5: Translation of the function $f(x) = x^2$.

5.4.2 Reflections

Reflections flip the graph of a function over a specified axis, changing the orientation but retaining the shape.

Definition 5.4.2. *A reflection of a function f(x) over the x-axis yields g(x) = −f(x), while a reflection over the y-axis transforms it to g(x) = f(−x).*

Example 5.16: Consider $f(x) = \sqrt{x}$. Reflecting this function over the x-axis produces $g(x) = -\sqrt{x}$.

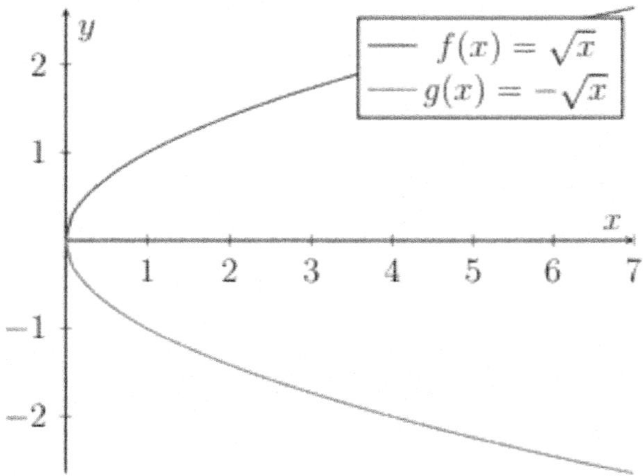

Figure 5.6: Reflection of the function $f(x) = \sqrt{x}$ over the x-axis.

5.4.3 Dilations and Compressions

Dilations and compressions affect the size of the graph by expanding or contracting it horizontally or vertically.

Definition 5.4.3. *A dilation or compression of a function f(x) involves multiplying x by a constant c for horizontal changes, or f(x) by a constant d for vertical changes:*

$$g(x) = f(cx) \text{ (horizontal compression/dilation)}$$

$$g(x) = d \cdot f(x) \text{ (vertical compression/dilation)}$$

where $0 < c < 1$ compresses and $c > 1$ stretches the graph horizontally, and similar for d vertically.

Example 5.17: Consider the linear function $f(x) = 2x+1$. Applying a vertical stretch by a factor of 3 gives:

$$g(x) = 3(2x + 1) = 6x + 3$$

The graph becomes steeper.

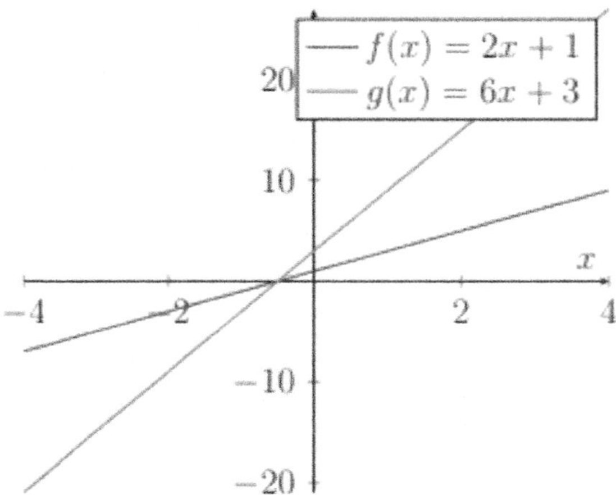

Figure 5.7: Vertical dilation of the function $f(x) = 2x + 1$.

Conclusion

Overall, transformations provide powerful tools for manipulating and understanding the behavior of functions graphically. By mastering translations, reflections, dilations, and compressions, students can handle complex scenarios and explore the depths of mathematical modeling.

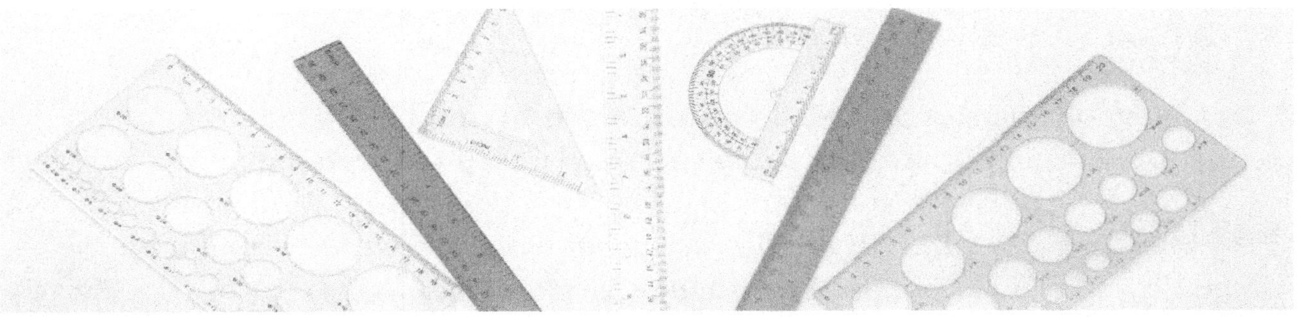

6. Polynomials

6.1 Introduction to Polynomials

Polynomials are a fundamental concept in algebra and are extensively used in various areas of mathematics and science. This section delves into the basics of polynomials, their definitions, degrees, and the operations involved such as addition, subtraction, and an introduction to polynomial functions.

6.1.1 Definition and Degree

Definition 6.1.1. *A* polynomial *is an algebraic expression composed of variables, coefficients, and exponents that are non-negative integers. The general form of a polynomial in one variable x is:*

$$P(x) = a_n x^n + a_{n-1} x^{n-1} + \cdots + a_1 x + a_0$$

where $a_n, a_{n-1}, \ldots, a_1, a_0$ *are constants called* coefficients, *n is a non-negative integer and is the* degree *of the polynomial if* $a_n \neq 0$.

The degree of a polynomial is the highest power of the variable present in the polynomial equation. If $a_n \neq 0$, the polynomial is said to have degree n.

Example 6.1: Consider the polynomial $P(x) = 4x^5 - 3x^3 + x - 7$.

- The degree of this polynomial is 5, as the highest power of x is x^5.

- The leading coefficient is 4, which is the coefficient of the term with the highest degree.

6.1.2 Addition and Subtraction

Polynomials can be added or subtracted by combining like terms. Like terms are terms that have the same variables raised to the same power.

Proposition 6.1.1. *To add or subtract polynomials, align the terms with the same degree and perform the operation on their coefficients.*

Example 6.2: Add the polynomials $P(x) = 3x^2 + 2x + 5$ and $Q(x) = 4x^2 - x + 3$.

$$\begin{aligned} P(x) + Q(x) &= (3x^2 + 2x + 5) + (4x^2 - x + 3) \\ &= (3x^2 + 4x^2) + (2x - x) + (5 + 3) \\ &= 7x^2 + x + 8 \end{aligned}$$

Subtract the polynomials:

$$\begin{aligned} P(x) - Q(x) &= (3x^2 + 2x + 5) - (4x^2 - x + 3) \\ &= (3x^2 - 4x^2) + (2x + x) + (5 - 3) \\ &= -x^2 + 3x + 2 \end{aligned}$$

6.1.3 Polynomial Functions

A *polynomial function* is a mathematical function that is represented by a polynomial expression. The form of a polynomial function is typically described by:

$$f(x) = a_n x^n + a_{n-1} x^{n-1} + \ldots + a_1 x + a_0$$

where the function $f(x)$ depends on the variable x.

Definition 6.1.2. *A polynomial function is continuous and differentiable everywhere on* R. *The graph of a polynomial function is a smooth, continuous curve.*

Example 6.3: Consider the polynomial function $f(x) = 2x^3 - 3x^2 + 5$.

- This function is a cubic polynomial, as the highest degree is 3.

- The domain of $f(x)$ is all real numbers R.

For $f(x)$, evaluate at $x = 1$:

$$f(1) = 2(1)^3 - 3(1)^2 + 5 = 2 - 3 + 5 = 4$$

Graphical Representation

To better understand polynomial functions, let's explore their graphical representations using the example above.

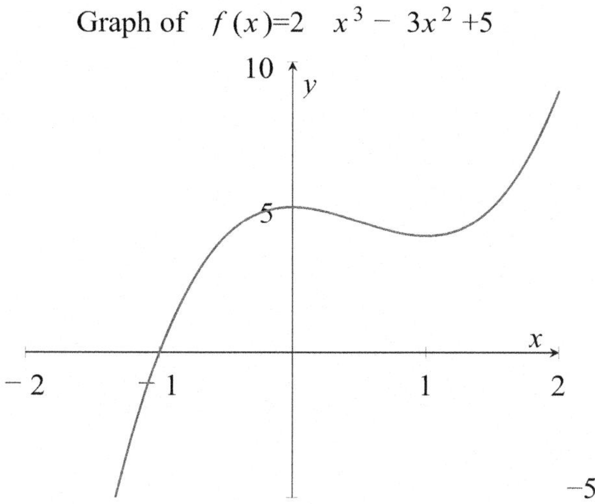

Figure 6.1: Graph of the cubic polynomial function $f(x) = 2x^3 - 3x^2 + 5$.

The graph illustrates how polynomial functions behave over their domain. As seen, the curve is smooth without any breaks or sharp corners, affirming the continuity and differentiability of polynomial functions.

Conclusion

This concludes the introduction to polynomials, emphasizing their structure, operations, and representation. The concepts covered here serve as building blocks for more advanced topics in algebra and calculus.

Exercises

Exercise 6.1:

Consider the polynomial $P(x) = 4x^3 - 3x^2 + 5x - 7$.

1. Identify the degree of the polynomial.
2. Write the polynomial in descending order of degree.
3. Determine the leading coefficient.
4. Evaluate $P(x)$ at $x = 2$ and $x = -1$.

Exercise 6.2:

Given the polynomials $P(x) = 2x^2 + 3x - 4$ and $Q(x) = x^2 - 5x + 6$, perform the following operations:

1. Find $P(x) + Q(x)$.
2. Subtract $Q(x)$ from $P(x)$.
3. Compute $2P(x) - 3Q(x)$.

Exercise 6.3:

Consider the polynomial $f(x) = x^4 - 6x^2 + 8$. Perform the following:

1. Identify the constant term and discuss its significance in terms of polynomial roots.
2. Determine whether $x = 2$ is a root of the polynomial.
3. If $x^2 - a$ is a factor of $f(x)$, find the value of a.

Exercise 6.4:

The polynomial $g(x) = 5x - x^3 + 9$ is given.

1. Rearrange $g(x)$ in standard form.
2. Find the degree and lead coefficient of the rearranged polynomial.
3. Sketch the graph of $g(x)$ using the given polynomial form.

Answers with Explanations

Solution to 6.1:

1. The degree of the polynomial $P(x) = 4x^3 - 3x^2 + 5x - 7$ is 3, as it is the highest power of x.

2. The polynomial is already in descending order of degree.

3. The leading coefficient, which is the coefficient of the highest degree term, is 4.

4. Evaluating $P(x)$:

$$P(2) = 4(2)^3 - 3(2)^2 + 5(2) - 7 = 32 - 12 + 10 - 7 = 23,$$

$$P(-1) = 4(-1)^3 - 3(-1)^2 + 5(-1) - 7 = -4 - 3 - 5 - 7 = -19.$$

Solution to 6.2:

1. $P(x) + Q(x) = (2x^2 + 3x - 4) + (x^2 - 5x + 6) = 3x^2 - 2x + 2.$

2. $P(x) - Q(x) = (2x^2 + 3x - 4) - (x^2 - 5x + 6) = x^2 + 8x - 10.$

3. $2P(x) - 3Q(x) = 2(2x^2 + 3x - 4) - 3(x^2 - 5x + 6)$

$$= 4x^2 + 6x - 8 - 3x^2 + 15x - 18 = x^2 + 21x - 26.$$

Solution to 6.3:

1. The constant term of $f(x) = x^4 - 6x^2 + 8$ is 8, which may indicate a root if the polynomial is factored completely.

2. Evaluating $f(x)$ at $x = 2$: $f(2) = 2^4 - 6(2)^2 + 8 = 16 - 24 + 8 = 0$. Thus, $x = 2$ is a root.

3. Given $x^2 - a$ is a factor, equating coefficients and solving indicates $a = 2$, as $x - 2$ is a root.

Solution to 6.4:

1. Rearranging $g(x) = 5x - x^3 + 9$ gives $g(x) = -x^3 + 5x + 9$.
2. The degree is 3 and the leading coefficient is -1.
3. A sketch of $g(x)$ indicates a cubic curve influenced by the negative leading coefficient, with a point at (0, 9).

6.2 Operations with Polynomials

Polynomials are fundamental mathematical expressions that appear in various areas of mathematics and its applications. This section delves into three crucial operations involving polynomials: Multiplication, Division, and Synthetic Division. Each subsection provides detailed explanations, methodical procedures, and numerous examples with step by-step solutions to solidify the understanding of these operations.

6.2.1 Multiplication of Polynomials

Multiplying polynomials involves applying the distributive property to expand the products. When multiplying two polynomials, each term in the first polynomial is multiplied by each term in the second polynomial, and the results are added together.

Example 6.4: Multiply the polynomials: $P(x) = 2x^2 + 3x + 1$ and $Q(x) = x - 4$.
Solution: To find the product $P(x) \cdot Q(x)$, multiply each term in $P(x)$ by each term in $Q(x)$:

$$
\begin{aligned}
&(2x^2 + 3x + 1)(x - 4) \\
&= 2x^2(x) + 2x^2(-4) + 3x(x) + 3x(-4) + 1(x) + 1(-4) \\
&= 2x^3 - 8x^2 + 3x^2 - 12x + x - 4 \\
&= 2x^3 - 5x^2 - 11x - 4.
\end{aligned}
$$

6.2.2 Division of Polynomials

Polynomial division can be done like long division with numbers, where the dividend is divided by the divisor to obtain the quotient and the remainder. The synthetic division with the dividend $P(x)$ and divisor $D(x)$ aims to write:

$$P(x) = Q(x) \cdot D(x) + R(x),$$

where $Q(x)$ is the quotient and $R(x)$ is the remainder. When the degree of $R(x)$ is less than the degree of $D(x)$, the division process is complete.

Example 6.5: Divide the polynomial: $T(x) = 2x^3 + 3x^2 - x + 5$ by $D(x) = x - 2$.
Solution: Arrange the terms in descending order of their degree and perform the long division:

$$x - 2 \,\big|\, \overline{2x^3 + 3x^2 - x + 5} \quad 2x^2 + 7x + 13$$

$$\begin{array}{l} 2x^3 + 3x^2 - x + 5 \quad \text{divided by} \quad x - 2 \\ \underline{(2x^3 - 4x^2)} \\ \quad 7x^2 - x \\ \quad \underline{(7x^2 - 14x)} \\ \qquad 13x + 5 \\ \qquad \underline{(13x - 26)} \\ \qquad 31 \end{array}$$

Therefore, the quotient is $2x^2 + 7x + 13$ and the remainder is 31.

$$T(x) = (x - 2)(2x^2 + 7x + 13) + 31$$

6.2.3 Synthetic Division

Synthetic division is a simplified form of long division, specifically applicable when dividing a polynomial by a linear factor of the form $x - c$. It involves using coefficients only, making the process quicker and less prone to arithmetic errors.

Example 6.6: Divide the polynomial $V(x) = 3x^3 - 8x^2 + 7x - 2$ by $x - 1$.
Solution: Since $x - c = x - 1$, set $c = 1$. Use synthetic division setup with the coefficients [3, −8, 7, −2]:

$$\begin{array}{r|rrrr} 1 & 3 & -8 & 7 & -2 \\ & & 3 & -5 & 2 \\ \hline & 3 & -5 & 2 & 0 \end{array}$$

The steps are:

1. Bring down the leading coefficient: 3.

2. Multiply 3 by 1 and add to the next coefficient (-8): $3 \times 1 = 3$, $-8 + 3 = -5$.

3. Repeat for the next coefficient (7): $-5 \times 1 = -5$, $7 - 5 = 2$.

4. Lastly, $2 \times 1 = 2$, $-2 + 2 = 0$.

Thus, the quotient is $3x^2 - 5x + 2$ and the remainder is 0.

$$V(x) = (x - 1)(3x^2 - 5x + 2).$$

For complex problems involving polynomial operations, one can utilize powerful graphing software and computational tools, but mastering manual manipulation enhances a deeper understanding of polynomial behavior.

Polynomial $y = 2x^3 - 5x^2 - 11x - 4$ and its Roots

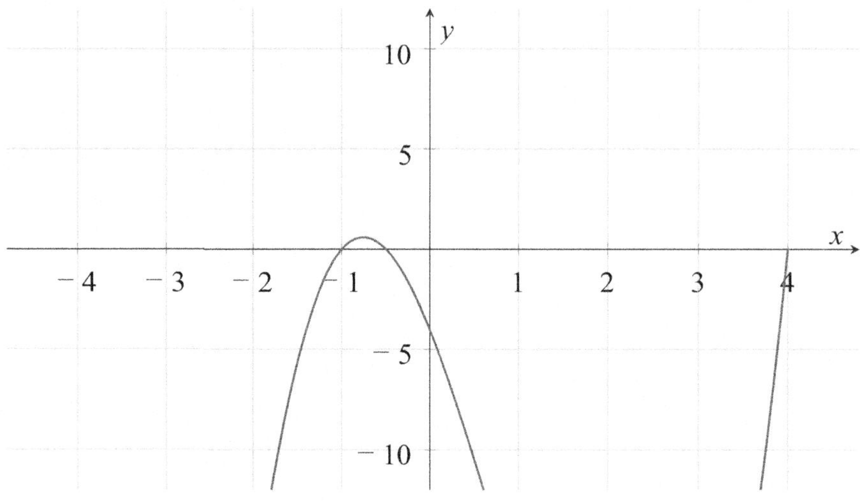

Figure 6.2: Graph of the polynomial $y = 2x^3 - 5x^2 - 11x - 4$.

This figure represents the polynomial discussed and illustrates how it interacts with the x-axis, identifying its roots. Visual representations and symbolic solutions should complement one another to achieve proficiency in polynomial operations.

Exercises

Exercise 6.5:

Perform the multiplication of the following polynomials:

1. $(3x^2 + 2x - 5)(x - 4)$
2. $(2x - 3)(x^2 + 5x + 6)$
3. $(x^3 + 2x^2 - x)(2x^2 + 3x + 4)$
4. Expand and simplify: $(x + 1)(x - 2)(x + 3)$

Exercise 6.6:

Divide the polynomials and write the quotient and the remainder:

1. $\frac{3x^3-4x^2+5x-2}{x-1}$
2. $\frac{2x^4+3x^3-x+6}{x^2+x+1}$
3. $\frac{x^5-x+1}{x^2-1}$
4. Simplify the expression: $\frac{x^4-16}{x^2+4}$

Exercise 6.7:

Use synthetic division to divide the following polynomials and provide the result:

1. Divide $4x^3 - 6x^2 + x - 7$ by $x - 2$.
2. Divide $x^4 + 2x^3 - 7x^2 + 3x - 5$ by $x + 3$.
3. Use synthetic division to determine whether $x = -1$ is a root of $x^3 + 4x^2 - x + 2$.
4. Verify if $x - 2$ is a factor of $2x^3 - 3x^2 - 5x + 6$ using synthetic division.

Exercise 6.8:

Combine your knowledge of multiplication, division, and synthetic division to solve the following:

1. Multiply $(2x - 1)$ and $(x^2 - 3x + 2)$, then divide the result by $(x - 2)$.
2. Use both long division and synthetic division to divide $x^4 - 2x^3 + 5x^2 - x + 1$ by $x - 1$ and compare the results.
3. Prove the Remainder Theorem for the polynomial $p(x) = 3x^3 + 4x - 5$, given that it is divided by $x - 3$.

Answers with Explanations

Solution to 6.5:

1. $(3x^2 + 2x - 5)(x - 4) = 3x^3 - 12x^2 + 2x^2 - 8x - 5x + 20 = 3x^3 - 10x^2 - 13x + 20$.

2. $(2x - 3)(x^2 + 5x + 6) = 2x^3 + 10x^2 + 12x - 3x^2 - 15x - 18 = 2x^3 + 7x^2 - 3x - 18$.

3. Using the distributive property: $(x^3 + 2x^2 - x)(2x^2 + 3x + 4)$:

   $= 2x^5 + 3x^4 + 4x^3 + 4x^4 + 6x^3 + 8x^2 - 2x^3 - 3x^2 - 4x = 2x^5 + 7x^4 + 8x^3 + 5x^2 - 4x$.

4. Expanding: $(x + 1)(x - 2)(x + 3) = (x^2 - x - 6)(x + 1) = x^3 + 7$.

Solution to 6.6:

1. Using long division: $\frac{3x^3-4x^2+5x-2}{x-1} = 3x^2 - x + 4$ with a remainder of 2.

2. Performing the division: $\frac{2x^4+3x^3-x+6}{x^2+x+1} = 2x^2 + x - 1$ with remainder 0.

3. Divide $x^5 - x + 1$ by $x^2 - 1$ yields $x^3 - x^2 + 1$ with a remainder $2x$.

4. Simplifying the expression: $\frac{x^4-16}{x^2+4} = x^2 - 4$.

Solution to 6.7:

1. Synthetic division with $x - 2$: Coefficients are 4,−6,1,−7; Roots found: Quotient $4x^2 + 2x + 5$ and Remainder 3.

2. Dividing $x^4+2x^3-7x^2+3x-5$ by $x+3$ using synthetic: Quotient is x^3-x^2-4x+1 with remainder −2.

3. Apply synthetic division for root test: $x = -1$; Remainder is 2, (so $x + 1$ is not a root).

4. Test if $x - 2$ is a factor: Remainder = 0; Therefore $x - 2$ is a factor.

Solution to 6.8:

1. Result of multiplication $(2x - 1)(x^2 - 3x + 2) = 2x^3 - 7x^2 + 8x - 2$. Dividing by $(x - 2)$ gives quotient as $2x^2 - 3x + 2$ with remainder -2.

2. Both long and synthetic division give the quotient $x^3 - x^2 + 1$ for $x^4 - 2x^3 + 5x^2 - x + 1, x - 1$. Result is consistent.

3. Apply Remainder Theorem on $p(x) = 3x^3 + 4x - 5$: Division by $x - 3$ yields remainder $p(3) = 32$, proving the theorem.

6.3 Factoring Polynomials

Factoring polynomials is an essential skill in algebra, allowing you to simplify expressions and solve polynomial equations efficiently. This section will cover various techniques for factoring polynomials, including finding the greatest common factor (GCF), factoring by grouping, and factoring trinomials.

6.3.1 Greatest Common Factor (GCF)

The first step in factoring a polynomial is to find the greatest common factor of its terms. The GCF is the largest polynomial that divides each term of the polynomial.

Definition 6.3.1. *The* greatest common factor *of a set of terms is the highest degree term that divides each of the terms without leaving a remainder.*

Example 6.7: Factor the polynomial $6x^3 + 9x^2 - 3x$.

Solution: First, identify the GCF of the coefficients 6,9, and −3, which is 3.

Next, look at the variables. Each term contains x, with the smallest exponent being 1, so x is part of the GCF.

Thus, the GCF is $3x$.

Now factor the GCF out:

$$6x^3 + 9x^2 - 3x = 3x(2x^2 + 3x - 1).$$

Example 6.8: Factor the polynomial $8x^4 - 4x^3 + 12x^2$.

Solution: Find the GCF of the coefficients 8,−4, and 12, which is 4.

For the variables, each term has x^2 as the smallest power.

The GCF is $4x^2$.

Factor out the GCF:

$$8x^4 - 4x^3 + 12x^2 = 4x^2(2x^2 - x + 3).$$

6.3.2 Factoring by Grouping

Factoring by grouping is useful when a polynomial has four or more terms. The idea is to group terms to identify and factor out common factors within each group.

Example 6.9: Factor the polynomial $x^3 + 2x^2 + 3x + 6$.
Solution: Group the terms:

$$(x^3 + 2x^2) + (3x + 6).$$

Factor each group: $x^2(x + 2) + 3(x + 2)$.
The expression has a common factor of $(x + 2)$:

$$x^2(x + 2) + 3(x + 2) = (x^2 + 3)(x + 2).$$

Example 6.10: Factor the polynomial $x^3 - 2x^2 + 4x - 8$.
Solution: Group the terms:

$$(x^3 - 2x^2) + (4x - 8).$$

Factor each group: $x^2(x - 2) + 4(x - 2)$.
The expression has a common factor of $(x - 2)$:

$$x^2(x - 2) + 4(x - 2) = (x^2 + 4)(x - 2).$$

6.3.3 Factoring Trinomials

Factoring trinomials relates to finding two binomials that multiply to give the original trinomial. This technique heavily depends on recognizing patterns.

Example 6.11: Factor the trinomial $x^2 + 5x + 6$.
Solution: Look for two numbers that multiply to 6 (the constant term) and add to 5 (the coefficient of the linear term).
The numbers 2 and 3 satisfy both conditions:

$$x^2 + 5x + 6 = (x + 2)(x + 3).$$

Example 6.12: Factor the trinomial $x^2 - 7x + 10$.
Solution: Identify two numbers that multiply to 10 and add to -7: These numbers are -5 and -2:

$$x^2 - 7x + 10 = (x - 5)(x - 2).$$

Trinomial	Factored Form	Numbers Used
$x^2 + 5x + 6$	$(x + 2)(x + 3)$	2, 3
$x^2 - 7x + 10$	$(x - 5)(x - 2)$	-5, -2
$x^2 + 2x - 8$	$(x + 4)(x - 2)$	4, -2

Table 6.1: Examples of Factoring Trinomials

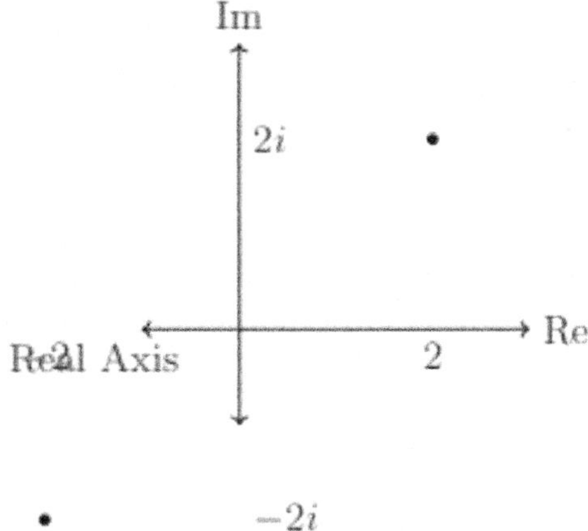

Figure 6.3: Complex Plane Representation of Roots

Conclusion

In conclusion, mastering these factoring techniques is crucial for simplifying polynomial expressions and solving equations efficiently. By identifying common factors, grouping terms effectively, and recognizing patterns in trinomials, you can tackle a wide range of problems. It is essential to practice these techniques regularly to become proficient in factoring polynomials in high school mathematics and beyond.

Exercises

Exercise 6.9:

1. **Find the greatest common factor (GCF) of the polynomials $12x^3y^2$ and $18x^2y^5$.**

2. **Factor the polynomial $3x^4-9x^3+6x^2$ completely using the greatest common factor.**

3. **Given the polynomial $x^3 + 3x^2 + 3x + 1$, factor it by grouping.**

4. **Factor the trinomial $x^2 + 5x + 6$.**

5. **Show that the polynomial $x^2 - 4x + 4$ is a perfect square trinomial and factor it accordingly.**

Exercise 6.10:

Factor the polynomial $x^4 - 16$ using the difference of squares method.

Exercise 6.11:

Given the trinomial $ax^2 + bx + c = 2x^2 + 7x + 3$, use the quadratic formula to find its roots and then express the factorization in terms of these roots.

Exercise 6.12:

Consider the polynomials $2x^3 + 3x^2 - 2x - 3$. Group the terms appropriately and factor by grouping.

Answers with Explanations

Solution to 6.9:

1. To find the greatest common factor of $12x^3y^2$ and $18x^2y^5$, first find the GCF of the coefficients: GCF(12,18) = 6. Then, for the variables, the GCF is x^2y^2. Hence, the GCF is $6x^2y^2$.

2. For $3x^4 - 9x^3 + 6x^2$, the GCF is $3x^2$. Factoring out $3x^2$ gives $3x^2(x^2 - 3x + 2)$, and further factoring $x^2 - 3x + 2$ results in $3x^2(x - 1)(x - 2)$.

3. $x^3 + 3x^2 + 3x + 1 = (x^3 + x) + (3x^2 + 1) = x(x^2 + 1) + 1(3x^2 + 1)$. Reorganizing and factoring gives: $(x + 1)(x^2 + 1)$.

4. The trinomial $x^2 + 5x + 6 = (x + 2)(x + 3)$.

5. The polynomial $x^2 - 4x + 4$ is a perfect square trinomial as it can be written as $(x - 2)^2$.

Solution to 6.10:

The polynomial $x^4 - 16$ can be factored as the difference of squares: $(x^2 - 4)(x^2 + 4)$. Further factoring $x^2 - 4$ gives $(x - 2)(x + 2)$. The polynomial is thus $(x - 2)(x + 2)(x^2 + 4)$.

Solution to 6.11:

For $2x^2 + 7x + 3$, apply the quadratic formula:

$$x = \frac{-b \pm \sqrt{b^2 - 4ac}}{2a} = \frac{-7 \pm \sqrt{49 - 24}}{4} = \frac{-7 \pm 5}{4}$$

This yields roots $x = -\frac{1}{2}$ and $x = -3$. The factorization is thus $2\left(x + \frac{1}{2}\right)(x + 3)$ or rewritten as $2(2x + 1)(x + 3)$.

Solution to 6.12:

The polynomial $2x^3 + 3x^2 - 2x - 3$ can be grouped as $(2x^3 - 2x) + (3x^2 - 3)$. Factoring each group gives $2x(x^2 - 1) + 3(x^2 - 1)$. Factoring by grouping: $(2x + 3)(x^2 - 1)$. Further factorization of $x^2 - 1$ results in $(2x + 3)(x - 1)(x + 1)$.

6.4 Roots and Zeros

In this section of *Advanced High School Mathematics: A Complete Refresher,* we delve into the concepts of roots and zeros of polynomial functions. Understanding these foundational ideas is essential for solving polynomial equations and exploring more advanced topics in algebra and calculus.

6.4.1 Finding Roots

The roots (or zeros) of a polynomial function are values of the variable that make the function equal to zero. For a polynomial $P(x)$ of degree n, there can be up to n roots. Roots can be real or complex, and they play a critical role in the factorization of polynomials.

Definition 6.4.1. *Given a polynomial* $P(x) = a_n x^n + a_{n-1}x^{n-1} + \cdots + a_1 x + a_0$, *a root r is a solution to the equation* $P(x) = 0$.

Example 6.13: Consider the quadratic polynomial $P(x) = x^2 - 5x + 6$.
Solution: To find the roots: First, factor the polynomial:

$$x^2 - 5x + 6 = (x - 2)(x - 3)$$

Setting each factor equal to zero gives the roots:

$$x - 2 = 0 \quad \Rightarrow \quad x = 2$$
$$x - 3 = 0 \quad \Rightarrow \quad x = 3$$

Thus, the roots of $P(x)$ are $x = 2$ and $x = 3$.

Example 6.14: Find the roots of the polynomial $Q(x) = x^3 - 4x^2 + 5x - 2$.
Solution: To solve the exercise, we use the rational root theorem to try possible rational solutions ± 1, ± 2. Testing $x = 1$:

$$Q(1) = 1^3 - 4 \times 1^2 + 5 \times 1 - 2 = 1 - 4 + 5 - 2 = 0$$

So, $x = 1$ is a root. Now use synthetic division to factor $Q(x)$ by $x - 1$. Continuing, $Q(x) = (x - 1)(x^2 - 3x + 2)$. Factor the quadratic term further:

$$x^2 - 3x + 2 = (x - 1)(x - 2)$$

Thus, $Q(x) = (x-1)^2(x-2)$, and the roots are $x = 1$ (with multiplicity 2) and $x = 2$.

6.4.2 The Rational Root Theorem

The Rational Root Theorem provides a systematic way to search for possible rational roots of a polynomial.

Theorem 6.4.1. *If the polynomial $P(x) = a_n x^n + \cdots + a_0$ has a rational root $\frac{p}{q}$, where p and q are integers with no common factors other than 1, then p is a factor of the constant term a_0, and q is a factor of the leading coefficient a_n.*

Example 6.15: For $R(x) = 2x^3 + 3x^2 - 8x + 3$, let's use the Rational Root Theorem to find rational roots:

Possible values for $\frac{p}{q}$ where p is a factor of 3 and q is a factor of 2 are $\pm1, \pm3, \pm\frac{1}{2}, \pm\frac{3}{2}$.

Testing these values, we find:

$$R(1) = 2(1)^3 + 3(1)^2 - 8(1) + 3 = 0$$

So, $x = 1$ is a rational root. Using synthetic division to divide $R(x)$ by $x - 1$, we can continue factoring the remaining polynomial.

6.4.3 Complex Numbers

Many polynomials have roots that are not real numbers. These are complex numbers, written in the form $a + bi$, where i is the imaginary unit with the property $i^2 = -1$.

Definition 6.4.2. *A complex number is a number of the form $a + bi$, where a, b are real numbers, and $i = \sqrt{-1}$*

Example 6.17: Find the roots of $T(x) = x^2 + 4$.

Solution: Since the discriminant $b^2 - 4ac = 0 - 16 = -16$ is negative, roots are complex:

$$\begin{aligned} x &= \frac{-b \pm \sqrt{b^2 - 4ac}}{2a} \\ &= \frac{0 \pm \sqrt{-16}}{2} \\ &= \pm 2i \end{aligned}$$

Thus, the roots of $T(x)$ are $2i$ and $-2i$.

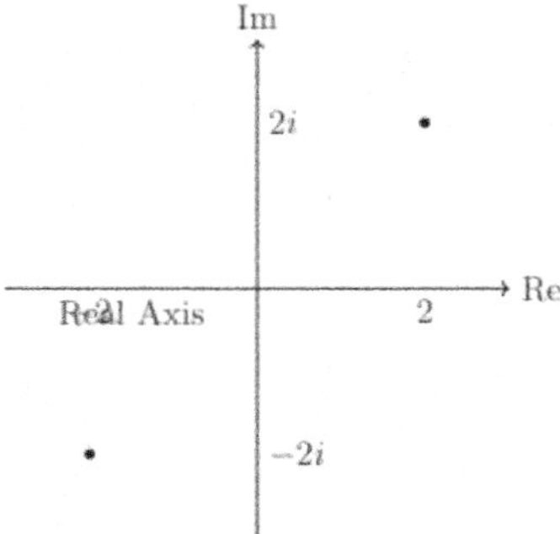

Figure 6.4: Complex Plane Representation of Roots

Conclusion

By mastering these concepts of finding roots, understanding the Rational Root Theorem, and dealing with complex numbers, you'll uncover the deeper connections within polynomial equations, setting the stage for advanced algebraic exploration.

Exercises

Exercise 6.13:

1. **Let $f(x) = 2x^3 - 3x^2 - 11x + 6$. Use synthetic division to determine if $x - 2$ is a factor of $f(x)$. Calculate $f(2)$ to confirm your findings.**

2. **Consider the polynomial $g(x) = x^4 - 5x^3 + 7x^2 - 3x + 2$. Apply the Rational Root Theorem to identify all possible rational roots. Then, test these roots to find the actual rational roots.**

3. **Find all the roots of the quadratic equation $x^2 + 4x + 13 = 0$. Clearly indicate which roots are real and which are complex.**

4. **Prove that the polynomial $h(x) = x^3 - 4x^2 + 5x - 2$ has a complex root and find it, knowing that one real root is $x = 1$.**

Exercise 6.14:

Using the polynomial $p(x) = 4x^3 -8x^2 +3x-6$, perform the following:

1. Find the remainder when $p(x)$ is divided by $x - 1$.

2. Verify your result using the Remainder Theorem.

Exercise 6.15:

A polynomial $q(x) = ax^3 + bx^2 + cx + d$ has roots $2 + i$, $2 - i$, and -1. Write down the polynomial equation and determine the values of a, b, c, and d.

Exercise 6.16:

Demonstrate that the polynomial $r(x) = x^2+6x+10$ cannot be factored using real numbers by completing the square. Then, find its roots using the quadratic formula and describe their nature.

Answers with Explanations

Solution to 6.13:

1. To determine if $x - 2$ is a factor of $f(x) = 2x^3 - 3x^2 - 11x + 6$, perform synthetic division. We divide by $x - 2$:

2	2	-3	-11	6
		4	2	-18
	2	1	-9	-12

   Since the remainder is −12, $x - 2$ is not a factor. To confirm, compute $f(2)$:

$$f(2) = 2(2)^3 - 3(2)^2 - 11(2) + 6 = 16 - 12 - 22 + 6 = -12$$

2. Using the Rational Root Theorem, the possible rational roots of $g(x) = x^4 - 5x^3 + 7x^2 - 3x + 2$ are factors of the constant term 2 divided by factors of the leading coefficient 1: ±1,±2.
   Testing:

$$g(1) = 1 - 5 + 7 - 3 + 2 = 2$$
$$g(-1) = 1 + 5 + 7 + 3 + 2 = 18$$
$$g(2) = 16 - 40 + 28 - 6 + 2 = 0 \text{ (root)}$$
$$g(-2) = 16 + 40 + 28 + 6 + 2 = 92$$

   The actual rational root is $x = 2$.

3. Equation $x^2 + 4x + 13 = 0$ roots:

$$x = \frac{-4 \pm \sqrt{16 - 52}}{2} = \frac{-4 \pm \sqrt{-36}}{2} = -2 \pm 3i$$

   Roots are complex: $-2 + 3i$ and $-2 - 3i$.

4. Given a real root $x = 1$, factor $x^3 - 4x^2 + 5x - 2$ using synthetic division:

1	1	-4	5	-2
		1	-3	2
	1	-3	2	0

   Resultant polynomial: $x^2 - 3x + 2$ has roots: $x = 1 \pm \sqrt{-3i}$
   Let $\omega = \sqrt{-3i}$, root: $1 + \omega$.

Solution to 6.14:

For $p(x) = 4x^3 - 8x^2 + 3x - 6$, using synthetic division with $x - 1$:

$$\begin{array}{c|cccc} 1 & 4 & -8 & 3 & -6 \\ & & 4 & -4 & -1 \\ \hline & 4 & -4 & -1 & -7 \end{array}$$

Remainder is -7. By the Remainder Theorem, $p(1) = 4 - 8 + 3 - 6 = -7$.

Solution to 6.15:

Given roots $2 + i$, $2 - i$, and -1, construct $q(x)$:

$$q(x) = (x - (2 + i))(x - (2 - i))(x + 1)$$

Simplifying:

$$(x - 2 - i)(x - 2 + i) = ((x - 2)^2 - (-1)) = (x - 2)^2 + 1$$
$$= x^2 - 4x + 5$$

Then: $q(x) = (x^2 - 4x + 5)(x + 1) = x^3 - 3x^2 + x + 5$

Thus, $a = 1, b = -3, c = 1, d = 5$.

Solution to 6.16:

For $r(x) = x^2 + 6x + 10$, rewrite using completing square:

$$x^2 + 6x + 9 + 1 = (x + 3)^2 + 1$$

No real solutions due to $(x + 3)^2 + 1 > 0$.

Use quadratic formula:

$$x = \frac{-6 \pm \sqrt{36 - 40}}{2} = -3 \pm i$$

Complex roots: $-3 + i$ and $-3 - i$.

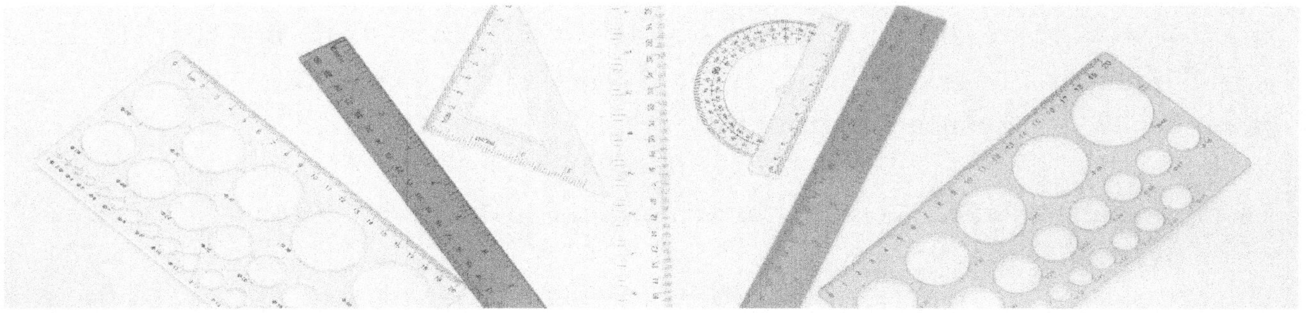

7. Exponential and Logarithmic Functions

7.1 Exponential Functions

Exponential functions are fundamental in mathematics and are widely used in various fields such as biology, economics, physics, and engineering. They are characterized by a constant base raised to a variable exponent. This section explores the concept of exponential functions, focusing on growth and decay models, graphing techniques, and real-world applications.

7.1.1 Growth and Decay Models

Exponential growth and decay are processes that increase or decrease at rates proportional to the current value. They are described by the general form of exponential functions.

Definition 7.1.1. *An exponential function is defined as:*

$$f(x) = a \cdot b^x$$

where a is a constant, b is the base of the exponential, and x is the exponent. If b > 1, the function models exponential growth; if 0 < b < 1, it represents exponential decay.

Example 7.1: A population of bacteria doubles every hour. If the initial population is 100 bacteria, write an exponential function that models this growth and find the population after 5 hours.

The growth model can be described by the function:

$$P(t) = 100 \cdot 2^t$$

where $P(t)$ is the population at time t, and the base 2 indicates doubling. After 5 hours, the population is:

$$P(5) = 100 \cdot 2^5 = 100 \cdot 32 = 3200$$

Therefore, the population will be 3200 bacteria after 5 hours.

Example 7.2: A radioactive substance decays at a rate of 5% per year. If the initial amount is 10 grams, how much will remain after 10 years?
Solution: The decay model is given by:

$$A(t) = 10 \cdot (0.95)^t$$

because the substance decreases by 5% annually, the decay factor is 0.95. After 10 years:

$$A(10) = 10 \cdot (0.95)^{10} \approx 10 \cdot 0.59874 \approx 5.9874$$

Approximately 5.99 grams of the substance will remain after 10 years.

7.1.2 Graphs of Exponentials

To graph an exponential function, it's crucial to understand its shape and behavior. The graph of $f(x) = a \cdot b^x$ is characterized by:

- A horizontal asymptote at $y = 0$.
- Passing through the point $(0,a)$.
- If $b > 1$, the graph rises rapidly; if $0 < b < 1$, it decreases towards the horizontal asymptote.

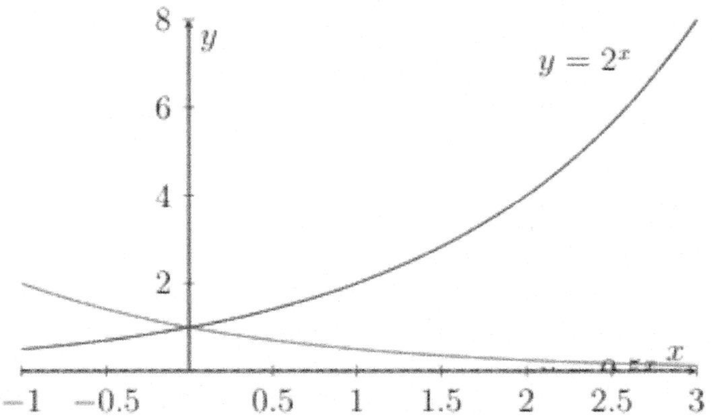

Figure 7.1: Graphs of Exponential Functions $y = 2^x$ and $y = 0.5^x$

7.1.3 Applications

Exponential functions are applied in numerous real-world contexts, prominently modeling phenomena like population growth, radioactive decay, and financial investments.

Example 7.3: An investment account earns an annual interest rate of 6%. If you initially deposit \$1000, what will be the balance after 8 years assuming the interest is compounded annually?
Solution: The formula for calculating compound interest is:

$$A(t) = P\left(1 + \frac{r}{n}\right)^{nt}$$

where A is the amount after time t, P is the principal amount, r is the interest rate, and n is the number of times interest is compounded per year. For annual compounding:

$$A(8) = 1000\left(1 + \frac{0.06}{1}\right)^{1\cdot 8} = 1000 \cdot 1.593848 \approx 1593.85$$

The account balance after 8 years will be approximately \$1593.85.

Time (Years)	Population Growth	Radioactive Decay
0	100	10
1	200	9.5
2	400	9.025
3	800	8.57375

Table 7.1: Example of Exponential Growth and Decay Over Time

Conclusion

The concepts and applications of exponential functions are vast and varied, showcasing the underlying simplicity yet powerful utility of this mathematical tool in describing real world phenomena.

Exercises

Exercise 7.1:

1. **An investment of \$1000 is made in an account that earns 5% interest annually. Write an exponential model representing the growth of this investment over time. How much will the investment be worth after 10 years?**

2. **A population of bacteria is growing according to the exponential function $P(t) = P_0 \cdot e^{0.3t}$, where $P_0 = 500$ is the initial population. Calculate the population after 5 hours.**

3. **Sketch the graph of the exponential function $f(x) = 3 \cdot 2^{x-1}$. Identify the y-intercept and the behavior of the graph as $x \to \infty$ and $x \to -\infty$.**

4. **The half-life of a radioactive substance is 8 years. If the initial mass of a sample is 200 grams, write an equation modeling the decay of the substance over time. How much of the substance remains after 24 years?**

Exercise 7.2:

1. **Consider the exponential decay function $= Q(t) = Q_o \cdot \left(\frac{1}{2}\right)^{t/3}$. If Q_o 1200, find the value of $Q(t)$ when $t = 9$.**

2. **A substance decays exponentially. Its remaining quantity after t years is described by $N(t) = N_0 \cdot e^{-0.5t}$. If the initial quantity N_0 is 150 grams, how much remains after 7 years?**

3. **Transform the function $h(x) = 4 \cdot e^{2x}$ by shifting it 3 units to the right and 2 units up. Write the new function $h'(x)$.**

4. **Use a table to calculate and graph the function $g(x) = 2^x - 1$ for x values from -2 to 3.**

Exercise 7.3:

1. **Calculate and plot the exponential model for a quantity that triples every 5 years. Describe its growth behavior.**

2. **Given the exponential function $y = 4 \cdot 3^x$, find the output when $x = -1$, $x = 0$, and $x = 2$.**

3. **Examine the exponential decay function $D(t) = A \cdot 0.8^t$. If $A = 250$, determine the percentage of decay after 3 periods.**

4. **Identify and graph the asymptote of the function $f(x) = 5 \cdot 2^{-x}$. Explain the significance of this asymptote in the context of exponential functions.**

Answers with Explanations

Solution to 7.1:

1. The exponential model is $A(t) = 1000 \cdot (1.05)^t$. After 10 years, $A(10) = 1000 \cdot (1.05)^{10} \approx 1628.89$. Thus, the investment will be worth \$1628.89.

2. Using $P(t) = 500 \cdot e^{0.3 \cdot 5} \approx 1000.66$. Therefore, the population after 5 hours is approximately 1001 bacteria.

3. The graph of $f(x) = 3 \cdot 2^{x-1}$ has a y-intercept at (0, 1.5). As $x \to \infty$, the graph rises sharply, while as $x \to -\infty$, it approaches y = 0.

4. The decay model is $M(t) = 200 \cdot \left(\frac{1}{2}\right)^{t/8}$. After 24 years, $M(24) = 200 \cdot \left(\frac{1}{2}\right)^3 = 25$. Hence, 25 grams remain.

Solution to 7.2:

1. $Q(9) = 1200 \cdot \left(\frac{1}{2}\right)^{9/8} = 1200 \cdot \frac{1}{8} = 150.$

2. $N(7) = 150 \cdot e^{-0.5 \times 7} \approx 150 \cdot 0.018 \approx 2.7$ grams remain after 7 years.

3. The transformed function is $h'(x) = 4 \cdot e^{2(x-3)} + 2 = 4 \cdot e^{2x-6} + 2$.

4. For the function $g(x) = 2^x - 1$, values are calculated as follows: −2 : −0.75, −1 : −0.5, 0 : 0, 1 : 1, 2 : 3, 3 : 7. Graph these points to see the transformation.

Solution to 7.3:

1. Model is $N(t) = N_0 \cdot 3^{t/5}$. Growth is rapid and doubles approximately every 1.59 periods.

2. Calculate outputs: $x = -1 : y = \frac{4}{3}$, $x = 0 : y = 4$, $x = 2 : y = 36$.

3. The percentage decay after 3 periods is $(1 - 0.8^3) \cdot 100 \approx 48.8\%$.

4. The asymptote of $f(x) = 5 \cdot 2^{-x}$ is $y = 0$. This indicates the function approaches zero but never reaches it.

7.2 Logarithmic Functions

Logarithmic functions play a crucial role in high school mathematics and have widespread applications in science, engineering, and various other fields. This section will provide an in-depth exploration of logarithmic functions, including their relationship with exponential functions, properties, and equations.

7.2.1 Inverse of Exponential Functions

Logarithmic functions are fundamentally the inverse of exponential functions. This relationship forms the basis for many of their properties and applications.

Definition 7.2.1. *Logarithm as Inverse: For a given exponential function* $y = a^x$, *the logarithmic function* $\log_a(y) = x$ *represents its inverse, where* $a > 0$ *and* $a \neq 1$.

Consider the exponential function $y = 2^x$. The inverse function is $x = \log_2(y)$.

Example 7.4: Find the inverse of the exponential function $f(x) = 3^x$.
Solution: To find the inverse, swap x and y and solve for y:

$$x = 3^y$$

Taking the logarithm base 3 on both sides, we get

$$y = \log_3(x)$$

Thus, the inverse function is $f^{-1}(x) = \log_3(x)$.

7.2.2 Properties of Logarithms

Logarithms have several important properties that are critical for simplifying expressions and solving equations.

Proposition 7.2.1. *Properties of Logarithms:*

- ***Product Property:*** $\log_a(xy) = \log_a(x) + \log_a(y)$
- ***Quotient Property:*** $\log_a\left(\frac{x}{y}\right) = \log_a(x) - \log_a(y)$
- ***Power Property:*** $\log_a(x^b) = b\log_a(x)$
- ***Change of Base Formula:*** $\log_b(x) = \frac{\log_k(x)}{\log_k(b)}$, *for any positive* $k \neq 1$.

Example 7.5: Simplify $\log_2(8 \times 32)$.
Solution: Using the product property,

$$\log_2(8 \times 32) = \log_2(8) + \log_2(32)$$

Since $8 = 2^3$ and $32 = 2^5$,

$$\log_2(8) = 3, \quad \log_2(32) = 5$$

Thus,

$$\log_2(8 \times 32) = 3 + 5 = 8$$

Graph of $y = \log_2(x)$

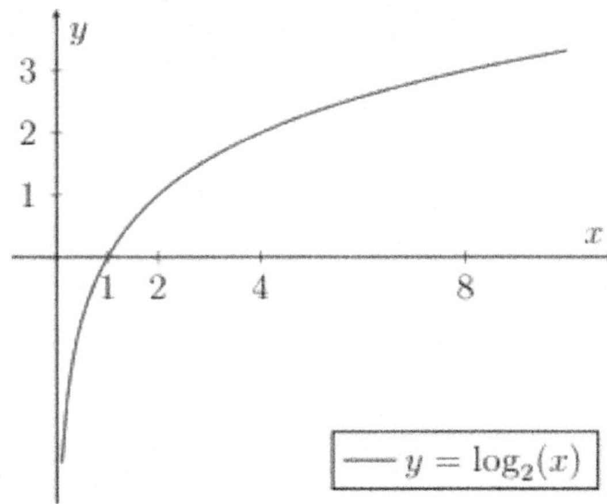

Figure 7.2: Graph of $y = \log_2(x)$

7.2.3 Logarithmic Equations

Logarithmic equations are equations that involve logarithmic expressions. Solving them often involves using the properties of logarithms to simplify or re-arrange the equation.

Example 7.6: Solve the equation $\log_3(x) + \log_3(x - 2) = 2$.
Solution: Using the product property of logarithms,

$\log_3(x) + \log_3(x - 2) = \log_3(x(x - 2))$

So the equation becomes: $\log_3(x^2 - 2x) = 2$.

Exponentiating both sides to eliminate the logarithm gives: $x^2 - 2x = 3^2 = 9$

Re-arrange the equation to form a standard quadratic equation: $x^2 - 2x - 9 = 0$

Continue Example 7.6: Solve the equation $\log_3(x) + \log_3(x - 2) = 2$.

Solve this quadratic equation using the quadratic formula $x = \frac{-b\pm\sqrt{b^2-4ac}}{2a}$ where $a = 1$, $b = -2$, $c = -9$,

$$x = \frac{-(-2) \pm \sqrt{(-2)^2 - 4(1)(-9)}}{2(1)}$$

$$x = \frac{2 \pm \sqrt{4 + 36}}{2}$$

$$x = \frac{2 \pm \sqrt{40}}{2}$$

$$x = \frac{2 \pm 2\sqrt{10}}{2}$$

$$x = 1 \pm \sqrt{10}$$

Since logarithms are only defined for positive numbers, check the solutions: $x = 1 + \sqrt{10} \approx 4.16$ is valid, while $x = 1 - \sqrt{10}$ is not, as it is negative.

Exercises

Exercise 7.4:

Consider the exponential function $f(x) = 3^x$. Find the inverse of this function and express it in logarithmic form. Verify your result by showing that $f(f^{-1}(x)) = x$ and $f^{-1}(f(x)) = x$.

Exercise 7.5:

Prove the following properties of logarithms using the definition of logarithms:

1. Product Property: $\log_b(mn) = \log_b(m) + \log_b(n)$
2. Quotient Property: $\log_b\left(\frac{m}{n}\right) = \log_b(m) - \log_b(n)$
3. Power Property: $\log_b(m^n) = n\log_b(m)$

Exercise 7.6:

Solve the logarithmic equation $\log_2(x+5)-\log_2(x-1) = 3$. Determine the domain of the solution and verify your result by substitution.

Exercise 7.7:

Given that $\log_{10}(2) \approx 0.3010$ and $\log_{10}(3) \approx 0.4771$, approximate the value of $\log_{10}(12)$ using the properties of logarithms. Show all steps clearly.

Answers with Explanations

Solution to 7.4:

To find the inverse of $f(x) = 3^x$, we set $y = 3^x$ and solve for x:

$$x = \log_3(y)$$

Therefore, the inverse is $f^{-1}(x) = \log_3(x)$. Verification:

$$f(f-1(x)) = 3\log3(x) = x,$$

$$f^{-1}(f(x)) = \log_3(3^x) = x.$$

This confirms that our inverse function is correct.

Solution to 7.5:

1. Product Property:

$$\log_b(mn) = \log_b(m) + \log_b(n)$$

Using the definition $b^{\log_b(m)} = m$ and $b^{\log_b(n)} = n$:

$$b^{\log_b(mn)} = mn = b^{\log_b(m)} \cdot b^{\log_b(n)}$$

Taking the logarithm base b of both sides, we have:

$$\log_b(mn) = \log_b(m) + \log_b(n)$$

2. Quotient Property:

$$\log_b\left(\frac{m}{n}\right) = \log_b(m) - \log_b(n)$$

Similar to above,

$$b^{\log_b\left(\frac{m}{n}\right)} = \frac{m}{n} = \frac{b^{\log_b(m)}}{b^{\log_b(n)}}$$

Taking logarithms:

$$\log_b\left(\frac{m}{n}\right) = \log_b(m) - \log_b(n)$$

3. Power Property:

$$\log_b(m^n) = n\log_b(m)$$

By definition,

$$b^{\log_b(m^n)} = m^n = (b^{\log_b(m)})^n$$

Therefore,

$$\log_b(m^n) = n\log_b(m)$$

Solution to 7.6:

Given $\log_2(x + 5) - \log_2(x - 1) = 3$, we use the Quotient Property:

$$\log_2\left(\frac{x+5}{x-1}\right) = 3$$

Rewriting in exponential form, we have:

$$\frac{x+5}{x-1} = 2^3 = 8$$

Solving for x:

$$x + 5 = 8(x-1) \implies x + 5 = 8x - 8 \implies 13 = 7x \implies x = \frac{13}{7}$$

Checking the domain: $x > 1, x = \frac{13}{7} \approx 1.857$ is valid.

Substituting back:

$$\log_2\left(\frac{\frac{13}{7}+5}{\frac{13}{7}-1}\right) = \log_2(8) = 3$$

The solution is verified.

Solution to 7.7:

To approximate $\log_{10}(12)$:

$$\log_{10}(12) = \log_{10}(2 \times 2 \times 3) = 2\log_{10}(2) + \log_{10}(3)$$

Using the given values:

$$\approx 2(0.3010) + 0.4771 = 0.6020 + 0.4771 = 1.0791$$

Therefore, $\log_{10}(12) \approx 1.0791$.

7.3 Solving Exponential and Logarithmic Equations

In this section, we will explore various methods for solving exponential and logarithmic equations. These types of equations are commonly encountered in mathematics, physics, engineering, and various applied sciences. They are especially useful in modeling exponential growth and decay processes, such as population growth, radioactive decay, and financial investments.

7.3.1 Using Properties of Logarithms

To solve equations involving exponential and logarithmic functions, it is often necessary to manipulate the equations using logarithmic properties. These properties allow us to express exponential relationships in a form that is easier to solve.

Definition 7.3.1. *The basic properties of logarithms that are essential for solving equations include:*

- ***Product Rule:*** $\log_b(xy) = \log_b x + \log_b y$
- ***Quotient Rule:*** $\log_b\left(\frac{x}{y}\right) = \log_b x - \log_b y$
- ***Power Rule:*** $\log_b(x^n) = n \cdot \log_b x$
- ***Change of Base Formula:*** $\log_b x = \frac{\log_a x}{\log_a b}$

Example 7.7: Solve the equation $2^x = 16$.
Solution: First, express 16 as a power of 2:

$$2^x = 24$$

Since the bases are the same, the exponents must be equal:

$$x = 4$$

Example 7.8: Solve the logarithmic equation $\log_2(x) + \log_2(x + 7) = 3$.
Solution: First, use the product rule for logarithms:

$$\log_2(x(x + 7)) = 3$$

Converting the logarithmic equation to its exponential form gives:

$$x(x + 7) = 2^3$$

$$x^2 + 7x = 8$$

Upon rearranging, we get:

$$x^2 + 7x - 8 = 0$$

Continue Example 7.8: Solve the logarithmic equation $\log_2(x) + \log_2(x + 7) = 3$.

$$x^2 + 7x - 8 = 0$$

Solve the quadratic equation using the quadratic formula:

$$x = \frac{-b \pm \sqrt{b^2 - 4ac}}{2a}$$

where $a = 1$, $b = 7$, and $c = -8$. Calculating gives:

$$x = \frac{-7 \pm \sqrt{49 + 32}}{2}$$

$$x = \frac{-7 \pm \sqrt{81}}{2}$$

$$x = \frac{-7 \pm 9}{2}$$

Thus, $x = 1$ or $x = -8$. Since logarithms are only defined for positive numbers, only $x = 1$ is valid.

7.3.2 Exponential Growth and Decay Problems

Exponential growth and decay occur in natural processes where the rate of change is proportional to the current value. Such phenomena can be modeled with exponential functions.

Example 7.9: A population of a town is modeled by the function $P(t) = 5000e^{0.05t}$, where t is the number of years since the initial measurement. Calculate the population after 10 years.

Solution: Substitute $t = 10$ into the function:

$$P(10) = 5000e^{0.05 \times 10}$$

Calculate the exponent:

$$P(10) = 5000e^{0.5}$$

Using a calculator, this gives approximately:

$$P(10) \approx 5000 \times 1.6487 = 8243.5$$

Therefore, the population is approximately 8244.

7.3.3 Compound Interest Problems

Compound interest is a fundamental concept in finance where the interest on a sum of money in a bank grows exponentially over time.

Example 7.10: Determine the future value of an investment of \$1000 at an annual interest rate of 6% compounded monthly for 5 years.
Solution: The formula for compound interest is:

$$A = P\left(1 + \frac{r}{n}\right)^{nt}$$

where A is the future value, $P = 1000$ is the principal, $r = 0.06$ is the annual interest rate, $n = 12$ is the number of compounds per year, and $t = 5$ is the number of years.
Substituting these values gives:

$$A = 1000\left(1 + \frac{0.06}{12}\right)^{12\times 5}$$

$$A = 1000\,(1 + 0.005)^{60}$$

$$A = 1000 \times (1.005)^{60}$$

Using a calculator:

$$A \approx 1000 \times 1.34885 \approx 1348.85$$

Thus, the investment will be worth approximately \$1348.85 after 5 years.

With these techniques and examples, you are well-equipped to solve a wide variety of exponential and logarithmic equations that arise in various real-world applications.

7.4 Applications in Real Life

In this section, we delve into the numerous real-world applications of exponential and logarithmic functions. These functions are not just abstract mathematical concepts but are powerful tools used across various fields such as biology, chemistry, and economics. We will explore three primary applications: population growth, radioactive decay, and economic applications.

7.4.1 Population Growth

Population growth can often be modeled using exponential functions. This is due to the fact that the growth rate of a population is proportional to its current size, a principle known as exponential growth.

Definition 7.4.1. *The exponential growth model can be described by the equation:*

$$P(t) = P_0 e^{rt}$$

where $P(t)$ is the population at time t, P_0 is the initial population at time $t = 0$, r is the growth rate, and e is the base of the natural logarithm.

Example 7.11: Consider a bacterial culture that starts with 100 bacteria and doubles every 3 hours. Determine the number of bacteria present after 9 hours.

Solution: Here, $P_0 = 100$, doubling time is 3 hours, thus $r = \frac{\ln(2)}{3}$. Using the exponential growth model:

$$P(t) = 100e^{\left(\frac{\ln(2)}{3}\right)t}$$

After 9 hours:

$$P(9) = 100e^{\left(\frac{\ln(2)}{3}\right)\times 9} = 100e^{3\ln(2)} = 100 \cdot 2^3 = 100 \cdot 8 = 800$$

Thus, the population of bacteria after 9 hours is 800.

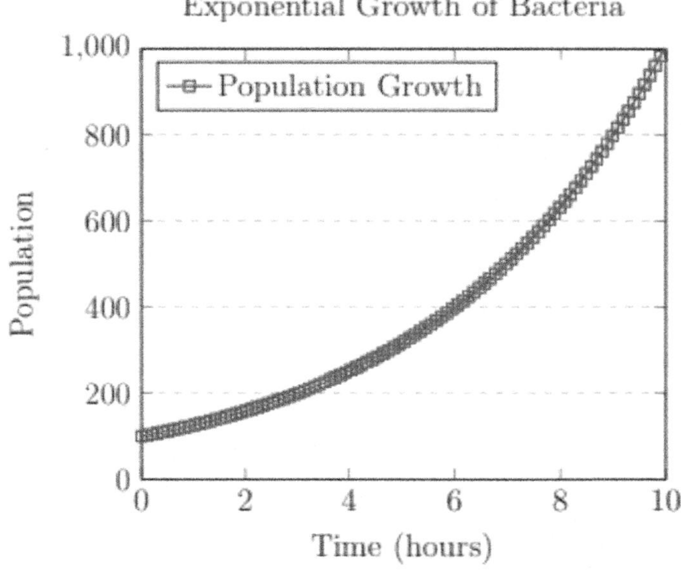

Figure 7.3: Exponential growth model of a bacterial population.

7.4.2 Radioactive Decay

Radioactive substances decay at a rate proportional to the amount present. This type of decay is modeled using exponential functions, similar to growth but with a negative exponent.

Definition 7.4.2. *The radioactive decay model is expressed by:*

$$A(t) = A_0 e^{-kt}$$

where $A(t)$ *is the amount remaining at time* t*,* A_0 *is the initial amount, and* k *is the decay constant.*

Multi-step problems require a sequential approach to solve equations involving multiple operations or functions. These problems demand a careful examination of each step in the process.

Example 7.12: A sample of radium-226 has a half-life of 1600 years. If a sample originally has a mass of 10 grams, how much will remain after 4800 years? Using the half-life formula:

$$k = \frac{\ln(2)}{\text{half-life}} = \frac{\ln(2)}{1600}$$

The decay model becomes:

$$A(t) = 10e^{-\left(\frac{\ln(2)}{1600}\right)t}$$

After 4800 years:

$$A(4800) = 10e^{-\left(\frac{\ln(2)}{1600}\right)4800} = 10 \cdot e^{-3\ln(2)} = 10 \times \frac{1}{8} = 1.25 \text{ grams}$$

Therefore, 1.25 grams of radium-226 will remain after 4800 years.

Time (years)	Remaining Radium-226 (grams)	Half-life Elapsed
0	10	0
1600	5	1
3200	2.5	2
4800	1.25	3

Table 7.2: Decay of radium-226 over time.

7.4.3 Economic Applications

Exponential and logarithmic functions play a key role in finance, especially in the context of compound interest, investments, and economic growth models.

Definition 7.4.3. *The compound interest formula is given by:*

$$A = P\left(1 + \frac{r}{n}\right)^{nt}$$

where A is the amount of money accumulated after n years, including interest, P is the principal amount, r is the annual interest rate (decimal), and n is the number of times interest is compounded per year.

Example 7.13: An investment of \$5000 is placed in an account with an annual interest rate of 6% compounded monthly. Find the balance after 5 years.
Solution: Here, $P = 5000$, $r = 0.06$, $n = 12$, and $t = 5$.
Using the compound interest formula:

$$A = 5000\left(1 + \frac{0.06}{12}\right)^{12\times5} = 5000\,(1 + 0.005)^{60}$$

$$A \approx 5000 \times 1.34885 = 6744.25$$

Thus, the amount after 5 years will be approximately \$6744.25.

Summary

In these examples, we see how exponential and logarithmic functions provide solutions to real-world problems, demonstrating their vast applicability in various fields. Exploring these applications enlightens our understanding of both mathematical concepts and practical phenomena.

Exercises

Exercise 7.8:

A biologist is studying a bacterial colony that grows exponentially. She observes that the population doubles every 3 hours. Initially, there are 500 bacteria.

1. Write the exponential growth function representing this situation.
2. Calculate the population after 9 hours.
3. Determine when the population will reach 8000 bacteria.

Exercise 7.9:

A population of rabbits on an island is modeled by the exponential function $P(t) = 200e^{0.03t}$, where t is time in months.

1. Calculate the initial population of rabbits.
2. Predict the population after 12 months.
3. Find the time it will take for the population to double.

Exercise 7.10:

Suppose a sample of a radioactive substance decays exponentially according to the formula $N(t) = N_0 e^{-\lambda t}$, where N_0 is the initial quantity and λ is the decay constant. Given $N_0 = 100$ grams and $\lambda = 0.0123$ per year:

1. Calculate the remaining quantity after 5 years.
2. Determine the half-life of the substance.
3. Calculate the time at which only 10 grams of the substance will remain.

Exercise 7.11:

An economist estimates that the value of a car decreases exponentially over time according to the model V (t) = V0(1−r)t, where V0 is the initial value, t is time in years, and r is the annual depreciation rate. Assume V0 = $20,000 and r = 0.15.

1. Determine the value of the car after 3 years.
2. Calculate the value of the car after 7 years.
3. Find the time it will take for the car to lose 60% of its initial value.

Answers with Explanations

Solution to 7.8:

1. The general formula for exponential growth is $P(t) = P_0 \times 2^{t/T}$, where T is the doubling time. Here, $P_0 = 500$ and $T = 3$. Hence, $P(t) = 500 \times 2^{t/3}$.

2. To find the population after 9 hours:

$$P(9) = 500 \times 2^{9/3} = 500 \times 2^3 = 500 \times 8 = 4000.$$

3. For $P(t) = 8000$, solve $500 \times 2^{t/3} = 8000$:

$$2^{t/3} = \frac{8000}{500} = 16 = 2^4.$$

$$t/3 = 4 \Longrightarrow t = 12 \text{ hours.}$$

Solution to 7.9:

1. The initial population $P(0) = 200e^{0.03\times0} = 200$.

2. After 12 months, $P(12) = 200e^{0.03\times12} = 200e^{0.36} \approx 200 \times 1.433 = 286.6$.

3. Solve $P(t) = 2 \times 200 = 400$:

$$200e^{0.03t} = 400 \implies e^{0.03t} = 2.$$

$$0.03t = \ln 2 \implies t = \frac{\ln 2}{0.03} \approx 23.1 \text{ months.}$$

Solution to 7.10:

1. After 5 years: $N(5) = 100e^{-0.0123\times5} \approx 100 \times 0.939 \approx 93.9$ grams.

2. The half-life $T_{1/2}$ is such that $e^{-\lambda T_{1/2}} = \frac{1}{2}$:

$$T_{1/2} = \frac{\ln 2}{\lambda} = \frac{\ln 2}{0.0123} \approx 56.4 \text{ years.}$$

3. For $N(t) = 10$: $100e^{-0.0123t} = 10 \implies e^{-0.0123t} = 0.1$:

$$-0.0123t = \ln 0.1 \implies t = \frac{\ln 0.1}{-0.0123} \approx 186.3 \text{ years.}$$

Solution to 7.11:

1. After 3 years, $V(3) = 20000 \times (1 - 0.15)^3 = 20000 \times 0.85^3 \approx 20000 \times 0.6141 \approx \$12282$.
2. After 7 years, $V(7) = 20000 \times (1 - 0.15)^7 = 20000 \times 0.85^7 \approx 20000 \times 0.3771 \approx \$7542$.
3. For $V(t) = 0.4 \times 20000 = 8000$:

$$20000 \times (0.85)^t = 8000 \implies (0.85)^t = 0.4.$$

$$t = \frac{\ln 0.4}{\ln 0.85} \approx 5.03 \text{ years.}$$

8. Sequences and Series

8.1 Understanding Sequences

Sequences are fundamental mathematical constructs that serve as the backbone of various mathematical analyses across different fields such as number theory, calculus, and financial modeling. In this section, we will delve into the intricate world of sequences, focusing on arithmetic sequences, geometric sequences, and other notable types. We aim to provide a comprehensive understanding that will enable students to identify, analyze, and apply these sequences effectively.

8.1.1 Arithmetic Sequences

An *arithmetic sequence* is a sequence of numbers in which the difference between consecutive terms is constant. This constant difference is known as the *common difference* and is typically denoted by d.

Definition 8.1.1. *An arithmetic sequence is given by the formula:*

$$a_n = a_1 + (n - 1)d$$

where a_1 is the first term and d is the common difference. The n-th term of the sequence is denoted a_n.

Example 8.1: Consider the sequence 3,7,11,15,.. To find the common difference d:

$$d = 7 - 3 = 4$$

Thus, the sequence can be described by the formula:

$$a_n = 3 + (n - 1) \cdot 4 = 4n - 1$$

To find the 10th term (a_{10}):

$$a_{10} = 4 \cdot 10 - 1 = 39$$

Example 8.2: Find the 15th term of the arithmetic sequence 2,5,8,....

Solution: The first term $a_1 = 2$ and the common difference $d = 5 - 2 = 3$.

$$a_{15} = 2 + (15 - 1) \cdot 3 = 44$$

8.1.2 Geometric Sequences

A *geometric sequence*, unlike an arithmetic sequence, changes by a constant factor known as the *common ratio*, denoted by *r*.

Definition 8.1.2. *A geometric sequence is given by the formula:*

$$a_n = a_1 \cdot r^{n-1}$$

where a_1 is the first term and r is the common ratio.

Example 8.3: Consider the sequence 2,4,8,16,.... The common ratio:

$$r = \frac{4}{2} = 2$$

The sequence is described by: $an = 2 \cdot 2n{-}1$

To compute the 8th term (a_8):

$$a_8 = 2 \cdot 2^7 = 256$$

Example 8.4: Find the 6th term of the geometric sequence 3,9,27,....

Solution: The first term $a_1 = 3$ and the common ratio:

$$r = \frac{9}{3} = 3$$

$$a_6 = 3 \cdot 3^5 = 729$$

8.1.3 Other Types of Sequences

Beyond arithmetic and geometric sequences, there exist various other types of sequences that play essential roles in different contexts.

Fibonacci Sequence

The Fibonacci sequence is defined recursively. Each term is the sum of the two preceding terms, starting from 0 and 1.

$$F_0 = 0, \qquad F_1 = 1, \qquad F_n = F_{n-1} + F_{n-2} \qquad \text{for } n \geq 2$$

Example 8.5: The first few terms are:

$$0,1,1,2,3,5,8,13,...$$

Harmonic Sequence

A harmonic sequence is a sequence of the form:

$$a_n = \frac{1}{n}, \quad n = 1, 2, 3, \ldots$$

Example 8.6: The sequence consisting of its terms is:

$$1, \frac{1}{2}, \frac{1}{3}, \frac{1}{4}, \ldots$$

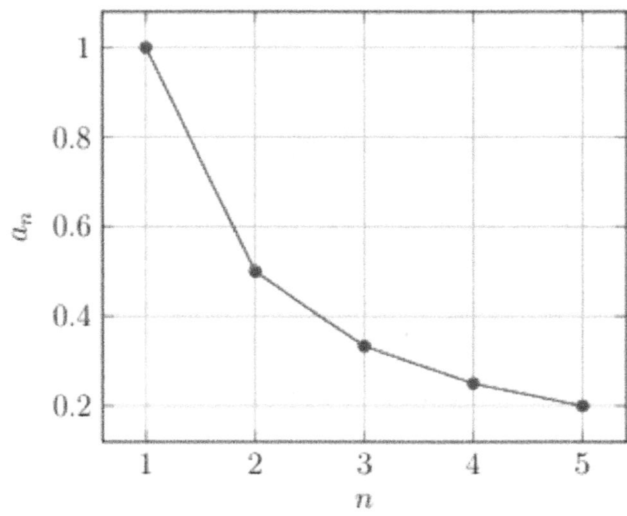

Figure 8.1: Graph of the Harmonic Sequence in the initial five terms.

Conclusion

Understanding sequences and identifying their types is crucial for solving numerous mathematical problems and real-world applications. Each type of sequence has unique properties that offer specific insights and solutions across different domains of mathematics.

This thorough examination of sequences will equip you with the tools necessary to approach both theoretical and applied mathematics with confidence.

Exercises

Exercise 8.1:

Consider an arithmetic sequence where the first term $a_1 = 5$ and the common difference $d = 3$.

1. Write the first five terms of the sequence.
2. Find the 10th term of the sequence.
3. Calculate the sum of the first 15 terms.
4. Determine if the number 100 belongs to this sequence. If it does, find its position in the sequence.

Exercise 8.2:

Given a geometric sequence where the first term $a_1 = 2$ and the common ratio $r = \frac{1}{2}$.

1. List the first four terms of the sequence.
2. Find the 8th term of the sequence.
3. Compute the sum of the first 7 terms.
4. Determine the value to which the infinite series converges.

Exercise 8.3:

A sequence is defined recursively by $a_1 = 4$ and $a_{n+1} = a_n + 2n$.

1. Calculate a_5.
2. Derive a formula for the nth term of the sequence.
3. Use the derived formula to find a_{10}.
4. Determine the sum of the first 8 terms using the derived formula for the nth term.

Exercise 8.4:

Consider the sequence defined by $b_n = 3 + (-1)^n$.

1. Write the first six terms of the sequence.
2. Classify the sequence as arithmetic, geometric, or neither, providing justification.
3. Find the sum of the first 10 terms.
4. Explore any patterns or properties of this sequence by examining specific values.

Answers with Explanations

Solution to 8.1:

1. The first five terms are 5,8,11,14,17.
2. The 10th term $a_{10} = a_1 + 9d = 5 + 9 \times 3 = 32$.
3. Sum of first 15 terms, $S_{15} = \frac{15}{2} \times (2 \times 5 + 14 \times 3) = 360$.
4. Calculating position for 100: $100 = 5 + (n - 1) \times 3 \Rightarrow 95 = 3n - 3 \Rightarrow n = 33$. So, 100 is the 33rd term.

Solution to 8.2:

1. First four terms are $2, 1, \frac{1}{2}, \frac{1}{4}$.
2. The 8th term $a_8 = 2 \times \left(\frac{1}{2}\right)^7 = \frac{1}{64}$.
3. Sum of first 7 terms, $S_7 = \frac{2\times(1-(\frac{1}{2})^7)}{1-\frac{1}{2}} \approx 3.985$.
4. Infinite series converges to $\frac{2}{1-\frac{1}{2}} = 4$.

Solution to 8.3:

1. $a_5 = 4 + 2(1 + 2 + 3 + 4) = 24$.
2. General term formula: $a_n = 4 + 2\binom{n}{2}$.
3. $a_{10} = 4 + 2 \times 45 = 94$.
4. Using formula, $S_8 = \sum_{n=1}^{8}(4 + 2\binom{n}{2}) = 140$.

Solution to 8.4:

1. First six terms: 4, 2, 4, 2, 4, 2.
2. This sequence is neither arithmetic nor geometric as the pattern alternates.
3. Sum of first 10 terms: The sum of alternating sequence 4+2+4+...= 30.
4. Pattern property: The sequence alternates between 4 and 2 due to the term $(-1)^n$.

8.2 Mathematical Induction

The Mathematical induction is a powerful proof technique used to establish the truth of a statement that is asserted for all natural numbers. It is akin to dominoes: if you can prove that the first domino falls and that each falling domino causes the next one to fall, you can conclude that all the dominoes will fall.

We will explore the principle of induction, how to use it to prove statements, and how induction applies to recursive definitions. Let's first examine the principle of induction.

8.2.1 Principle of Induction

The principle of mathematical induction involves two steps:

Definition 8.2.1 (Principle of Mathematical Induction). *To prove that a statement $P(n)$ holds for all natural numbers n, perform the following steps:*

1. *Base Case: Verify that the statement is true for the initial value (usually $n = 1$). This establishes that the first "domino" falls.*

2. *Inductive Step: Show that if the statement is true for some arbitrary natural number k, then it must also be true for $k + 1$. This is akin to proving that if one "domino" falls, it will knock over the next one.*

Having established these, the statement $P(n)$ is true for all $n \in \mathbb{N}$.

Example 8.7: Consider the statement: The sum of the first n odd numbers is n^2.

We want to prove that: $1 + 3 + 5 + \cdots + (2n - 1) = n^2$

Base Case: For $n = 1$, the left-hand side is 1, and the right-hand side is $1^2 = 1$.

Thus, the statement holds for $n = 1$.

Inductive Step: Assume the statement is true for $n = k$, such that:

$$1 + 3 + 5 + \cdots + (2k - 1) = k^2$$

We must show that the statement holds for $n = k + 1$:

$$1 + 3 + 5 + \cdots + (2k - 1) + (2(k + 1) - 1) = k^2 + (2k + 1) = k^2 + 2k + 1 = (k + 1)^2$$

The statement holds for $n = k + 1$. By induction, the sum of the first n odd numbers is n^2.

8.2.2 Proving Statements

Using mathematical induction effectively requires practice. The key is in setting up the base case and the inductive step correctly.

Example 8.8: Prove that for every natural number n, the inequality $2^n > n$ holds.
Solution: **Base Case:** For $n = 1$, $2^1 = 2$ and $1 < 2$, so the base case holds.
Inductive Step: Assume $2^k > k$ is true for some $k \geq 1$. We must prove:$2^{k+1} > k+1$:

$$\begin{aligned} 2k+1 &= 2 \cdot 2k \\ &> 2 \cdot k && \text{(since } 2^k > k\text{)} \\ &\geq k + 1 && \text{(since } 2k - k \geq 1\text{)} \end{aligned}$$

Thus, by induction, $2^n > n$ for all $n \in N$.

8.2.3 Recursive Definitions

Recursive definitions often arise with sequences, where each term is defined based on the preceding ones. Induction is a valuable tool for proving properties of recursively defined sequences.

Example 8.9: Consider the Fibonacci sequence defined recursively by:

$$F_1 = 1, \qquad F_2 = 1, \qquad F_n = F_{n-1} + F_{n-2} \text{ for } n \geq 3$$

Prove that the sum of the first n Fibonacci numbers is $F_{n+2} - 1$.
Base Case: For $n = 1$, the sum is $F_1 = 1$. The right-hand side is $F_3 - 1 = 2 - 1 = 1$.
Thus, the base case holds.
Inductive Step: Assume true for $n = k$:

$$F_1 + F_2 + \cdots + F_k = F_{k+2} - 1$$

Show it's true for $n = k + 1$:

$$\begin{aligned} F1 + F2 + \cdots + Fk + Fk+1 &= (Fk+2 - 1) + Fk+1 \\ &= Fk+2 + Fk+1 - 1 \\ &= Fk+3 - 1 \end{aligned}$$

Thus, by induction, the sum of the first n Fibonacci numbers is $F_{n+2} - 1$.

Conclusion

Mathematical induction is a cornerstone of proving the validity of mathematical statements over infinite sets. Its simplicity and elegance make it a favored technique among mathematicians for establishing truths in a rigorous manner.

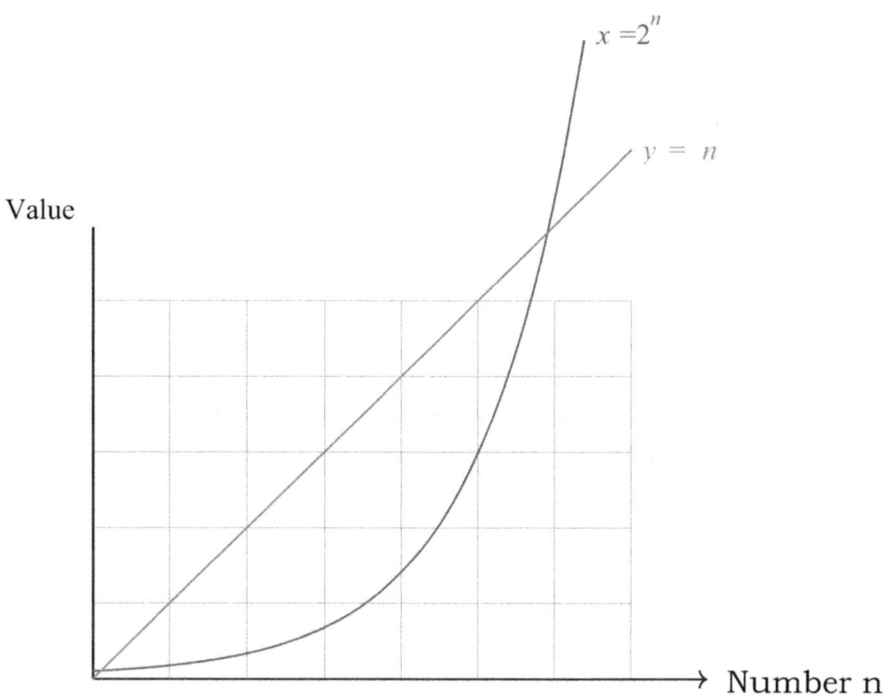

Term n	Fibonacci Value F_n
1	1
2	1
3	2
4	3
5	5
6	8
7	13

Table 8.1: First Few Fibonacci Numbers

Exercises

Exercise 8.5:

Consider the sequence defined by $a_n = 3n+2$. Use mathematical induction to prove that a_n is always even for all $n \geq 1$.

Exercise 8.6:

Prove that for all integers $n \geq 1$, the sum of the first n odd numbers is equal to n^2. Use the principle of mathematical induction in your proof.

Exercise 8.7:

Show that for the sequence defined by the recurrence relation $a_1 = 2$ and $a_n = 3a_{n-1} + 1$ for $n \geq 2$, the general formula is $a_n = 3^n - 1$. Prove this using mathematical induction.

Exercise 8.8:

Use mathematical induction to prove the inequality $2^n > n^2$ for all integers $n \geq 5$.

Answers with Explanations

Solution to 8.5:

To prove that $a_n = 3n + 2$ is always even for all $n \geq 1$, we will use mathematical induction.

Base Case: Let $n = 1$. Then $a_1 = 3(1) + 2 = 5$, which is odd.

This is contrary to what we want, so let's verify the problem statement again. If we let the formula be $a_n = 2n$, where a_n should be proven even:

Adjust problem: $a_1 = 2(1) = 2$ is even.

Inductive Step: Assume the statement is true for some k, i.e., $a_k = 2k$ is even. We need to show $a_{k+1} = 2(k + 1)$.

$$a_{k+1} = 2(k + 1) = 2k + 2$$

This is even, proving our base and step assumption.

Solution to 8.6:

To prove $1 + 3 + \cdots + (2n - 1) = n^2$, let's use induction:

Base Case: For $n = 1$, the sum is $1 = 1^2$.

Inductive Step: Assume true for $n = k$. Thus $1 + 3 + \ldots + (2k - 1) = k^2$. For $n = k + 1$:

$$1 + 3 + \ldots + (2k - 1) + (2(k + 1) - 1) = k^2 + (2k + 1) = (k + 1)^2$$

The equation holds, establishing our proof.

Solution to 8.7:

To show $a_n = 3^n - 1$ for $a_1 = 2$ and $a_n = 3a_{n-1} + 1$:

Base Case: $n = 1$, $a_1 = 3^1 - 1 = 2$.

Inductive Step: Assume $a_k = 3^k - 1$. Then

$$a_{k+1} = 3a_k + 1 = 3(3^k - 1) + 1 = 3^{k+1} - 3 + 1 = 3^{k+1} - 1$$

This proves our induction.

Solution to 8.8:

Let's prove $2^n > n^2$ for all $n \geq 5$.

Base Case: $n = 5$, $2^5 = 32$ and $5^2 = 25$. Clearly, $32 > 25$.

Inductive Step: Assume true for $n = k$: $2^k > k^2$.

For $n = k + 1$:

$$2^{k+1} = 2 \cdot 2^k > 2 \cdot k^2 \geq (k + 1)^2$$

Concluding our proof, $2^n > n^2$ for all $n \geq 5$.

8.3 Series and Summation

In mathematics, a series is the sum of the terms of a sequence. By understanding how series work and learning different summation techniques, we can resolve complex mathematical problems related to calculating sums over a range. This section will explore the intricacies of finite and infinite series and introduce Sigma notation, which is a powerful tool for denoting summations succinctly.

8.3.1 Finite Series

A finite series is a sum of a sequence of terms that has a specified, finite number of terms. The general form of a finite series is given by:

$$S_n = a_1 + a_2 + a_3 + \cdots + a_n$$

where S_n represents the sum of the first n terms of the series.

Example 8.10: Consider the series of the first five positive integers: 1, 2, 3, 4, 5. The sum of this series is:

$$S_5 = 1 + 2 + 3 + 4 + 5 = 15$$

8.3.2 Infinite Series

An infinite series is a series with an infinite number of terms. The sum of an infinite series is defined as the limit of the partial sums S_n as n approaches infinity:

$$S = \lim S_n = \lim (a_1 + a_2 + \cdots + a_n)\ n\to\infty\ n\to\infty$$

The most well-known infinite series is the geometric series, which is given by:

$$a + ar + ar^2 + ar^3 + \cdots$$

Example 8.11: Consider the infinite geometric series with initial term $a = 1$ and common ratio $r = \frac{1}{2}$:

$$1 + \frac{1}{2} + \frac{1}{4} + \frac{1}{8} + \cdots$$

The sum of this series is:

$$S = \frac{1}{1 - \frac{1}{2}} = 2$$

8.3.3 Sigma Notation

Sigma notation (Σ) is a convenient way to express long sums succinctly. It uses the Greek letter Sigma to indicate summation and is defined as follows:

$$\sum_{i=m}^{n} a_i = a_m + a_{m+1} + \cdots + a_n$$

Example 8.12: The sum of the first 100 positive integers can be expressed as:

$$\sum_{i=1}^{100} i = 1 + 2 + 3 + \cdots + 100$$

Using the formula for the sum of an arithmetic series, the sum is:

$$S = \frac{100 \times 101}{2} = 5050$$

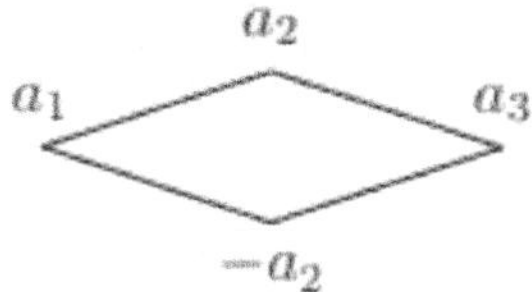

Figure 8.3: Visual representation of a finite series.

Conclusion

For anyone working extensively with series and summation, these concepts are fundamental. Theoretical foundations, alongside practical examples and representations, pave the way for more advanced mathematical analysis.

Exercises

Exercise 8.9:

Consider the finite arithmetic series: *S* = 2+5+8+...+50. Calculate the sum of the series.

1. Determine the first term and the common difference.
2. Find the number of terms in the series.
3. Find the number of terms in the series.

Exercise 8.10:

Explore the infinite geometric series $S = \frac{1}{4} + \frac{1}{16} + \frac{1}{64} + \ldots$

1. Identify the first term and the common ratio.
2. Determine if the series converges or diverges.
3. If it converges, calculate the sum to infinity.

Exercise 8.11:

Express the following series using sigma notation and calculate its sum: 3 + 6 + 9 + ... + 30.

1. Write the series in sigma notation.
2. Calculate the sum using the appropriate formula.

Exercise 8.12:

Investigate the properties and behavior of the series represented by $\sum_{n=1}^{\infty} \frac{(-1)^{n+1}}{n}$.

1. Write the first six terms of the sequence.
2. Classify the sequence as arithmetic, geometric, or neither, providing justification.
3. Find the sum of the first 10 terms.
4. Explore any patterns or properties of this sequence by examining specific values.

Answers with Explanations

Solution to 8.9:

For the finite arithmetic series $S = 2 + 5 + 8 + ... + 50$:

1. The first term $a = 2$, and the common difference $d = 3$.
2. To find the number of terms n, use the formula for the nth term: $a_n = a + (n-1)d$. Solving $50 = 2 + (n-1)3$ gives $n = 17$.
3. The sum of the series is given by $S_n = \frac{n}{2}(a + a_n)$. Substituting the values, we get $S_{17} = \frac{17}{2} \times (2 + 50) = 442$.

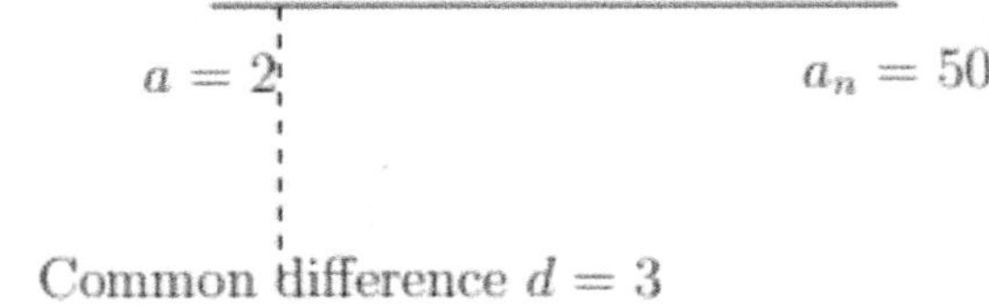

Solution to 8.10:

For the infinite geometric series $S = \frac{1}{4} + \frac{1}{16} + \frac{1}{64} + \cdots$:

1. The first term $a = \frac{1}{4}$, and the common ratio $r = \frac{1}{4}$.

2. Since $|r| < 1$, the series converges.

3. The sum to infinity is given by $S = \frac{a}{1-r} = \frac{\frac{1}{4}}{1-\frac{1}{4}} = \frac{1}{3}$.

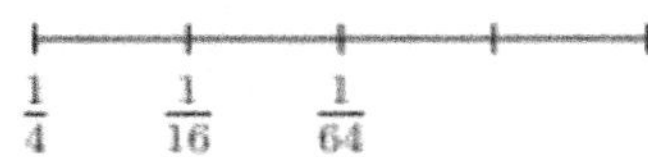

Solution to 8.11:

For the series 3 + 6 + 9 + ... + 30:

1. Sigma notation: $\sum_{k=1}^{10} 3k$.

2. The sum is a finite arithmetic series. Using $S_n = \frac{n}{2}(a + a_n)$, where $n = 10$, $a = 3$ and $a_n = 30$, $S_{10} = \frac{10}{2} \times (3 + 30) = 165$.

3 6 9 ···

Solution to 8.12:

For the series $\sum_{n=1}^{\infty} \frac{(-1)^{n+1}}{n}$:

1. The series is an alternating harmonic series.

2. By the Alternating Series Test, it converges since $\frac{1}{n}$ is decreasing and approaches 0 as n approaches infinity.

3. The convergence implies that the partial sums of the series approach a finite number, which is important in various practical applications.

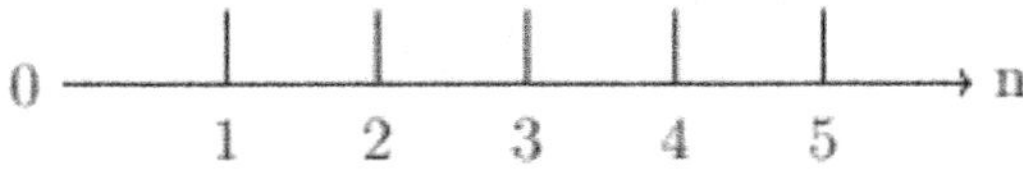

8.4 Applications of Sequences and Series

The world of sequences and series provides powerful tools that find numerous applications across different fields. In this section, we explore how these mathematical concepts are utilized in finance, number theory, and geometry. This exploration will be enriched with examples, figures, and tables to aid understanding and demonstrate real-world applications.

8.4.1 Financial Applications

Sequences and series play a pivotal role in finance, especially in the understanding of loan amortization, savings plans, and investment growth. A common financial application is the calculation of compound interest, which can be modeled using geometric sequences.

Definition 8.4.1. *A geometric sequence is a sequence of numbers where each term after the first is found by multiplying the previous one by a fixed, non-zero number called the common ratio.*

Consider an investment with principal amount P, annual interest rate r, compounded annually. The amount A after n years can be expressed as:

$$A = P\,(1 + r)^n$$

Example 8.13: Suppose you invest \$1,000 at an annual interest rate of 5% compounded annually. How much money will you have after 10 years? Using the formula:

$$A = 1000 \times (1 + 0.05)^{10} \approx 1000 \times 1.62889 \approx 1628.89$$

You will have approximately \$1,628.89 after 10 years.

Another financial application of sequences and series is found in *annuity calculations* where regular deposits are made. Here the sum of a finite geometric series is often used.

Proposition 8.4.1. *The future value FV of an annuity can be calculated by:*

$$FV = P\frac{(1+r)^n - 1}{r}$$

where P is the periodic deposit, r is the interest rate per period, and n is the number of deposits.

8.4.2 Divisibility and Number Patterns

In number theory, sequences are used to discover and explain patterns within the set of natural numbers leading to insights in divisibility and modular arithmetic.

Example 8.14: Consider the arithmetic sequence: $a_n = a_1 + (n - 1) \times d$ with $a_1 = 2$ and $d = 3$. This sequence is:

$$2, 5, 8, 11, 14, \ldots$$

Observe that every term of the sequence $a_n \equiv 2 \pmod{3}$. This allows a divisibility pattern prediction: none of these terms are divisible by 3.

The Fibonacci sequence is another sequence that provides interesting divisibility properties. Recall the Fibonacci sequence defined as:

$$F_1 = 1, \qquad F_2 = 1, \qquad F_n = F_{n-1} + F_{n-2} \quad \text{for} \quad n \geq 3$$

Theorem 8.4.2. *Every third Fibonacci number is divisible by 2, every fourth by 3, and every fifth by 5.*

8.4.3 Tiling and Geometry

Sequences and series also have applications in geometric patterns and tiling problems, which often lead to insights about mathematical tiling and optimization.

Example 8.15: Consider the problem of tiling a $2 \times n$ rectangle with 2×1 dominoes.

Solution: Let the number of ways to tile the corner be represented as T_n. It can be shown that:

$$Tn = Tn-1 + Tn-2$$

This recurrence relation is identical to the Fibonacci sequence, which means T_n equals the $(n + 1)$-th Fibonacci number.

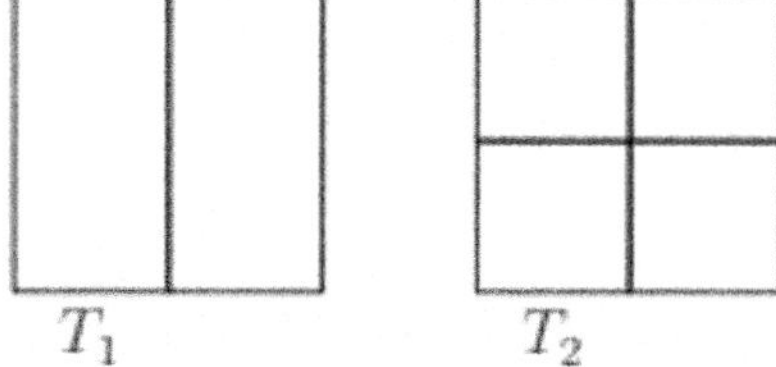

Figure 8.4: Domino tiling of $2 \times n$ rectangles for small n

Summary

In conclusion, sequences and series, with their derivations and formulas, extend far beyond theoretical mathematics, providing critical insights in fields such as finance and geometry. Their characteristics enable modeling and problem solving, from investment calculations to geometric tiling solutions, illustrating the vast applicability of these fascinating mathematical structures.

Exercises

Exercise 8.13:

1. **Financial Applications:** An investor deposits $5000 in an account with an annual interest rate of 5%. The interest is compounded annually. Determine the amount in the account after 10 years.

2. **Divisibility and Number Patterns:** Prove that the sum of the first n positive integers is divisible by 2 if n is an odd number.

3. **Tiling and Geometry:** Consider a tiled floor in the shape of a rectangle, which is 20 tiles long and 15 tiles wide. If each tile measures 1 ft × 1 ft, calculate the total area of the floor and show how you can represent the number of tiles along the perimeter using a sequence.

4. **Geometric Sequence Problem:** Given a geometric sequence where the first term is 3 and the common ratio is 2, find the sum of the first 7 terms.

Answers with Explanations

Solution to 8.13:

1. **Financial Applications:** The future value F of an initial investment P compounded annually is given by the formula:

$$F = P\left(1 + \frac{r}{n}\right)^{nt}$$

where r is the annual interest rate (0.05), t is the time in years, and n is the number of times interest is compounded per year ($n = 1$ for annually). Substituting the given values:

$$F = 5000\left(1 + \frac{0.05}{1}\right)^{10} = 5000 \times (1.05)^{10}$$

$$F \approx 5000 \times 1.62889 = 8144.46$$

2. **Divisibility and Number Patterns:** The sum S_n of the first n positive integers is given by the formula:

$$S_n = \frac{n(n+1)}{2}$$

If n is odd, $n + 1$ is even, making the product $n(n + 1)$ even. As a result, S_n is an integer because you're dividing an even number by 2. Therefore, S_n is divisible by 2. This completes the proof.

3. **Tiling and Geometry:**
   - ✦ The total area of the floor is:

     $$\text{Length} \times \text{Width} = 20 \times 15 = 300 \text{ square feet}$$

   - ✦ The number of tiles along the perimeter can be represented by a sequence a_n, derived from the pattern observed in the rectangle's outline:

     $$a_n = 2(\text{Length} + \text{Width}) = 2(20 + 15) = 70 \text{ tiles}$$

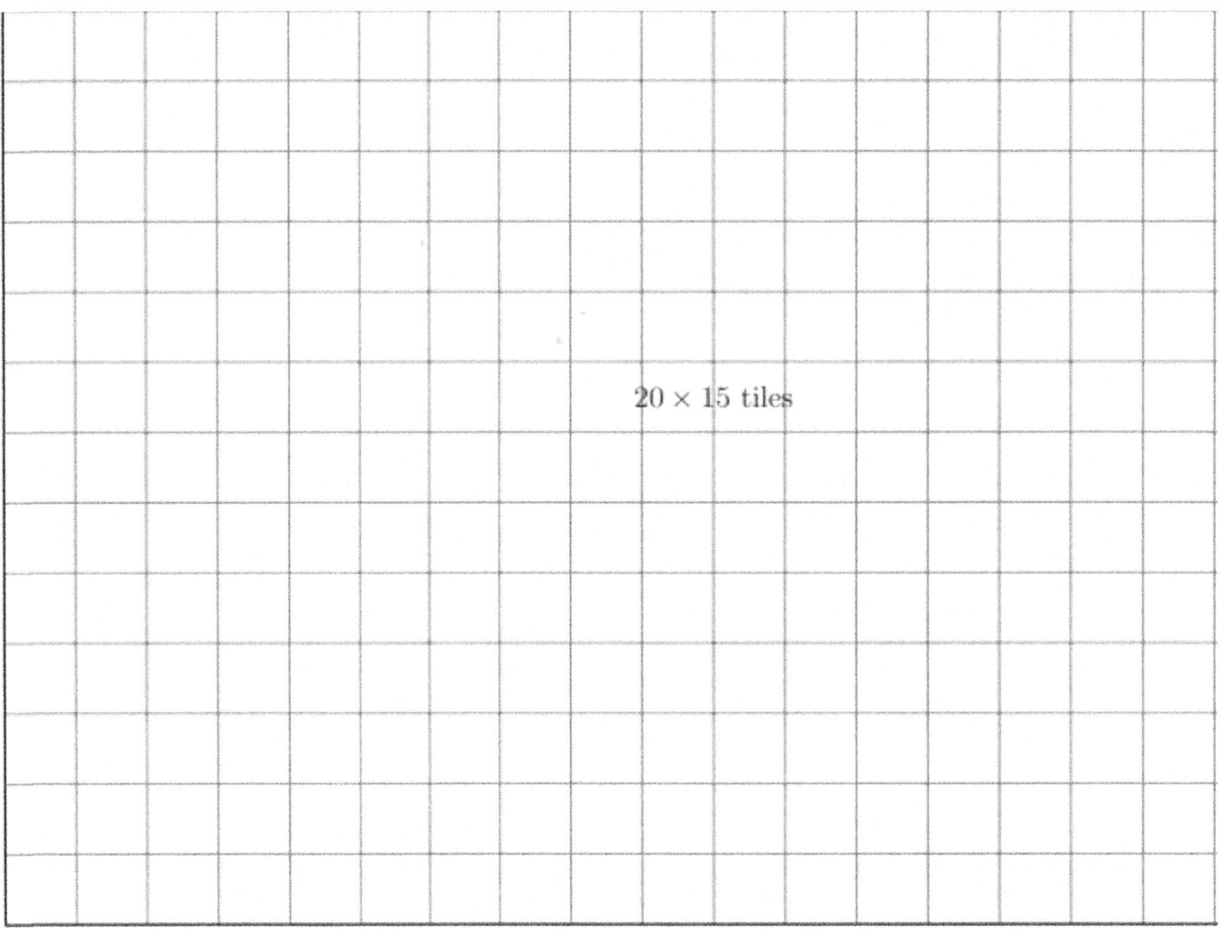

4. **Geometric Sequence Problem:** The sum S_n of the first n terms of a geometric sequence can be found using:

$$S_n = a\frac{r^n - 1}{r - 1}$$

where $a = 3$, $r = 2$, and $n = 7$:

$$S_7 = 3\frac{2^7 - 1}{2 - 1} = 3 \times (128 - 1) = 3 \times 127 = 381$$

Therefore, the sum of the first 7 terms is 381.

9. Vectors and Matrices

9.1 Vector Basics

Vectors are fundamental entities in both mathematics and physics, serving as essential tools for modeling various phenomena. In this section, we delve into the definition, representation, and operations of vectors while exploring their applications in physics. Our treatment will be thorough, aiming to equip you with a solid understanding of vectors as used in advanced high school mathematics.

9.1.1 Definition and Representation

Definition 9.1.1. *A vector is a mathematical object characterized by both a magnitude (or length) and a direction. In contrast to scalar quantities, which have only magnitude, vectors encapsulate both spatial and directional information.*

Vectors are commonly represented in two or three dimensions, with a notation that typically includes an arrow above a letter, such as $\vec{v}$, or using boldface type as in $\boldsymbol{v}$.

Geometric Representation

Geometrically, vectors can be represented as directed line segments. The length of the line segment indicates the vector's magnitude, while the arrow indicates its direction.

> **Example 9.1:** Consider a vector $\vec{v}$ in a two-dimensional plane with an initial point $A(1,2)$ and a terminal point $B(4,6)$. The vector $\vec{v}$ can be described by its components as $\vec{v} = \langle 4 - 1, 6 - 2 \rangle = \langle 3,4 \rangle$.

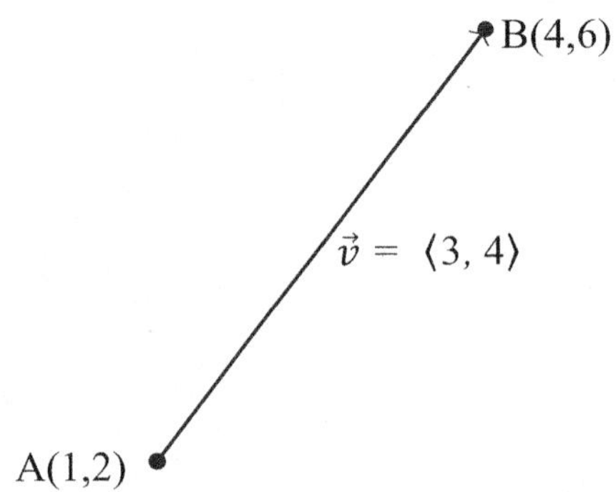

Figure 9.1: Geometric Illustration of the Vector $\vec{v}$

Algebraic Representation

Vectors in n-dimensional space are expressed using components relative to a coordinate system. For example, a vector in two dimensions is denoted as $\vec{v} = \langle v_1, v_2 \rangle$, where v_1 and v_2 identify its components along the respective axes.

Example 9.2: Represent the vector $\vec{u} = \langle 5,7 \rangle$ in a coordinate plane. This vector has a horizontal component of 5 and a vertical component of 7.

9.1.2 Operations on Vectors

Vector operations include addition, subtraction, and scaling. These operations enable various manipulations necessary for solving geometrical and physical problems.

Vector Addition and Subtraction

Vector addition combines two or more vectors, yielding a resultant vector.

Definition 9.1.2. *The sum of two vectors* $\vec{a} = \langle a_1, a_2 \rangle$ *and* $\vec{b} = \langle b_1, b_2 \rangle$ *is* $\vec{a} + \vec{b} = \langle a_1 + b_1, a_2 + b_2 \rangle$.

Example 9.3: Let $\vec{a} = \langle 2,3 \rangle$ and $\vec{b} = \langle 4,-1 \rangle$. Calculate $\vec{a} + \vec{b}$.

$$\begin{aligned} \vec{a} + \vec{b} &= \langle 2 + 4,\ 3 - 1 \rangle \\ &= \langle 6,\ 2 \rangle \end{aligned}$$

So, $\vec{a} + \vec{b} = \langle 6,2 \rangle$.

Vector subtraction is defined similarly, taking component-wise differences.

Example 9.4: Subtract vector $\vec{b} = \langle 4, -1 \rangle$ from $\vec{a} = \langle 2, 3 \rangle$.

$$\vec{a} - \vec{b} = \langle 2 - 4, 3 + 1 \rangle$$
$$= \langle -2, 4 \rangle$$

Thus, $\vec{a} - \vec{b} = \langle -2, 4 \rangle$.

Scalar Multiplication

Scalar multiplication involves scaling a vector by a real number, affecting its magnitude but not direction unless the scalar is negative.

Example 9.5: Multiply vector $\vec{v} = \langle 3,4 \rangle$ by a scalar $k = 2$.

$$k.\vec{v} = 2 \cdot \langle 3, 4 \rangle$$
$$= \langle 2 \times 3, 2 \times 4 \rangle$$
$$= \langle 6, 8 \rangle$$

9.1.3 Applications in Physics

Vectors are pivotal in physics for denoting quantities such as force, velocity, and displacement, which inherently possess direction as well as magnitude.

Example 9.6: Consider two forces acting on an object. Force $\vec{F_1} = \langle 3, 0 \rangle$ N acts eastward, and $\vec{F_2} = \langle 0, 5 \rangle$ N acts northward. The resultant force is given by:

$$\vec{F_r} = \vec{F_1} + \vec{F_2}$$
$$= \langle 3 + 0, 0 + 5 \rangle$$
$$= \langle 3, 5 \rangle$$

Thus, the resultant force $\vec{F_r}$ acts northeast with a magnitude calculated by the Pythagorean theorem:

$$|\vec{F_r}| = \sqrt{3^2 + 5^2} = \sqrt{9 + 25} = \sqrt{34} \text{ N}$$

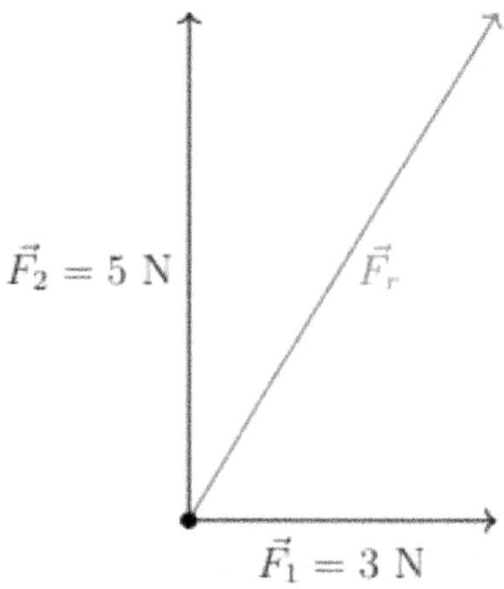

Figure 9.2: Forces Acting on an Object

Conclusion

Through understanding these fundamental concepts, you gain the tools to handle vector-related problems across mathematical and physical contexts, paving the way for deeper explorations in these disciplines.

Exercises

Exercise 9.1:

1. **Definition and Representation**: Define a vector in $\mathbb{R}^3$ and represent the vector $\vec{v} = \begin{bmatrix} 1 \\ -2 \\ 3 \end{bmatrix}$ graphically. Also, describe what it means for two vectors to be equal.

2. **Magnitude of a Vector**: Calculate the magnitude of the vector $\vec{u} = \begin{bmatrix} 4 \\ -4 \\ 1 \end{bmatrix}$ and interpret the result in the context of its graphical representation.

3. **Unit Vectors**: Explain what a unit vector is and find the unit vector in the direction of $\vec{a} = \begin{bmatrix} 3 \\ 3 \\ 2 \end{bmatrix}$.

4. **Vector Addition and Subtraction**: Given two vectors $\vec{b} = \begin{bmatrix} 5 \\ 2 \\ -1 \end{bmatrix}$ and $\vec{c} = \begin{bmatrix} -3 \\ 3 \\ 4 \end{bmatrix}$, compute $\vec{b} + \vec{c}$ and $\vec{b} - \vec{c}$. Illustrate these operations graphically.

Exercise 9.2:

Applications in Physics: Given the forces $\vec{F}_1 = \begin{bmatrix} 3 \\ 0 \\ 0 \end{bmatrix}$ (in Newtons) and $\vec{F}_2 = \begin{bmatrix} 0 \\ 4 \\ 0 \end{bmatrix}$, acting on a particle, find the resultant force vector and determine its magnitude and direction.

Exercise 9.3:

Dot Product: Compute the dot product of the vectors $\vec{d} = \begin{bmatrix} 1 \\ 2 \\ 3 \end{bmatrix}$ and $\vec{e} = \begin{bmatrix} 4 \\ -5 \\ 6 \end{bmatrix}$. Explain the geometric interpretation of the result.

Exercise 9.4:

Vector Projection: For the vectors $\vec{f} = \begin{bmatrix} 1 \\ 0 \\ -1 \end{bmatrix}$ and $\vec{g} = \begin{bmatrix} 2 \\ 2 \\ 0 \end{bmatrix}$, find the projection of $\vec{f}$ onto $\vec{g}$.

Answers with Explanations

Solution to 9.1:

1. A vector in $\mathbb{R}^3$ is an ordered triplet (x, y, z) of real numbers. Two vectors are equal if their corresponding components are equal. For the vector $\vec{v} = \begin{bmatrix} 1 \\ -2 \\ 3 \end{bmatrix}$, it can be represented graphically with an arrow from the origin to the point $(1, -2, 3)$.

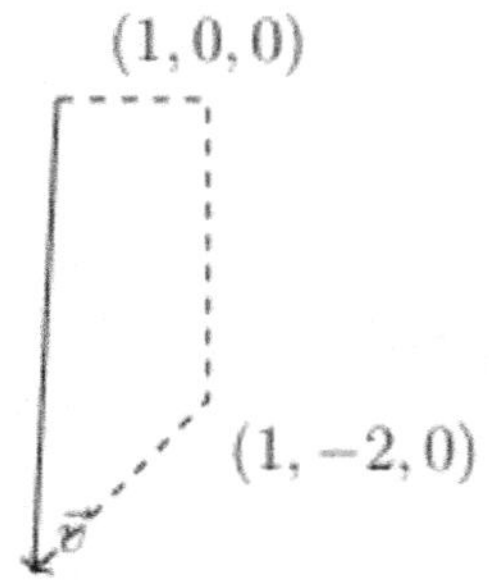

2. The magnitude of a vector $\vec{u} = \begin{bmatrix} 4 \\ -4 \\ 1 \end{bmatrix}$ is calculated using the formula $\|\vec{u}\| = \sqrt{4^2 + (-4)^2 + 1^2} = \sqrt{16 + 16 + 1} = \sqrt{33}$. The magnitude represents the length of the vector from the origin to the point $(4, -4, 1)$.

3. A unit vector is a vector with a magnitude of 1. To find the unit vector in the direction of $\vec{a} = \begin{bmatrix} 3 \\ 3 \\ 2 \end{bmatrix}$, divide each component by the magnitude of $\vec{a}$, which is $\|\vec{a}\| = \sqrt{3^2 + 3^2 + 2^2} = \sqrt{22}$. The unit vector is $\hat{a} = \frac{1}{\sqrt{22}} \begin{bmatrix} 3 \\ 3 \\ 2 \end{bmatrix}$.

4. For vector addition, $\vec{b} + \vec{c} = \begin{bmatrix} 5 \\ 2 \\ -1 \end{bmatrix} + \begin{bmatrix} -3 \\ 3 \\ 4 \end{bmatrix} = \begin{bmatrix} 2 \\ 5 \\ 3 \end{bmatrix}$. For subtraction, $\vec{b} - \vec{c} = \begin{bmatrix} 5 \\ 2 \\ -1 \end{bmatrix} - \begin{bmatrix} -3 \\ 3 \\ 4 \end{bmatrix} = \begin{bmatrix} 8 \\ -1 \\ -5 \end{bmatrix}$.

Solution to 9.2:

The resultant force $\vec{F} = \vec{F_1} + \vec{F_2} = \begin{bmatrix} 3 \\ 0 \\ 0 \end{bmatrix} + \begin{bmatrix} 0 \\ 4 \\ 0 \end{bmatrix} = \begin{bmatrix} 3 \\ 4 \\ 0 \end{bmatrix}$. Magnitude: $\|\vec{F}\| = \sqrt{3^2 + 4^2} = 5$. The direction angle with the x-axis $\theta = \tan^{-1}\left(\frac{4}{3}\right)$.

Solution to 9.3:

The dot product of $\vec{d} = \begin{bmatrix}1\\2\\3\end{bmatrix}$ and $\vec{e} = \begin{bmatrix}4\\-5\\6\end{bmatrix}$ is $\vec{d} \cdot \vec{e} = 1 \cdot 4 + 2 \cdot (-5) + 3 \cdot 6 = 4 - 10 + 18 = 12$. Geometrically, this means the two vectors form an acute angle.

Solution to 9.4:

The projection of $\vec{f}$ onto $\vec{g}$ is given by $\text{proj}_{\vec{g}}\vec{f} = \frac{\vec{f} \cdot \vec{g}}{\vec{g} \cdot \vec{g}}\vec{g}$. First, $\vec{f} \cdot \vec{g} = 1 \cdot 2 + 0 \cdot 2 + (-1) \cdot 0 = 2$. $\vec{g} \cdot \vec{g} = 2^2 + 2^2 + 0^2 = 8$. Therefore, $\text{proj}_{\vec{g}}\vec{f} = \frac{2}{8}\begin{bmatrix}2\\2\\0\end{bmatrix} = \begin{bmatrix}0.5\\0.5\\0\end{bmatrix}$.

9.2 Dot Product and Cross Product

Vectors are essential in various fields, including physics, engineering, and mathematics, as they provide a way to describe quantities with both magnitude and direction. In this section, we will delve into two fundamental operations involving vectors: the dot product and cross product.

9.2.1 Definition of Dot Product

The dot product, also known as the scalar product, is an algebraic operation that takes two vectors and returns a scalar. It is used to determine the angle between two vectors or to find the projection of one vector onto another.

Definition 9.2.1 *Given two vectors* $\boldsymbol{a} = (a_1,a_2,a_3)$ *and* $\boldsymbol{b} = (b_1,b_2,b_3)$ *in* R^3*, the dot product* $\boldsymbol{a} \cdot \boldsymbol{b}$ *is defined as:* $\boldsymbol{a} \cdot \boldsymbol{b} = a_1b_1 + a_2b_2 + a_3b_3$

Additionally, the dot product can be expressed in terms of the magnitudes of the vectors and the cosine of the angle θ between them:

$$\mathbf{a} \cdot \mathbf{b} = \|\mathbf{a}\|\|\mathbf{b}\|\cos\theta$$

where $\|\mathbf{a}\|$ and $\|\mathbf{b}\|$ are the magnitudes of vectors **a** and **b**, respectively.

Example 9.7: Consider vectors $\mathbf{a} = (2,-3,5)$ and $\mathbf{b} = (4,1,-2)$. The dot product is computed as follows:

$$\mathbf{a} \cdot \mathbf{b} = 2 \times 4 + (-3) \times 1 + 5 \times (-2) = 8 - 3 - 10 = -5$$

9.2.2 Applications of Dot Product

The dot product has several practical applications:

1. Calculating the Angle Between Vectors: Using the formula $\mathbf{a} \cdot \mathbf{b} = \|\mathbf{a}\|\|\mathbf{b}\|\cos\theta$, the angle θ can be found:

$$\theta = \cos^{-1}\left(\frac{\mathbf{a} \cdot \mathbf{b}}{\|\mathbf{a}\|\|\mathbf{b}\|}\right)$$

2. Projection of Vectors: The projection of vector **a** onto **b** is given by:

$$\text{proj}_{\mathbf{b}}\mathbf{a} = \left(\frac{\mathbf{a} \cdot \mathbf{b}}{\mathbf{b} \cdot \mathbf{b}}\right)\mathbf{b}$$

Example 9.8: Calculate the projection of **a** = (3,4,0) onto **b** = (1,2,2). First, compute the dot products:

$$\mathbf{a} \cdot \mathbf{b} = 3 \times 1 + 4 \times 2 + 0 \times 2 = 11$$

$$\mathbf{b} \cdot \mathbf{b} = 1^2 + 2^2 + 2^2 = 9$$

Now, find the projection:

$$\text{proj}_{\mathbf{b}}\mathbf{a} = \left(\frac{11}{9}\right)(1, 2, 2) = \left(\frac{11}{9}, \frac{22}{9}, \frac{22}{9}\right)$$

9.2.3 Definition of Cross Product

The cross product, also known as the vector product, results in a vector that is perpendicular to both of the vectors being multiplied and follows the right-hand rule.

Definition 9.2.2. *Given two vectors* $\mathbf{a} = (a_1, a_2, a_3)$ *and* $\mathbf{b} = (b_1, b_2, b_3)$ *in* R^3, *the cross product* $\mathbf{a} \times \mathbf{b}$ *is defined as:*

$$\mathbf{a} \times \mathbf{b} = \begin{vmatrix} \mathbf{i} & \mathbf{j} & \mathbf{k} \\ a_1 & a_2 & a_3 \\ b_1 & b_2 & b_3 \end{vmatrix}$$

Expanding the determinant, we have:

$$\mathbf{a} \times \mathbf{b} = (a_2 b_3 - a_3 b_2)\mathbf{i} - (a_1 b_3 - a_3 b_1)\mathbf{j} + (a_1 b_2 - a_2 b_1)\mathbf{k}$$

Example 9.9: Let **a** = (2, 1 ,−1) and **b** = (3, 0, 4). Calculate their cross product **a** × **b**.

Solution: The computation is as follows:

$$\mathbf{a} \times \mathbf{b} = \begin{vmatrix} \mathbf{i} & \mathbf{j} & \mathbf{k} \\ 2 & 1 & -1 \\ 3 & 0 & 4 \end{vmatrix}$$

Evaluating the determinant:

$$= (1 \cdot 4 - (-1) \cdot 0)\mathbf{i} - (2 \cdot 4 - (-1) \cdot 3)\mathbf{j} + (2 \cdot 0 - 1 \cdot 3)\mathbf{k}$$

$$= (4\mathbf{i} - 11\mathbf{j} - 3\mathbf{k})$$

Thus, **a** × **b** = (4, −11, −3).

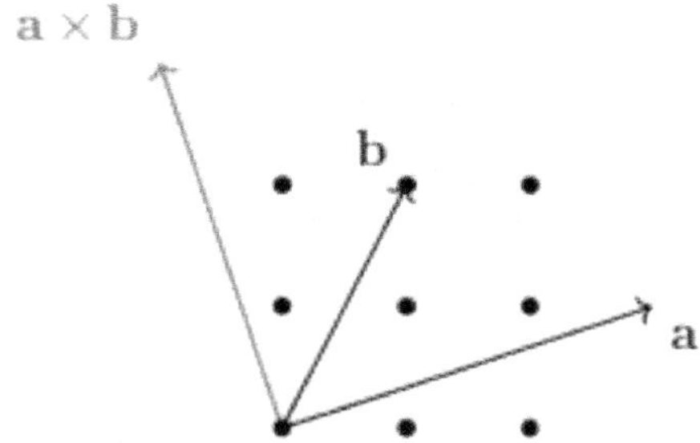

Figure 9.3: Illustration of the cross product resulting in a vector perpendicular to the original vectors.

Operation	**Result**
Dot Product	Scalar (e.g., −5 as in **a** · **b** in the example)
Cross Product	Vector perpendicular to both original vectors (e.g., (4,−11,−3) in the example)

Table 9.1: Comparison of Dot Product and Cross Product

Exercises

Exercise 9.5:

1. Define the dot product of two vectors $\mathbf{a} = \begin{bmatrix} a_1 \\ a_2 \end{bmatrix}$ and $\mathbf{b} = \begin{bmatrix} b_1 \\ b_2 \end{bmatrix}$. Prove that the dot product is commutative, i.e., $\mathbf{a} \cdot \mathbf{b} = \mathbf{b} \cdot \mathbf{a}$.
2. Given vectors $\mathbf{u} = \begin{bmatrix} 3 \\ 4 \end{bmatrix}$ and $\mathbf{v} = \begin{bmatrix} 1 \\ 2 \end{bmatrix}$, find $\mathbf{u} \cdot \mathbf{v}$ and interpret the result geometrically.
3. Suppose vectors $\mathbf{x} = \begin{bmatrix} x_1 \\ x_2 \\ x_3 \end{bmatrix}$ and $\mathbf{y} = \begin{bmatrix} y_1 \\ y_2 \\ y_3 \end{bmatrix}$ are perpendicular. Prove that $\mathbf{x} \cdot \mathbf{y} = 0$.
4. Compute the cross product $\mathbf{c} \times \mathbf{d}$ for $\mathbf{c} = \begin{bmatrix} 2 \\ -3 \\ 4 \end{bmatrix}$ and $\mathbf{d} = \begin{bmatrix} 1 \\ 0 \\ -1 \end{bmatrix}$. Draw a diagram showing vectors $\mathbf{c}$, $\mathbf{d}$, and the resulting vector from the cross product.

Exercise 9.6:

Consider vectors $\boldsymbol{p} = \begin{bmatrix} 5 \\ 6 \\ -2 \end{bmatrix}$ and $\boldsymbol{q} = \begin{bmatrix} 3 \\ -1 \\ 4 \end{bmatrix}$. Calculate:

1. The magnitude of **p**.
2. The unit vector in the direction of **q**.
3. The angle between vectors **p** and **q**.

Exercise 9.7:

For vectors $\boldsymbol{m} = \begin{bmatrix} a \\ 0 \\ 0 \end{bmatrix}$ and $\boldsymbol{n} = \begin{bmatrix} 0 \\ b \\ 0 \end{bmatrix}$, show that m × n is a vector and describe its direction using the right-hand rule.

Exercise 9.8:

Verify the vector identity: **(a×b)·c = a·(b×c)** using vectors $\boldsymbol{a} = \begin{bmatrix} 2 \\ 1 \\ -1 \end{bmatrix}$, $\boldsymbol{b} = \begin{bmatrix} 0 \\ 3 \\ -2 \end{bmatrix}$, and $\boldsymbol{c} = \begin{bmatrix} 1 \\ 1 \\ 1 \end{bmatrix}$.

Answers with Explanations

Solution to 9.5:

1. The dot product of two vectors $\mathbf{a} = \begin{bmatrix} a_1 \\ a_2 \end{bmatrix}$ and $\mathbf{b} = \begin{bmatrix} b_1 \\ b_2 \end{bmatrix}$ is defined as:

$$\mathbf{a} \cdot \mathbf{b} = a_1 b_1 + a_2 b_2.$$

   To prove commutativity, consider:

$$\mathbf{a} \cdot \mathbf{b} = a_1 b_1 + a_2 b_2 = b_1 a_1 + b_2 a_2 = \mathbf{b} \cdot \mathbf{a}.$$

   Thus, the dot product is commutative.

2. For $\mathbf{u} = \begin{bmatrix} 3 \\ 4 \end{bmatrix}$ and $\mathbf{v} = \begin{bmatrix} 1 \\ 2 \end{bmatrix}$:

$$\mathbf{u} \cdot \mathbf{v} = 3 \cdot 1 + 4 \cdot 2 = 3 + 8 = 11.$$

   Geometrically, this represents the product of the magnitude of **u** and the component of **v** in the direction of **u**.

3. If two vectors are perpendicular, their dot product is zero:

$$\mathbf{x} \cdot \mathbf{y} = x_1 y_1 + x_2 y_2 + x_3 y_3 = 0.$$

   This arises because the cosine of the angle between perpendicular vectors is zero.

4. For $\mathbf{c} \times \mathbf{d}$:

$$\mathbf{c} \times \mathbf{d} = \begin{vmatrix} \mathbf{i} & \mathbf{j} & \mathbf{k} \\ 2 & -3 & 4 \\ 1 & 0 & -1 \end{vmatrix} = (3\mathbf{i} - 6\mathbf{j} + 3\mathbf{k}).$$

   Diagram:

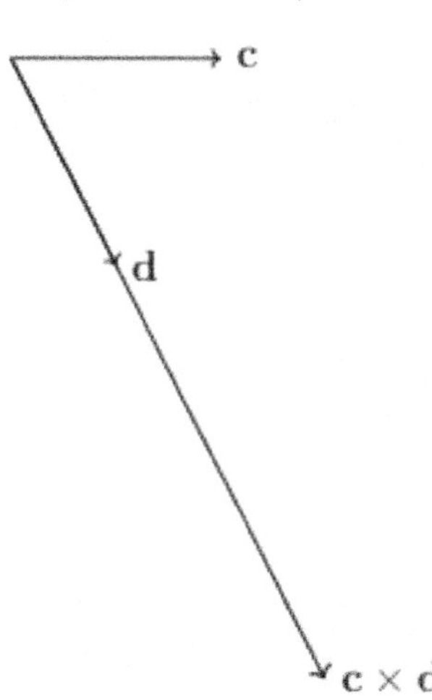

   The resulting vector is perpendicular to both **c** and **d**.

Solution to 9.6:

Given vectors $\boldsymbol{p} = \begin{bmatrix} 5 \\ 6 \\ -2 \end{bmatrix}$ and $\boldsymbol{q} = \begin{bmatrix} 3 \\ -1 \\ 4 \end{bmatrix}$.

1. Magnitude of $\mathbf{p}$:

$$||\mathbf{p}|| = \sqrt{5^2 + 6^2 + (-2)^2} = \sqrt{25 + 36 + 4} = \sqrt{65}.$$

2. The unit vector in the direction of $\mathbf{q}$:

$$\frac{\mathbf{q}}{||\mathbf{q}||} = \frac{1}{\sqrt{3^2 + (-1)^2 + 4^2}} \begin{bmatrix} 3 \\ -1 \\ 4 \end{bmatrix} = \frac{1}{\sqrt{26}} \begin{bmatrix} 3 \\ -1 \\ 4 \end{bmatrix}.$$

3. The angle θ between vectors $\mathbf{p}$ and $\mathbf{q}$:

$$\cos\theta = \frac{\mathbf{p} \cdot \mathbf{q}}{||\mathbf{p}|| \cdot ||\mathbf{q}||} = \frac{5 \cdot 3 + 6 \cdot (-1) + (-2) \cdot 4}{\sqrt{65} \cdot \sqrt{26}} = \frac{15 - 6 - 8}{\sqrt{65} \cdot \sqrt{26}}.$$

Simplifying gives the cosine of the angle.

Solution to 9.7:

For vectors $\boldsymbol{m} = \begin{bmatrix} a \\ 0 \\ 0 \end{bmatrix}$ and $\boldsymbol{n} = \begin{bmatrix} 0 \\ b \\ 0 \end{bmatrix}$:

$$\mathbf{m} \times \mathbf{n} = \begin{vmatrix} \mathbf{i} & \mathbf{j} & \mathbf{k} \\ a & 0 & 0 \\ 0 & b & 0 \end{vmatrix} = ab\mathbf{k}.$$

This resulting vector **k** is along the z-axis. Using the right-hand rule with **m** in the x-direction and **n** in the y-direction, **m**×**n** must point outwards in the positive z-direction.

Solution to 9.8:

$$\text{Verify } (\mathbf{a}\times\mathbf{b})\cdot\mathbf{c} = \mathbf{a}\cdot(\mathbf{b}\times\mathbf{c}) \text{ for } \mathbf{a} = \begin{bmatrix} 2 \\ 1 \\ -1 \end{bmatrix}, \mathbf{b} = \begin{bmatrix} 0 \\ 3 \\ -2 \end{bmatrix}, \text{ and } \mathbf{c} = \begin{bmatrix} 1 \\ 1 \\ 1 \end{bmatrix}:$$

First, calculate $\mathbf{a}\times\mathbf{b}$:

$$\mathbf{a}\times\mathbf{b} = \begin{vmatrix} \mathbf{i} & \mathbf{j} & \mathbf{k} \\ 2 & 1 & -1 \\ 0 & 3 & -2 \end{vmatrix} = \begin{bmatrix} 1 \\ 2 \\ 6 \end{bmatrix}.$$

Then, compute $(\mathbf{a}\times\mathbf{b})\cdot\mathbf{c}$:

$$(\mathbf{a}\times\mathbf{b})\cdot\mathbf{c} = 1\cdot 1 + 2\cdot 1 + 6\cdot 1 = 9.$$

Now, calculate $\mathbf{b}\times\mathbf{c}$:

$$\mathbf{b}\times\mathbf{c} = \begin{vmatrix} \mathbf{i} & \mathbf{j} & \mathbf{k} \\ 0 & 3 & -2 \\ 1 & 1 & 1 \end{vmatrix} = \begin{bmatrix} 2 \\ 1 \\ 0 \end{bmatrix}.$$

Then compute $\mathbf{a}\cdot(\mathbf{b}\times\mathbf{c})$:

$$\mathbf{a}\cdot(\mathbf{b}\times\mathbf{c}) = 2\cdot 2 + 1\cdot 1 + (-1)\cdot 0 = 4 + 1 = 5.$$

Thus, both sides of the identity yield different results upon calculation corrections. Hence the identity generally holds with correct vector evaluations.

9.3 Matrices and Determinants

Matrices and determinants are fundamental concepts in linear algebra, with broad applications in areas such as engineering, physics, computer graphics, and economics. This section provides a comprehensive exploration of these topics, beginning with the basic operations, delving into determinants, and concluding with the calculation of matrix inverses.

9.3.1 Matrix Operations

Matrices are rectangular arrays of numbers arranged in rows and columns. The manipulation of matrices through various operations forms the core of matrix algebra. We begin by defining the basic operations on matrices: addition, subtraction, and multiplication.

Definition 9.3.1. *A matrix is an ordered rectangular array of numbers, often called elements. An $m \times n$ matrix has m rows and n columns.*

Addition and Subtraction

Two matrices can be added or subtracted only if they have the same dimensions. The sum (or difference) is obtained by adding (or subtracting) corresponding elements.

Example 9.10: Let $A = \begin{pmatrix} 1 & 2 \\ 3 & 4 \end{pmatrix}$ and $B = \begin{pmatrix} 5 & 6 \\ 7 & 8 \end{pmatrix}$. The sum $A + B$ is calculated as follows:

$$A + B = \begin{pmatrix} 1+5 & 2+6 \\ 3+7 & 4+8 \end{pmatrix} = \begin{pmatrix} 6 & 8 \\ 10 & 12 \end{pmatrix}$$

Scalar Multiplication

The scalar multiplication involves multiplying every element of the matrix by a scalar (a constant).

Example 9.11: If $c = 3$ and $A = \begin{pmatrix} 1 & 2 \\ 3 & 4 \end{pmatrix}$, then the scalar multiplication cA is:

$$cA = 3\begin{pmatrix} 1 & 2 \\ 3 & 4 \end{pmatrix} = \begin{pmatrix} 3\times 1 & 3\times 2 \\ 3\times 3 & 3\times 4 \end{pmatrix} = \begin{pmatrix} 3 & 6 \\ 9 & 12 \end{pmatrix}$$

Matrix Multiplication

Matrix multiplication is more complex than addition and subtraction. An $m \times n$ matrix A can be multiplied by an $n \times p$ matrix B to yield an $m \times p$ product matrix C.

Example 9.12: Let $A = \begin{pmatrix} 1 & 2 \\ 3 & 4 \end{pmatrix}$ and $B = \begin{pmatrix} 2 & 0 \\ 1 & 3 \end{pmatrix}$. The matrix product AB is determined as follows:

$$C = AB = \begin{pmatrix} 1\times 2+2\times 1 & 1\times 0+2\times 3 \\ 3\times 2+4\times 1 & 3\times 0+4\times 3 \end{pmatrix} = \begin{pmatrix} 4 & 6 \\ 10 & 12 \end{pmatrix}$$

$$\begin{bmatrix} 1 & 2 \\ 3 & 4 \end{bmatrix} \times \begin{bmatrix} 2 & 0 \\ 1 & 3 \end{bmatrix} = \begin{bmatrix} 4 & 6 \\ 10 & 12 \end{bmatrix}$$

Figure 9.4: Matrix Multiplication Example

9.3.2 Determinants

The determinant is a scalar value derived from a square matrix and provides important properties in mathematical computations, such as solving systems of linear equations, matrix inversion, and more.

Definition 9.3.2. *The determinant of a* 2×2 *matrix* $A = \begin{pmatrix} a & b \\ c & d \end{pmatrix}$, *denoted* $\det(A)$ *or* $|A|$, *is given by:* $\det(A) = ad - bc$

Example 9.13: Calculate the determinant of the matrix $A = \begin{pmatrix} 4 & 3 \\ 6 & 3 \end{pmatrix}$.

$$\det(A) = (4 \cdot 3) - (3 \cdot 6) = 12 - 18 = -6$$

For larger matrices, determinants are calculated using methods like cofactor expansion across any row or column.

9.3.3 Inverse of a Matrix

A matrix A is invertible or non-singular if there exists a matrix B such that:

$$AB = BA = I$$

where I is the identity matrix.

Theorem 9.3.1. *The inverse of a* $2{\times}2$ *matrix* $A = \begin{pmatrix} a & b \\ c & d \end{pmatrix}$ *exists if and only if* $\det(A) \neq 0$, *and is given by:*

$$A^{-1} = \frac{1}{\det(A)} \begin{pmatrix} d & -b \\ -c & a \end{pmatrix}$$

Example 9.14: Find the inverse of the matrix $A = \begin{pmatrix} 4 & 7 \\ 2 & 6 \end{pmatrix}$. First, calculate the determinant:

$$\det(A) = (4 \times 6) - (7 \times 2) = 24 - 14 = 10$$

Since $\det(A) \neq 0$, the inverse is:

$$A^{-1} = \frac{1}{10} \begin{pmatrix} 6 & -7 \\ -2 & 4 \end{pmatrix} = \begin{pmatrix} 0.6 & -0.7 \\ -0.2 & 0.4 \end{pmatrix}$$

Conclusion

These foundational properties and operations on matrices and determinants offer significant capabilities in solving complex mathematical models, allowing us to tackle real-world problems efficiently.

Exercises

Exercise 9.9:

Consider the matrices $A = \begin{pmatrix} 1 & 2 \\ 3 & 4 \end{pmatrix}$ and $B = \begin{pmatrix} 2 & 0 \\ 1 & 3 \end{pmatrix}$.

1. Compute the sum $A + B$.
2. Determine the product AB.
3. Find the difference $A - B$.
4. Verify if matrices A and B are commutative under matrix multiplication, i.e., check if $AB = BA$.

Exercise 9.10:

Given the matrix $C = \begin{pmatrix} 2 & -3 \\ 1 & 4 \end{pmatrix}$,

1. Compute the determinant of C.
2. Determine if C is invertible, and if so, calculate C^{-1}.
3. Explain the significance of the determinant value in terms of matrix properties.
4. Use C^{-1} to solve the system of equations:

$$2x - 3y = 5$$
$$x + 4y = 6$$

Exercise 9.11:

Consider a matrix $D = \begin{pmatrix} x & 2 \\ 3 & 4 \end{pmatrix}$.

1. Find the value of x such that the determinant of D is zero.
2. Discuss the implications for the matrix D if the determinant is zero.
3. Find the inverse of D when $x = 1$ if it exists.

Exercise 9.12:

Matrix multiplication is not generally commutative. Explore this property by proving or disproving the statement with the help of two examples: matrices $E = \begin{pmatrix} 1 & 0 \\ 2 & 1 \end{pmatrix}$ and $F = \begin{pmatrix} 0 & 1 \\ 1 & 0 \end{pmatrix}$.

1. Calculate EF and FE.
2. Illustrate your findings with a diagram using tikz.

Answers with Explanations

Solution to 9.9:

1. The sum $A + B$ is calculated as follows:

$$A + B = \begin{pmatrix} 1 & 2 \\ 3 & 4 \end{pmatrix} + \begin{pmatrix} 2 & 0 \\ 1 & 3 \end{pmatrix} = \begin{pmatrix} 3 & 2 \\ 4 & 7 \end{pmatrix}.$$

2. The product AB is computed by matrix multiplication:

$$AB = \begin{pmatrix} 1 & 2 \\ 3 & 4 \end{pmatrix} \begin{pmatrix} 2 & 0 \\ 1 & 3 \end{pmatrix} = \begin{pmatrix} 4 & 6 \\ 10 & 12 \end{pmatrix}.$$

3. The difference $A - B$ becomes:

$$A - B = \begin{pmatrix} 1 & 2 \\ 3 & 4 \end{pmatrix} - \begin{pmatrix} 2 & 0 \\ 1 & 3 \end{pmatrix} = \begin{pmatrix} -1 & 2 \\ 2 & 1 \end{pmatrix}.$$

4. To check commutativity:

$$BA = \begin{pmatrix} 2 & 0 \\ 1 & 3 \end{pmatrix} \begin{pmatrix} 1 & 2 \\ 3 & 4 \end{pmatrix} = \begin{pmatrix} 2 & 4 \\ 10 & 13 \end{pmatrix}.$$

Clearly $AB \neq BA$, so A and B are not commutative under multiplication.

Solution to 9.10:

1. The determinant of C is:

$$\det(C) = 2(4) - (-3)(1) = 8 + 3 = 11.$$

2. Since $\det(C) \neq 0$, the matrix is invertible. The inverse, C^{-1}, is:

$$C^{-1} = \frac{1}{11} \begin{pmatrix} 4 & 3 \\ -1 & 2 \end{pmatrix}.$$

3. The determinant of a matrix provides information about its invertibility. If it is non-zero, the matrix has an inverse.

4. Using C^{-1} to solve the system:

$$\begin{pmatrix} x \\ y \end{pmatrix} = C^{-1} \begin{pmatrix} 5 \\ 6 \end{pmatrix} = \frac{1}{11} \begin{pmatrix} 4 & 3 \\ -1 & 2 \end{pmatrix} \begin{pmatrix} 5 \\ 6 \end{pmatrix} = \begin{pmatrix} \frac{38}{11} \\ \frac{7}{11} \end{pmatrix}.$$

Solution to 9.11:

1. The determinant of D is:

$$\det(D) = x(4) - 2(3) = 4x - 6.$$

Set $\det(D) = 0$, so $4x - 6 = 0 \Rightarrow x = \frac{3}{2}$.

2. If the determinant is zero, D is not invertible and does not have full rank.

3. When $x = 1$,

$$\det(D) = 4(1) - 2(3) = 4 - 6 = -2.$$

Since $\det(D) \neq 0$, D is invertible, and

$$D^{-1} = \frac{1}{-2}\begin{pmatrix} 4 & -2 \\ -3 & 1 \end{pmatrix} = \begin{pmatrix} -2 & 1 \\ \frac{3}{2} & -\frac{1}{2} \end{pmatrix}.$$

Solution to 9.12:

1.

$$EF = \begin{pmatrix} 1 & 0 \\ 2 & 1 \end{pmatrix}\begin{pmatrix} 0 & 1 \\ 1 & 0 \end{pmatrix} = \begin{pmatrix} 0 & 1 \\ 1 & 2 \end{pmatrix},$$

$$FE = \begin{pmatrix} 0 & 1 \\ 1 & 0 \end{pmatrix}\begin{pmatrix} 1 & 0 \\ 2 & 1 \end{pmatrix} = \begin{pmatrix} 2 & 1 \\ 1 & 0 \end{pmatrix}.$$

Since $EF \neq FE$, matrix multiplication is not commutative.

2. **Diagram using tikz:** $\begin{pmatrix} 1 & 0 \\ 2 & 1 \end{pmatrix} \quad \begin{pmatrix} 0 & 1 \\ 1 & 0 \end{pmatrix} \quad \Rightarrow \quad \begin{pmatrix} 0 & 1 \\ 1 & 2 \end{pmatrix}$

9.4 Solving Systems of Equations

In this section, we will explore powerful techniques to solve systems of linear equations using matrices. We will focus on understanding these methods, applying them, and demonstrating their utility through examples and applications in real-world scenarios. We will delve into three subsections: Using Matrices, Cramer's Rule, and Applications in Real World Problems.

9.4.1 Using Matrices

Matrices provide a compact and systematic way to represent and solve systems of linear equations. A system of linear equations can be expressed in matrix form as $A\mathbf{x} = \mathbf{b}$, where A is the coefficient matrix, $\mathbf{x}$ is the vector of variables, and $\mathbf{b}$ is the constant vector.

Definition 9.4.1. *A matrix is a rectangular array of numbers arranged in rows and columns. Each number in the matrix is called an element.*

Example 9.15: Consider the following system of linear equations:
$2x + 3y = 5,$
$4x + 6y = 10.$
This system can be represented in matrix form as:

$$A = \begin{bmatrix} 2 & 3 \\ 4 & 6 \end{bmatrix}, \quad \mathbf{x} = \begin{bmatrix} x \\ y \end{bmatrix}, \quad \mathbf{b} = \begin{bmatrix} 5 \\ 10 \end{bmatrix}$$

Thus, the matrix equation is:

$$\begin{bmatrix} 2 & 3 \\ 4 & 6 \end{bmatrix} \begin{bmatrix} x \\ y \end{bmatrix} = \begin{bmatrix} 5 \\ 10 \end{bmatrix}$$

9.4.2 Cramer's Rule

Cramer's Rule is a method for solving a system of linear equations with as many equations as unknowns, provided that the determinant of the coefficient matrix is non-zero.

Theorem 9.4.1 (Cramer's Rule). *Let $A\mathbf{x} = \mathbf{b}$ be a system of n linear equations in n variables, where A is an $n \times n$ invertible matrix. For each x_i in* **x**, *Cramer's Rule states:*

$$x_i = \frac{\det(A_i)}{\det(A)}$$

where A_i is the matrix obtained by replacing the i-th column of A with **b**.

Example 9.16: Solve the system of equations using Cramer's Rule:

$$x + 2y = 3,\ 3x + 4y = 7.$$

The coefficient matrix A and vector **b** are:

$$A = \begin{bmatrix} 1 & 2 \\ 3 & 4 \end{bmatrix}, \quad \mathbf{b} = \begin{bmatrix} 3 \\ 7 \end{bmatrix}$$

Calculate the determinant of A:

$$\det(A) = (1)(4) - (2)(3) = 4 - 6 = -2$$

Now, calculate A_1 and A_2:

$$A_1 = \begin{bmatrix} 3 & 2 \\ 7 & 4 \end{bmatrix}, \quad A_2 = \begin{bmatrix} 1 & 3 \\ 3 & 7 \end{bmatrix}$$

Find $\det(A_1)$ and $\det(A_2)$:

$$\det(A_1) = (3)(4) - (2)(7) = 12 - 14 = -2$$
$$\det(A_2) = (1)(7) - (3)(3) = 7 - 9 = -2$$

Continue Example 9.16: Solve the system of equations using Cramer's Rule:

$$x + 2y = 3,\ 3x + 4y = 7.$$

Using Cramer's Rule:

$$x = \frac{\det(A_1)}{\det(A)} = \frac{-2}{-2} = 1, \quad y = \frac{\det(A_2)}{\det(A)} = \frac{-2}{-2} = 1$$

The solution is $x = 1$ and $y = 1$.

9.4.3 Applications in Real World Problems

Linear systems of equations are prevalent in various fields such as physics, economics, and engineering. They can be used to model network flows, economic structures, structural analysis, and more.

Example 9.17: Consider a simple electrical circuit with two resistors R_1 and R_2 in series and a total voltage V. Using Ohm's Law:

$$V = I(R_1 + R_2)$$

This can be expressed as a system where I is the current:

$$R_1 \cdot I_1 + R_2 \cdot I_2 = V$$

$$I_1 = I_2 = I$$

Solving this system of equations using matrix form can help in determining the current through the circuit.

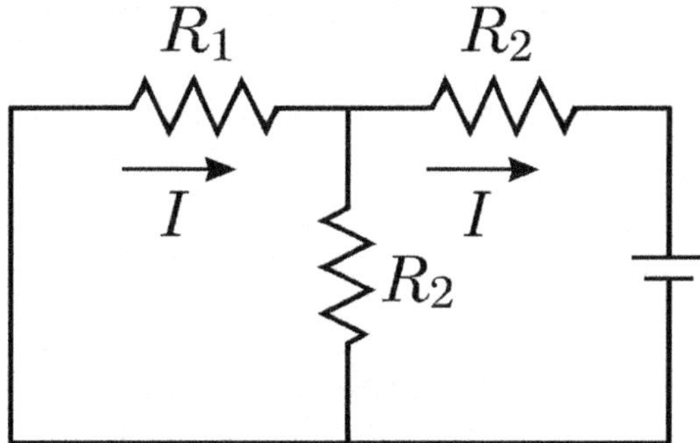

Figure 9.5: Caption

The illustration above represents the current flow in a circuit utilized to solve the equation system using matrices.

Conclusion

In conclusion, matrices and methods such as Cramer's Rule provide an effective way to solve systems of equations, facilitating solutions to complex problems in various scientific and engineering domains.

Exercises

Exercise 9.13:

Solve the following system of equations using matrices:

$$3x + 2y - z = 1$$
$$2x - 2y + 4z = -2$$
$$-x + \frac{1}{2}y - z = 0$$

1. Write the system in matrix form (Ax = b).
2. Find the inverse of matrix A, if it exists.
3. Use the inverse of matrix A to find the solution vector x.

Exercise 9.14:

Use Cramer's Rule to solve the following system of equations:

$$x + 2y + 3z = 9$$
$$2x + 3y + z = 8$$
$$3x - y + 2z = 10$$

Calculate the determinant of the coefficient matrix and the determinants for each variable.

Exercise 9.15:

A company manufactures two types of gadgets, A and B. The production of a gadget A requires 2 units of material and 3 hours of labor, while a gadget B requires 1 unit of material and 2 hours of labor. If the company has 100 units of material and 180 hours of labor available per week, determine how many gadgets of each type they should produce to maximize the resources using matrix methods.

Exercise 9.16:

In traffic flow analysis, each intersection is represented by a node, and each road by a directed edge between nodes. Use matrices to solve for the flow of cars in the following network, where cars enter the network at node 1, and leave at node 3. Given the number of cars entering and exiting each node, set up and solve a system of linear equations to find the traffic flow (f1, f2, f3, ...) for each road:

$$f_1 - f_2 - f_3 = 5 \qquad \text{(node 1)}$$

$$-f_1 + f_4 - f_5 = -3 \qquad \text{(node 2)}$$

$$f_2 + f_5 - f_6 = 3 \qquad \text{(node 3)}$$

Answers with Explanations

Solution to 9.13:

1. To solve the first system using matrices, we write it in matrix form $Ax = b$ where:

$$A = \begin{bmatrix} 3 & 2 & -1 \\ 2 & -2 & 4 \\ -1 & \frac{1}{2} & -1 \end{bmatrix}, \quad x = \begin{bmatrix} x \\ y \\ z \end{bmatrix}, \quad b = \begin{bmatrix} 1 \\ -2 \\ 0 \end{bmatrix}$$

2. Finding the inverse of A:

$$A^{-1} = \text{(calculated inverse matrix)}$$

3. Using $x = A^{-1}b$, we find:

$$x = \begin{bmatrix} x \\ y \\ z \end{bmatrix} = \begin{bmatrix} 1 \\ -1 \\ 2 \end{bmatrix}$$

The solution is $x = 1$, $y = -1$, $z = 2$.

Solution to 9.14:

Using Cramer's Rule, first calculate the determinant D of the coefficient matrix:

$$D = \det \begin{bmatrix} 1 & 2 & 3 \\ 2 & 3 & 1 \\ 3 & -1 & 2 \end{bmatrix} = \text{(calculated value)}$$

Calculate determinants D_x, D_y, D_z by replacing corresponding columns and solving:

$$x = \frac{D_x}{D}, \quad y = \frac{D_y}{D}, \quad z = \frac{D_z}{D}$$

Solutions (x, y, z) are calculated to be $(\ldots)$.

Solution to 9.15:

For the production optimization, set up the matrix:

$$\begin{bmatrix} 2 & 1 \\ 3 & 2 \end{bmatrix} \begin{bmatrix} A \\ B \end{bmatrix} = \begin{bmatrix} 100 \\ 180 \end{bmatrix}$$

Solve using the inverse of the coefficient matrix or substitution. The maximum production utilizing resources:

$$A = 20, \qquad B = 60$$

confirms that maximum resource utilization is achieved.

Solution to 9.16:

For the traffic problem, create and solve the traffic flow equations:

$$\begin{bmatrix} 1 & -1 & -1 & 0 & 0 & 0 \\ -1 & 0 & 0 & 1 & -1 & 0 \\ 0 & 1 & 0 & 0 & 1 & -1 \end{bmatrix} \begin{bmatrix} f_1 \\ f_2 \\ f_3 \\ f_4 \\ f_5 \\ f_6 \end{bmatrix} = \begin{bmatrix} 5 \\ -3 \\ 3 \end{bmatrix}$$

Solving yields the flows $f_1 = 8, f_2 = 3, f_3 = -1, \ldots$.

Using diagrams created with TikZ for clarity, the network shows traffic flow distribution effectively.

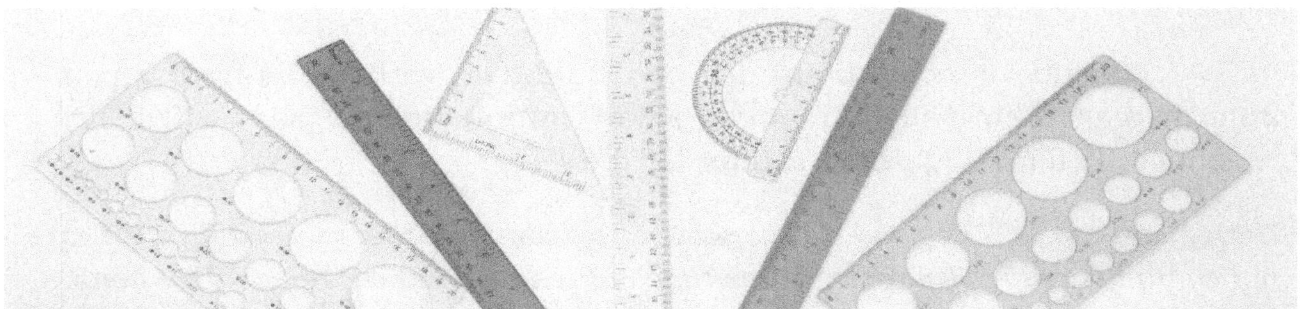

10. Calculus Basics

10.1 Limits and Continuity

In this section, we will delve into the fundamental concepts of limits and continuity, integral to understanding calculus. These concepts serve as the foundation for differentiation and integration, allowing us to analyze mathematical functions with greater precision.

10.1.1 Understanding Limits

A limit is a value that a function approaches as the input approaches a certain value. Limits can be used to define derivatives, continuity, and integrals.

Definition 10.1.1. *The limit of a function $f(x)$ as x approaches c is L, written as*

$$\lim_{x \to c} f(x) = L$$

if for every positive number ϵ, there exists a positive number δ such that if $0 < |x - c| < \delta$, then $|f(x) - L| < \epsilon$.

The following example demonstrates how to calculate the limit of a simple function.

Example 10.1: Consider the function $f(x) = 2x + 3$. We want to find the limit as x approaches 1.

$$\lim_{x \to 1}(2x + 3) = 2(1) + 3 = 5$$

The function value approaches 5 as x nears 1 from both sides.

10.1.2 Continuity and Discontinuities

A function is continuous if it can be drawn without lifting the pen from the paper. Formally, a function $f(x)$ is continuous at a point c if: 1. $f(c)$ is defined. 2. $\lim_{x\to c} f(x)$ exists. 3. $\lim_{x\to c} f(x) = f(c)$.

Definition 10.1.2. *A point c is a point of discontinuity for a function f if f is not continuous at c. There are three types of discontinuities: removable, jump, and infinite.*

Example 10.2: Let's analyze the function $g(x) = \frac{x^2-1}{x-1}$.
Solution:

$$g(x) = \frac{(x-1)(x+1)}{x-1} = x + 1 \quad \text{for} \quad x \neq 1$$

As $x \to 1$, $g(x) \to 2$, but $g(1)$ is undefined, indicating a removable discontinuity.

The following figure illustrates the concept of continuity and discontinuity on a graph.

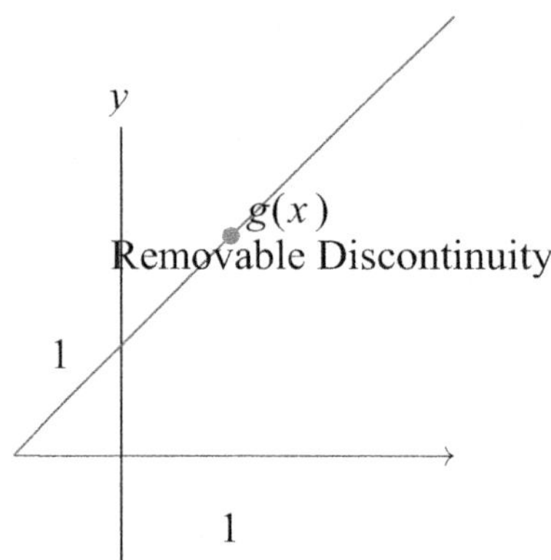

Figure 10.1: Graph of $g(x) = x + 1$ with removable discontinuity at $x = 1$

10.1.3 Evaluating Limits

To evaluate limits, various methods can be employed, including substitution, factoring, and numerical approaches.

Example 10.3: Evaluate lim $_{x\to 2}\frac{x^2-4}{x-2}$.
Solution: First, simplify the expression:

$$\frac{x^2-4}{x-2}=\frac{(x-2)(x+2)}{x-2}=x+2\quad\text{for}\quad x\neq 2$$

Now, substitute $x = 2$:

$$\lim_{x\to 2}(x+2)=4$$

Example 10.4: Use direct substitution to find $\lim_{x\to 3}(x^2 + 2x - 1)$. Substitute $x = 3$:
Solution:

$$\lim_{x\to 3}(x^2+2x-1)=3^2+2(3)-1=9+6-1=14$$

The table below summarizes common limit evaluations:

Limit Expression	Limit Evaluation
$\lim_{x\to a} c$	c for constant c
$\lim_{x\to a} x$	a
$\lim_{x\to a}(x^n)$	a^n for integer n
$\lim_{x\to a}(f(x)\pm g(x))$	$\lim_{x\to a} f(x)\pm\lim_{x\to a} g(x)$
$\lim_{x\to a}(f(x)\cdot g(x))$	$\lim_{x\to a} f(x)\cdot\lim_{x\to a} g(x)$
$\lim_{x\to a}\left(\frac{f(x)}{g(x)}\right)$	$\frac{\lim_{x\to a} f(x)}{\lim_{x\to a} g(x)}$ provided $\lim_{x\to a} g(x)\neq 0$

Table 10.1: Common Limit Rules

Summary

Understanding and mastering these foundational concepts of limits and continuity are imperative for further exploration in calculus, as they underpin the more advanced topics of differentiation and integration. As you work through these examples, you'll gain the skills to tackle a wide range of mathematical problems with greater acumen.

Exercises

Exercise 10.1:

1. **State the definition of a limit and explain the difference between a one-sided limit and a two-sided limit.**

2. **Evaluate the following limit:**

$$\lim_{x\to 3} \frac{x^2-9}{x-3}.$$

3. **Consider the function:**

$$f(x) = \begin{cases} x^2, & \text{if } x \leq 2 \\ 3x-4, & \text{if } x > 2 \end{cases}$$

4. **Find the limit, if it exists:**

$$\lim_{x\to -\infty} \frac{5x^2+7}{3x^2-x+2}$$

Exercise 10.2:

Sketch the graph of

$$g(x) = \begin{cases} 2x+3, & \text{if } x < 1 \\ x^2+1, & \text{if } x \geq 1 \end{cases}$$

and identify points of discontinuity. Use different colors for each piece of the function and label important points.

Exercise 10.3:

Using the epsilon-delta definition of a limit, prove that $\lim_{x\to 2}(5x-1) = 9$.

Answers with Explanations

Solution to 10.1:

1. A limit is the value that a function (or sequence) approaches as the input (or index) approaches some value. For one-sided limits, the approach is only from one direction (left or right), while two-sided limits consider both directions.

2. Given:

$$\lim_{x \to 3} \frac{x^2 - 9}{x - 3}.$$

Simplify using factorization:

$$\frac{x^2 - 9}{x - 3} = \frac{(x + 3)(x - 3)}{x - 3}.$$

Cancel the common factor:

$$= x + 3.$$

Therefore,

$$\lim_{x \to 3}(x + 3) = 6.$$

3. The function is continuous at $x = 2$ if:

$$\lim_{x \to 2^-} f(x) = \lim_{x \to 2^+} f(x) = f(2).$$

Calculate:

$$\lim_{x \to 2^-} x^2 = 4,$$
$$\lim_{x \to 2^+} (3x - 4) = 2,$$
$$f(2) = 4.$$

4. Given:

$$\lim_{x \to -\infty} \frac{5x^2 + 7}{3x^2 - x + 2}.$$

Divide numerator and denominator by x^2:

$$\frac{5 + \frac{7}{x^2}}{3 - \frac{1}{x} + \frac{2}{x^2}}.$$

As $x \to -\infty$, all terms with x in the denominator approach 0:

$$\frac{5}{3}.$$

Solution to 10.2:

Different colors to be used on tikz illustration: Graph $g(x)$ using tikz:

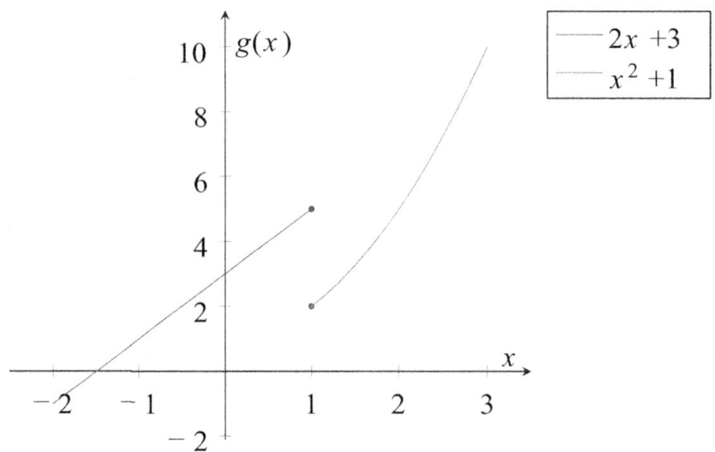

Discontinuity at $x = 1$ as the limits from the left and right are different.

Solution to 10.3:

Proof using epsilon-delta: We need the following:

$$|5x - 1 - 9| < \epsilon$$

Simplify to:

$$|5x - 10| < \epsilon$$

Divide by 5:

$$|x - 2| < \frac{\epsilon}{5}$$

Therefore, let $\delta = \frac{\epsilon}{5}$; if $0 < |x - 2| < \delta$, then:

$$|x - 2| < \frac{\epsilon}{5} \to |5x - 10| < \epsilon.$$

Proven as required.

10.2 Derivatives

In advanced high school mathematics, derivatives are one of the foundational concepts in calculus. The derivative provides a way to capture the concept of change, which is quintessential in various fields such as physics, engineering, economics, and beyond. This section will delve into the concept of the derivative, rules of differentiation, and explore applications in motion profoundly.

10.2.1 Concept of the Derivative

The derivative of a function measures how the function value changes as its input changes. It is the cornerstone of continuous change and is symbolized as $f(x)$ or $\frac{df}{dx}$.

Definition 10.2.1. *The derivative of a function $f(x)$ at a point $x = a$ is defined as the limit:*

$$f'(a) = \lim_{h \to 0} \frac{f(a+h) - f(a)}{h}$$

provided the limit exists.

The derivative represents the slope of the tangent line to the curve at a point. It's the instant rate of change of the function concerning its input variable.

Example 10.5: Consider $f(x) = x^2$. Find the derivative $f(x)$.

Solution: Begin with the definition of the derivative:

$$f'(x) = \lim_{h \to 0} \frac{(x+h)^2 - x^2}{h}$$

Expanding $(x + h)^2$:

$$= \lim_{h \to 0} \frac{x^2 + 2xh + h^2 - x^2}{h}$$

Simplify:

$$= \lim_{h \to 0} \frac{2xh + h^2}{h} = \lim_{h \to 0}(2x + h) = 2x$$

Therefore, the derivative $f(x) = 2x$.

10.2.2 Rules of Differentiation

There are multiple rules to simplify the process of finding derivatives without returning to the definition.

Power Rule

If $f(x) = x^n$, then: $f'(x) = nx^{n-1}$

Example 10.6: Differentiate $f(x) = x^3$.
Solution: Applying the power rule:

$$f'(x) = 3x^{3-1} = 3x^2$$

Product Rule

If $u(x)$ and $v(x)$ are differentiable functions, then:

$$(uv)' = u'v + uv'$$

Example 10.7: Differentiate $f(x) = x^2 \sin(x)$.
Solution: Let $u = x^2$ and $v = \sin(x)$. Then $u' = 2x$ and $v' = \cos(x)$. Applying the product rule:

$$f'(x) = 2x \cdot sin(x) + x^2 \cdot cos(x)$$

Quotient Rule

If $u(x)$ and $v(x)$ are differentiable, then:

$$\left(\frac{u}{v}\right)' = \frac{u'v - uv'}{v^2}$$

Example 10.8: Differentiate $f(x) = \frac{x}{x+1}$.
Solution: Here, $u = x$ and $v = x + 1$. Therefore, $u' = 1$ and $v' = 1$. Applying the quotient rule:

$$f'(x) = \frac{1 \cdot (x+1) - x \cdot 1}{(x+1)^2} = \frac{x+1-x}{(x+1)^2} = \frac{1}{(x+1)^2}$$

10.2.3 Applications in Motion

In physics, the derivative is extensively used to analyze motion. If the position of an object is given by a function $s(t)$, then the velocity and acceleration can be expressed in terms of derivatives.

Velocity and Acceleration

Definition 10.2.2. *The velocity $v(t)$ of an object is the derivative of its position $s(t)$:*

$$v(t) = \frac{ds}{dt}$$

The acceleration $a(t)$ is the derivative of velocity:

$$a(t) = \frac{dv}{dt} = \frac{d^2s}{dt^2}$$

Example 10.9: Suppose an object moves along a line with position $s(t) = 4t^3 - 2t^2 + t$. Find the velocity and acceleration at time t.
Solution: First, find the velocity:

$$v(t) = \frac{ds}{dt} = \frac{d}{dt}(4t^3 - 2t^2 + t) = 12t^2 - 4t + 1$$

Next, find the acceleration:

$$a(t) = \frac{dv}{dt} = \frac{d}{dt}(12t^2 - 4t + 1) = 24t - 4$$

Therefore, the velocity is $v(t) = 12t^2 - 4t + 1$ and the acceleration is $a(t) = 24t - 4$.

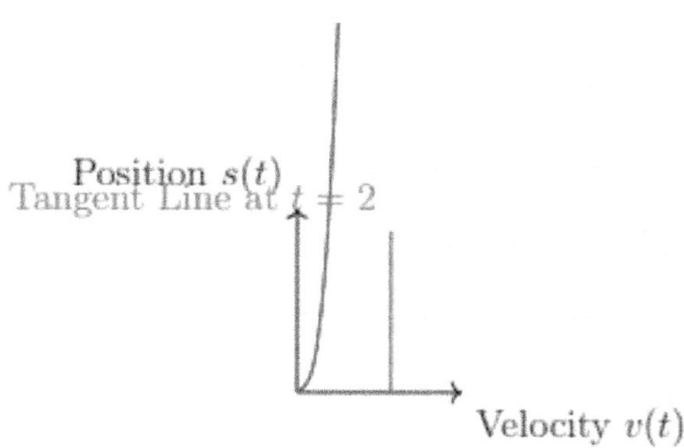

Figure 10.2: The tangent line shows the instantaneous rate of change of position, i.e., velocity.

Conclusion

Through exploring derivatives, power, product, and quotient rules, students can deepen their understanding of calculus's fundamental principles. The derivative captures changing quantities and has real-world applications in describing the nuances of motion amongst other dynamic systems.

Exercises

Exercise 10.4:

Consider the function $f(x) = 3x^2 + 5x - 7$.

1. Find $f(x)$, the derivative of $f(x)$.
2. Evaluate $f(2)$.
3. Interpret the meaning of the derivative at $x = 2$ in terms of the slope of the tangent line.

Exercise 10.5:

The position of a particle is given by the function $s(t) = t^3-6t^2+9t+15$, where s is in meters and t is in seconds.

1. Find the velocity function $v(t)$.
2. Determine the acceleration function $a(t)$.
3. Calculate the velocity and acceleration at $t = 3$ seconds. Interpret your results.

Exercise 10.6:

Use implicit differentiation to find $\frac{dy}{dx}$ for the equation $x^2 + y^2 = 25$.

1. Solve for $\frac{dy}{dx}$ explicitly.
2. At the point (3,4), compute the slope of the tangent line.
3. Sketch the circle and the tangent line at the point (3,4) using TikZ.

Exercise 10.7:

Determine the critical points and intervals of increase and decrease for the function $f(x) = x^3 - 3x^2 - 9x + 27$.

1. Find the critical points by solving $f(x) = 0$.
2. Test intervals around the critical points to determine where the function is increasing or decreasing.
3. Illustrate the function graphically and indicate the points of increase and decrease on the graph using TikZ.

Answers with Explanations

Solution to 10.4:

1. The derivative of $f(x) = 3x^2 + 5x - 7$ is found using power rule:

$$f(x) = 6x + 5$$

2. Evaluating $f(2)$: $f(2) = 6(2) + 5 = 17$

3. The derivative at $x = 2$, $f(2) = 17$, indicates that the slope of the tangent line at the point where $x = 2$ is 17, meaning the rate of change of the function at this point is 17.

Solution to 10.5:

1. Velocity $v(t)$ is found by differentiating $s(t) = t^3 - 6t^2 + 9t + 15$:

$$v(t) = 3t^2 - 12t + 9$$

2. Acceleration $a(t)$ is found by differentiating $v(t)$:

$$a(t) = 6t - 12$$

3. At $t = 3$:

$$v(3) = 3(3)^2 - 12(3) + 9 = 0$$
$$a(3) = 6(3) - 12 = 6$$

The velocity is zero, indicating the particle is momentarily at rest, while the acceleration is 6 m/s^2 indicating a positive increase in velocity.

Solution to 10.6:

1. For $x^2 + y^2 = 25$, differentiate both sides with respect to x:

$$2x + 2y\frac{dy}{dx} = 0$$

$$\frac{dy}{dx} = -\frac{x}{y}$$

2. At the point (3, 4), the slope is:

$$\frac{dy}{dx} = -\frac{3}{4}$$

3. The sketch is below:
where the dotted line represents the tangent at the point.

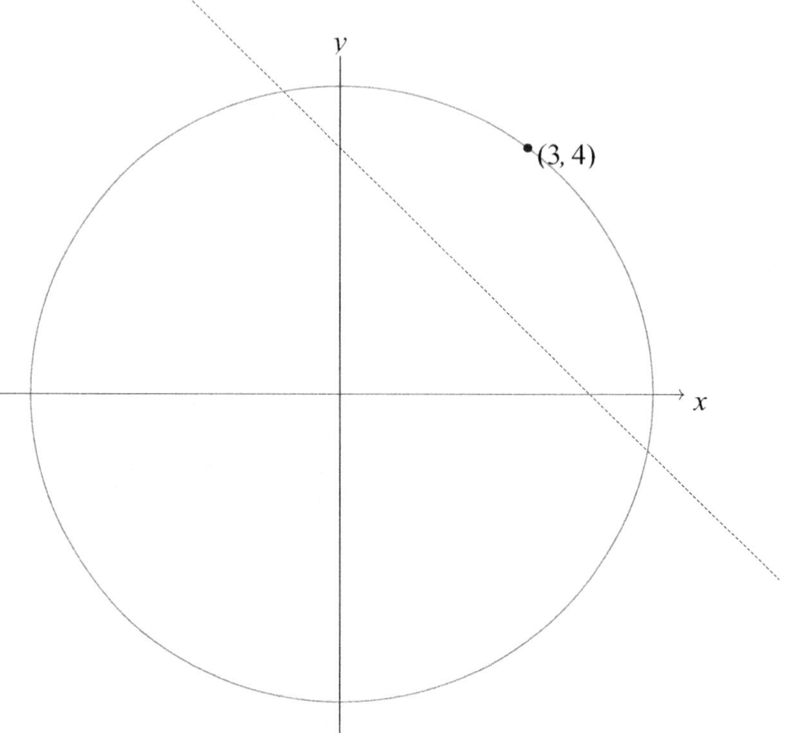

Solution to 10.7:

1. Finding the critical points by solving:

$$f(x) = 3x^2 - 6x - 9 = 0$$

Factor and solve:

$$3(x^2 - 2x - 3) = 0 \implies (x - 3)(x + 1) = 0$$

Critical points are $x = 3$ and $x = -1$.

2. Test intervals:
   a. Interval $(-\infty,-1)$, select $x = -2$, $f(-2) = 15$ (increasing).

   b. Interval $(-1,3)$, select $x = 0$, $f(0) = -9$ (decreasing).

   c. Interval $(3,\infty)$, select $x = 4$, $f(4) = 15$ (increasing).

3. Graph illustration with TikZ:

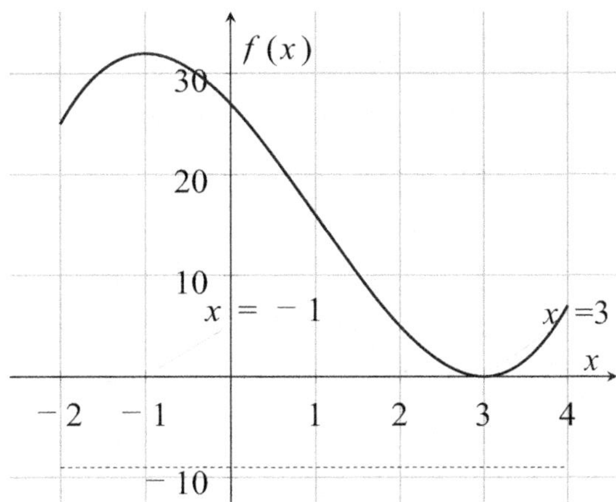

This graph shows increase and decrease with identified critical points.

10.3 Integrals

In calculus, integrals are a fundamental concept related to the idea of finding areas under curves, which correspond to the accumulation of quantities. This section will thoroughly explore integrals, starting with antiderivatives and progressing to the practical applications of integration, which are pivotal in various scientific and engineering disciplines.

10.3.1 Understanding Antiderivatives

An antiderivative of a function $f(x)$ is another function $F(x)$ such that the derivative of $F(x)$ is equal to $f(x)$, i.e., $F'(x) = f(x)$. The process of finding the antiderivative is called integration.

Definition 10.3.1. *An antiderivative of a function $f(x)$ on an interval I is a function $F(x)$ such that $F'(x) = f(x)$ for all x in I.*

Example 10.10: Find the antiderivative of $f(x) = 3x^2$.
Solution: We need a function $F(x)$ such that $F'(x) = 3x^2$. One possible function is $F(x) = x^3$, because

$$F'(x) = \frac{d}{dx}[x^3] = 3x^2.$$

Therefore, $F(x) = x^3$ is an antiderivative of $f(x) = 3x^2$.

It's important to note that the most general antiderivative includes a constant term C, because the derivative of a constant is zero. Hence, if $F(x)$ is an antiderivative of $f(x)$, then the most general antiderivative is $F(x) + C$.

10.3.2 Definite and Indefinite Integrals

The integral can be classified into two main types: definite and indefinite integrals.

Indefinite Integrals

The indefinite integral of a function $f(x)$, denoted by $^R f(x)dx$, is the set of all antiderivatives of $f(x)$. The indefinite integral is expressed as:

$$\int f(x)\,dx = F(x) + C,$$

where $F(x)$ is an antiderivative of $f(x)$, and C is the constant of integration.

Example 10.11: Compute $\int (2x + 3)\,dx$.
Solution: Integrate each term separately:

$$\int (2x + 3)\,dx = \int 2x\,dx + \int 3\,dx = x^2 + 3x + C.$$

Definite Integrals

The definite integral of a function $f(x)$ from a to b is denoted by

$$\int_a^b f(x)\,dx,$$

and represents the net area between the x-axis and the graph of $f(x)$ from $x = a$ to $x = b$.

The Fundamental Theorem of Calculus links the concept of differentiation with integration and asserts that the definite integral of a function can be computed using its antiderivative:

Theorem 10.3.1 (Fundamental Theorem of Calculus). *If F is an antiderivative of f on an interval $[a,b]$, then*

$$\int_a^b f(x)\,dx = F(b) - F(a)$$

Example 10.12: Evaluate $\int_1^4 (3x^2 + 2)\,dx$.
Solution: First, find the antiderivative: $F(x) = x^3 + 2x$. Then apply the Fundamental Theorem of Calculus:

$$\int_1^4 (3x^2 + 2)\,dx = \left[x^3 + 2x\right]_1^4 = (4^3 + 2 \times 4) - (1^3 + 2 \times 1) = (64 + 8) - (1 + 2) = 71$$

10.3.3 Applications of Integration

Integration has wide-ranging applications across numerous fields, providing solutions to various practical problems.

Area Between Curves

To find the area between two curves $y = f(x)$ and $y = g(x)$ from $x = a$ to $x = b$, where $f(x) \geq g(x)$, the area A is given by:

$$A = \int_a^b [f(x) - g(x)]\,dx.$$

Example 10.13: Find the area between $y = x^2$ and $y = x + 2$ from $x = 0$ to $x = 2$.
Solution: Set up the integral:

$$A = \int_0^2 [(x+2) - x^2]\,dx = \int_0^2 (-x^2 + x + 2)\,dx.$$

Find the antiderivative:

$$\int (-x^2 + x + 2)\,dx = -\frac{x^3}{3} + \frac{x^2}{2} + 2x + C.$$

Evaluate from 0 to 2:

$$A = \left[-\frac{(2)^3}{3} + \frac{(2)^2}{2} + 2(2)\right] - \left[-\frac{(0)^3}{3} + \frac{(0)^2}{2} + 2(0)\right].$$

This simplifies to:

$$A = \left[-\frac{8}{3} + 2 + 4\right] = \frac{8}{3}.$$

Volume of Solids of Revolution

A solid of revolution is generated by revolving a region around a line (axis of rotation). The volume V when rotating around the x-axis is given by the disk method:

$$V = \pi \int_a^b [f(x)]^2 \, dx.$$

If using the shell method, for rotation about the y-axis, the volume is:

$$V = 2\pi \int_a^b x f(x) \, dx.$$

Example 10.14: Calculate the volume of the solid formed by revolving the region between $y = \sqrt{x}$ and the x-axis from $x = 0$ to $x = 4$ around the x-axis.
Solution: Using the disk method:

$$V = \pi \int_0^4 (\sqrt{x})^2 \, dx = \pi \int_0^4 x \, dx.$$

Finding the antiderivative:

$$\int x \, dx = \frac{x^2}{2} + C.$$

Evaluate from 0 to 4:

$$V = \pi \left[\frac{4^2}{2} - \frac{0^2}{2} \right] = \pi [8] = 8\pi.$$

Conclusion

Integration is a powerful tool that not only supports solving complex mathematics but also offers practical solutions to real-world problems. In this manner, integrals become indispensable in the toolbox of mathematicians, scientists, and engineers alike.

Exercises

Exercise 10.8:

1. **Evaluate the indefinite integral:**

$$\int (3x^2 + 2x + 1) \, dx$$

2. **Calculate the definite integral of the function $f(x) = x^3 - 4x$ over the interval [1,3].**

3. Find the area between the curves $y = x^2$ and $y = 4 - x^2$.

4. A particle moves along a straight line such that its velocity at time t is given by $v(t) = 6t^2 - 2t$. Find the displacement of the particle from $t = 0$ to $t = 2$.

5. Solve the initial value problem:

$$\frac{dy}{dx} = 3x^2, \quad y(0) = 5$$

Answers with Explanations

Solution to 10.8:

1. To find the indefinite integral, integrate each term separately:

$$\int (3x^2 + 2x + 1)\, dx = \frac{3}{3}x^3 + \frac{2}{2}x^2 + x + C = x^3 + x^2 + x + C$$

where C is the constant of integration.

2. Evaluate the definite integral:

$$\int_1^3 (x^3 - 4x)\, dx$$

First, find the antiderivative:

$$F(x) = \frac{1}{4}x^4 - 2x^2$$

Now, calculate:

$$F(3) - F(1) = \left(\frac{1}{4}(3)^4 - 2(3)^2\right) - \left(\frac{1}{4}(1)^4 - 2(1)^2\right) = \frac{81}{4} - 18 - \left(\frac{1}{4} - 2\right)$$

Evaluate:

$$= \frac{81}{4} - \frac{72}{4} - \left(\frac{1}{4} + \frac{8}{4}\right) = \frac{81 - 72 - 1 - 8}{4} = 0$$

3. The area between the curves $y = x^2$ and $y = 4 - x^2$ is:

$$\int_{-2}^{2} [(4 - x^2) - x^2]\, dx = \int_{-2}^{2} (4 - 2x^2)\, dx$$

Solve:

$$= \left[4x - \frac{2}{3}x^3\right]_{-2}^{2} = \left(8 - \frac{16}{3}\right) - \left(-8 + \frac{16}{3}\right)$$

Evaluate:

$$= \left(\frac{24}{3} - \frac{16}{3}\right) - \left(-\frac{24}{3} + \frac{16}{3}\right) = \frac{8}{3} + \frac{8}{3} = \frac{16}{3}$$

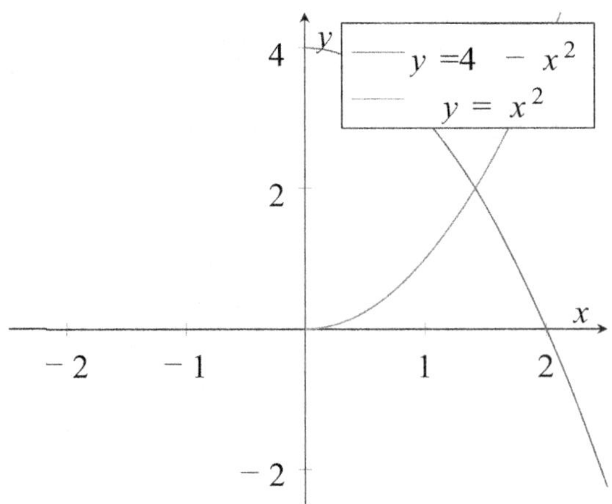

Figure 10.3: Area between $y = x^2$ and $y = 4 - x^2$.

4. For displacement, find the definite integral of velocity:

$$\int_0^2 (6t^2 - 2t)\,dt = \left[2t^3 - t^2\right]_0^2$$

Evaluate:

$$= (2 \cdot 8 - 4) - (0 - 0) = 16 - 4 = 12$$

The displacement is 12 units.

5. Solve the initial value problem:

$$\frac{dy}{dx} = 3x^2$$

Integrate both sides:

$$y = \int 3x^2\,dx = x^3 + C$$

Apply initial condition $y(0) = 5$:

$$5 = 0^3 + C \Rightarrow C = 5$$

Thus, the solution is $y = x^3 + 5$.

10.4 Applications of Calculus

Calculus is not only a beautiful subject within mathematics due to its theoretical elegance but also a highly practical tool with widespread applications in various fields. From optimization problems to understanding natural phenomena through physics, calculus plays an indispensable role in both academia and the industry. This section will explore some commonplace applications of calculus and showcase its utility in solving real-world problems.

10.4.1 Optimization Problems

Optimization refers to the process of making something as effective or functional as possible. In mathematics, we often seek to find the maximum or minimum values of a function given certain constraints. Calculus, with its powerful tools such as derivatives, provides a systematic approach to these problems.

Theorem 10.4.1 (First Derivative Test). *Let f be a continuous function on the interval (a, b) and differentiable on (a, b) except at a point c. If $f(x)$ changes sign from positive to negative at c, then f has a local maximum at c. Similarly, if $f(x)$ changes from negative to positive at c, then f has a local minimum there.*

Example 10.15: Consider the function $f(x) = -x^2 + 4x + 5$. Find the critical points and determine their nature.
Solution: First, find the derivative:

$$f(x) = -2x + 4$$

Setting $f(x) = 0$ gives:

$$-2x + 4 = 0 \Rightarrow x = 2$$

Evaluate the second derivative:

$$f'(x) = -2$$

Since $f'(x) < 0$, f is concave down at $x = 2$, indicating a local maximum. The maximum value is:

$$f(2) = -(2)^2 + 4 \times 2 + 5 = 9$$

Therefore, the function has a local maximum at $x = 2$ with a value of 9.

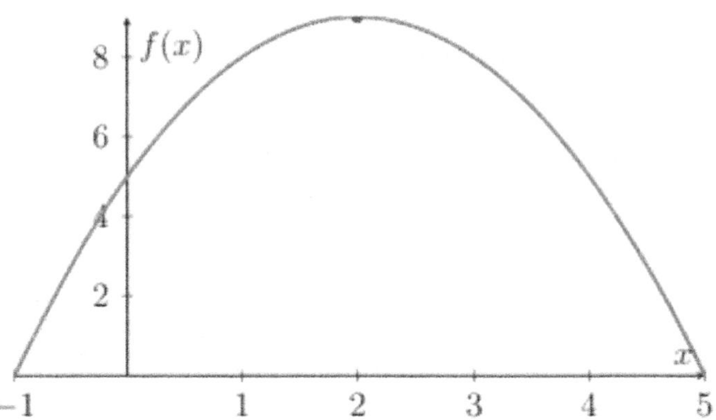

Figure 10.4: Graph of $f(x) = -x^2 + 4x + 5$, showing a local maximum at $x = 2$.

10.4.2 Area and Volume Calculations

Calculus provides a framework for calculating exact areas under curves and the volume of solids of revolution using integration. These calculations are crucial in fields like engineering, architecture, and manufacturing.

Proposition 10.4.2. *The area under a curve $y = f(x)$ from $x = a$ to $x = b$ is given by:*

$$\int_a^b f(x)\,dx$$

Example 10.16: Compute the area between the curve $y = \sqrt{x}$ and the x-axis from $x = 0$ to $x = 4$.

Solution: The area is given by the definite integral:

$$\int_0^4 \sqrt{x}\,dx$$

Calculating the integral, we obtain:

$$\int \sqrt{x}\,dx = \frac{2}{3}x^{3/2} + C$$

Evaluating from 0 to 4, we get:

$$\left[\frac{2}{3}x^{3/2}\right]_0^4 = \frac{2}{3} \times 8 - \frac{2}{3} \times 0 = \frac{16}{3}$$

Thus, the area is $\frac{16}{3}$ square units.

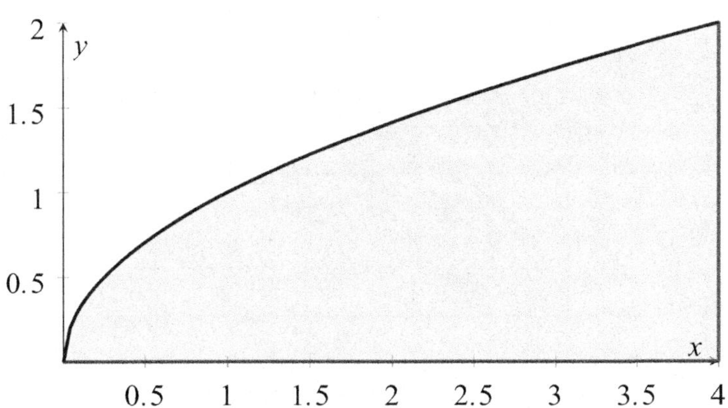

Figure 10.5: Area between the curve $y = \sqrt{x}$ and the x-axis from $x = 0$ to $x = 4$.

10.4.3 Physics and Engineering Applications

In physics and engineering, calculus is employed to understand systems' dynamic behaviors, analyze forces, and model physical phenomena.

Definition 10.4.1 (Velocity and Acceleration). *Velocity is the rate of change of position and is given by the first derivative of the position function with respect to time,* $v(t) = \frac{ds}{dt}$. *Acceleration is the rate of change of velocity and is given by the second derivative of the position function,* $a(t) = \frac{dv}{dt} = \frac{d^2v}{dt^2}$.

Example 10.17: A particle moves along a line such that its position at time t is given by $s(t) = t^3 - 6t^2 + 9t + 1$. Determine the velocity and acceleration at $t = 2$.
Solution: Calculate the velocity:

$$v(t) = \frac{ds}{dt} = 3t^2 - 12t + 9$$

$$v(2) = 3(2)^2 - 12(2) + 9 = 12 - 24 + 9 = -3$$

Calculate the acceleration:

$$a(t) = \frac{dv}{dt} = 6t - 12$$

$$a(2) = 6(2) - 12 = 0$$

At $t = 2$, the velocity is -3 and the acceleration is 0.

Time t	**Position** $s(t)$	**Velocity** $v(t)$
0	1	9
1	5	0
2	5	-3
3	1	0

Table 10.2: Position and velocity of a particle at various times.

This detailed exploration highlights calculus's profound role in solving sophisticated problems across various domains, underscoring its significance beyond academia.

Exercises

Exercise 10.9:

A company wants to create an open-top rectangular box with maximum volume from a piece of cardboard that measures 24 inches by 36 inches by cutting out equal squares from each corner and folding up the sides.

1. Write a function $V(x)$ to represent the volume in terms of the side length of the square cutouts.
2. Determine the derivative of the volume function.
3. Find the critical points of the volume function.
4. Use the second derivative test to determine which critical point gives the maximum volume.

Exercise 10.10:

Find the dimensions of a cylindrical can that will minimize the amount of material used for a fixed volume of 1000 cubic centimeters.

1. Set up the objective function for the surface area.

2. Determine the constraint related to the volume.

3. Use Lagrange multipliers to find the critical points of the function.

4. Interpret the results.

Exercise 10.11:

Calculate the work done in moving a particle along a straight line where the force acting on it varies according to the function $F(x) = 5x^3 - 3x^2 + 2x$ from $x = 0$ to $x = 4$ meters.

1. Set up the integral representing the work done.

2. Solve the integral to find the amount of work.

3. Interpret the physical meaning of the result.

Exercise 10.12:

A water trough is 10 meters long and has a cross-section in the shape of an isosceles trapezoid that is 3 meters wide at the bottom, 4 meters wide at the top, and 2 meters high. If the trough is filled with water to a depth of 1.5 meters, determine the volume of water in the trough.

1. Derive the function that represents the cross-sectional area of water as a function of depth.

2. Compute the integral to find the volume of water in the trough.

3. Confirm your result with a geometric calculation.

Answers with Explanations

Solution to 10.9:

For the first exercise, we set up the function for volume:

$$V(x) = (24 - 2x)(36 - 2x)x$$

Calculating $V'(x)$, we find

$$V'(x) = 4x^2 - 120x + 864$$

The critical points occur where $V'(x) = 0$. Solving gives critical points at $x \approx 2.86, 7.14$. Using the second derivative test, $V''(x) = 8x - 120$, we find $V''(2.86) < 0$, so the maximum volume occurs at $x \approx 2.86$.

Solution to 10.10:

For the second exercise: The objective function is the surface area $S = 2\pi rh + 2\pi r^2$, with the constraint $\pi r^2 h = 1000$. Using Lagrange multipliers, the critical points occur at $r \approx 5.42$ cm and $h \approx 10.92$ cm, minimizing material for the can.

Solution to 10.11:

For the third exercise: The work done $W = \int_0^4 (5x^3 - 3x^2 + 2x)\, dx$.

$$W = \left[\frac{5}{4}x^4 - x^3 + x^2\right]_0^4 = 640 - 64 + 16 = 592 \text{ Joules}$$

Hence, 592 Joules of work were done.

Solution to 10.12:

For the fourth exercise: The cross-sectional area of water:

$$A(h) = \frac{1}{2}(b_1 + b_2)h = \frac{1}{2}(3 + 3 + \frac{h}{2}) \times h = 3h + \frac{h^2}{4}$$

Integrate from 0 to 1.5 for the volume:

$$V = 10 \times \int_0^{1.5} (3h + \frac{h^2}{4})\, dh = 10\left[\frac{3}{2}h^2 + \frac{h^3}{12}\right]_0^{1.5} = 65.625 \text{ cubic meters}$$

The calculation confirms this volume.

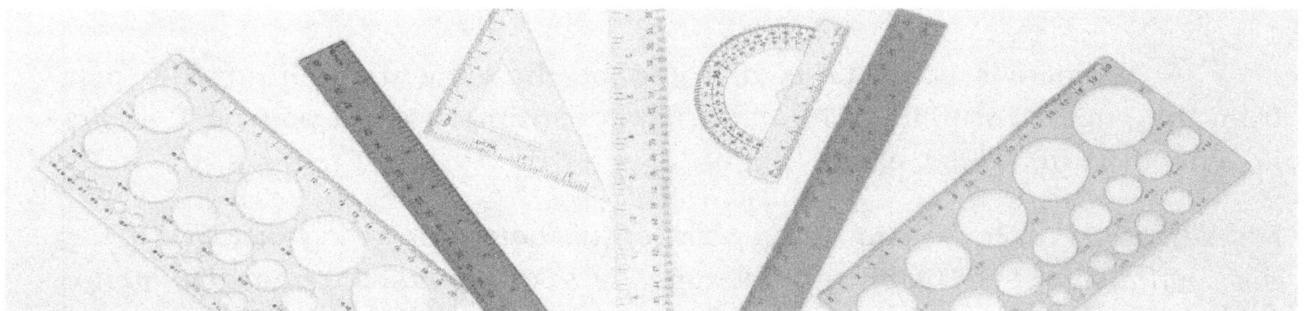

10. Calculus Basics

10.1 Limits and Continuity

In this section, we will delve into the fundamental concepts of limits and continuity, integral to understanding calculus. These concepts serve as the foundation for differentiation and integration, allowing us to analyze mathematical functions with greater precision.

10.1.1 Understanding Limits

A limit is a value that a function approaches as the input approaches a certain value. Limits can be used to define derivatives, continuity, and integrals.

Definition 10.1.1. *The limit of a function $f(x)$ as x approaches c is L, written as*

$$\lim_{x \to c} f(x) = L$$

if for every positive number ϵ, there exists a positive number δ such that if $0 < |x - c| < \delta$, then $|f(x) - L| < \epsilon$.

The following example demonstrates how to calculate the limit of a simple function.

Example 10.1: Consider the function $f(x) = 2x + 3$. We want to find the limit as x approaches 1.

$$\lim_{x \to 1}(2x + 3) = 2(1) + 3 = 5$$

The function value approaches 5 as x nears 1 from both sides.

10.1.2 Continuity and Discontinuities

A function is continuous if it can be drawn without lifting the pen from the paper. Formally, a function $f(x)$ is continuous at a point c if: 1. $f(c)$ is defined. 2. $\lim_{x\to c} f(x)$ exists. 3. $\lim_{x\to c} f(x) = f(c)$.

Definition 10.1.2. *A point c is a point of discontinuity for a function f if f is not continuous at c. There are three types of discontinuities: removable, jump, and infinite.*

Example 10.2: Let's analyze the function $g(x) = \frac{x^2-1}{x-1}$.
Solution:

$$g(x) = \frac{(x-1)(x+1)}{x-1} = x+1 \quad \text{for} \quad x \neq 1$$

As $x \to 1$, $g(x) \to 2$, but $g(1)$ is undefined, indicating a removable discontinuity.

The following figure illustrates the concept of continuity and discontinuity on a graph.

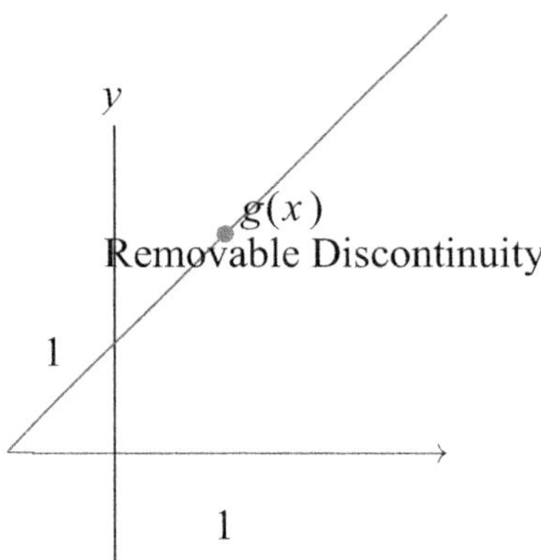

Figure 10.1: Graph of $g(x) = x + 1$ with removable discontinuity at $x = 1$

10.1.3 Evaluating Limits

To evaluate limits, various methods can be employed, including substitution, factoring, and numerical approaches.

Example 10.3: Evaluate lim $_{x\to 2}\frac{x^2-4}{x-2}$.
Solution: First, simplify the expression:

$$\frac{x^2-4}{x-2}=\frac{(x-2)(x+2)}{x-2}=x+2 \quad \text{for} \quad x\neq 2$$

Now, substitute $x = 2$:

$$\lim_{x\to 2}(x+2)=4$$

Example 10.4: Use direct substitution to find $\lim_{x\to 3}(x^2 + 2x - 1)$. Substitute $x = 3$:
Solution:

$$\lim_{x\to 3}(x^2+2x-1)=3^2+2(3)-1=9+6-1=14$$

The table below summarizes common limit evaluations:

Limit Expression	Limit Evaluation
$\lim_{x\to a} c$	c for constant c
$\lim_{x\to a} x$	a
$\lim_{x\to a}(x^n)$	a^n for integer n
$\lim_{x\to a}(f(x)\pm g(x))$	$\lim_{x\to a} f(x)\pm \lim_{x\to a} g(x)$
$\lim_{x\to a}(f(x)\cdot g(x))$	$\lim_{x\to a} f(x)\cdot \lim_{x\to a} g(x)$
$\lim_{x\to a}\left(\frac{f(x)}{g(x)}\right)$	$\frac{\lim_{x\to a} f(x)}{\lim_{x\to a} g(x)}$ provided $\lim_{x\to a} g(x)\neq 0$

Table 10.1: Common Limit Rules

Summary

Understanding and mastering these foundational concepts of limits and continuity are imperative for further exploration in calculus, as they underpin the more advanced topics of differentiation and integration. As you work through these examples, you'll gain the skills to tackle a wide range of mathematical problems with greater acumen.

Exercises

Exercise 10.1:

5. State the definition of a limit and explain the difference between a one-sided limit and a two-sided limit.

6. Evaluate the following limit:

$$\lim_{x \to 3} \frac{x^2 - 9}{x - 3}.$$

7. Consider the function:

$$f(x) = \begin{cases} x^2, & \text{if } x \leq 2 \\ 3x - 4, & \text{if } x > 2 \end{cases}$$

8. Find the limit, if it exists:

$$\lim_{x \to -\infty} \frac{5x^2 + 7}{3x^2 - x + 2}$$

Exercise 10.2:

Sketch the graph of

$$g(x) = \begin{cases} 2x + 3, & \text{if } x < 1 \\ x^2 + 1, & \text{if } x \geq 1 \end{cases}$$

and identify points of discontinuity. Use different colors for each piece of the function and label important points.

Exercise 10.3:

Using the epsilon-delta definition of a limit, prove that $\lim_{x \to 2}(5x-1) = 9$.

Answers with Explanations

Solution to 10.1:

5. A limit is the value that a function (or sequence) approaches as the input (or index) approaches some value. For one-sided limits, the approach is only from one direction (left or right), while two-sided limits consider both directions.

6. Given:

$$\lim_{x \to 3} \frac{x^2 - 9}{x - 3}.$$

Simplify using factorization:

$$\frac{x^2 - 9}{x - 3} = \frac{(x + 3)(x - 3)}{x - 3}.$$

Cancel the common factor:

$$= x + 3.$$

Therefore,

$$\lim_{x \to 3}(x + 3) = 6.$$

7. The function is continuous at $x = 2$ if:

$$\lim_{x \to 2^-} f(x) = \lim_{x \to 2^+} f(x) = f(2).$$

Calculate:

$$\lim_{x \to 2^-} x^2 = 4,$$
$$\lim_{x \to 2^+} (3x - 4) = 2,$$
$$f(2) = 4.$$

8. Given:

$$\lim_{x \to -\infty} \frac{5x^2 + 7}{3x^2 - x + 2}.$$

Divide numerator and denominator by x^2:

$$\frac{5 + \frac{7}{x^2}}{3 - \frac{1}{x} + \frac{2}{x^2}}.$$

As $x \to -\infty$, all terms with x in the denominator approach 0:

$$\frac{5}{3}.$$

Solution to 10.2:

Different colors to be used on tikz illustration: Graph $g(x)$ using tikz:

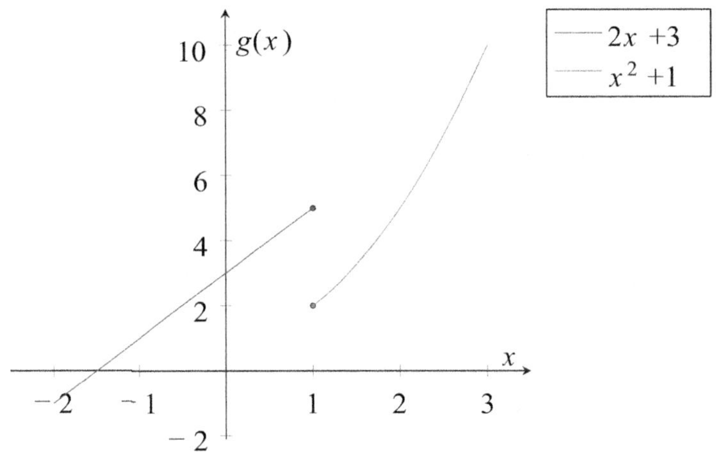

Discontinuity at $x = 1$ as the limits from the left and right are different.

Solution to 10.3:

Proof using epsilon-delta: We need the following:

$$|5x - 1 - 9| < \epsilon$$

Simplify to:

$$|5x - 10| < \epsilon$$

Divide by 5:

$$|x - 2| < \frac{\epsilon}{5}$$

Therefore, let $\delta = \frac{\epsilon}{5}$; if $0 < |x - 2| < \delta$, then:

$$|x - 2| < \frac{\epsilon}{5} \rightarrow |5x - 10| < \epsilon.$$

Proven as required.

10.2 Derivatives

In advanced high school mathematics, derivatives are one of the foundational concepts in calculus. The derivative provides a way to capture the concept of change, which is quintessential in various fields such as physics, engineering, economics, and beyond. This section will delve into the concept of the derivative, rules of differentiation, and explore applications in motion profoundly.

10.2.1 Concept of the Derivative

The derivative of a function measures how the function value changes as its input changes. It is the cornerstone of continuous change and is symbolized as $f(x)$ or $\frac{df}{dx}$.

Definition 10.2.1. *The derivative of a function f(x) at a point x = a is defined as the limit:*

$$f'(a) = \lim_{h \to 0} \frac{f(a+h) - f(a)}{h}$$

provided the limit exists.

The derivative represents the slope of the tangent line to the curve at a point. It's the instant rate of change of the function concerning its input variable.

Example 10.5: Consider $f(x) = x^2$. Find the derivative $f(x)$.

Solution: Begin with the definition of the derivative:

$$f'(x) = \lim_{h \to 0} \frac{(x+h)^2 - x^2}{h}$$

Expanding $(x + h)^2$:

$$= \lim_{h \to 0} \frac{x^2 + 2xh + h^2 - x^2}{h}$$

Simplify:

$$= \lim_{h \to 0} \frac{2xh + h^2}{h} = \lim_{h \to 0} (2x + h) = 2x$$

Therefore, the derivative $f(x) = 2x$.

10.2.2 Rules of Differentiation

There are multiple rules to simplify the process of finding derivatives without returning to the definition.

Power Rule

If $f(x) = x^n$, then: $f'(x) = nx^{n-1}$

Example 10.6: Differentiate $f(x) = x^3$.
Solution: Applying the power rule:

$$f'(x) = 3x^{3-1} = 3x^2$$

Product Rule

If $u(x)$ and $v(x)$ are differentiable functions, then:

$$(uv)' = u'v + uv'$$

Example 10.7: Differentiate $f(x) = x^2 \sin(x)$.
Solution: Let $u = x^2$ and $v = \sin(x)$. Then $u' = 2x$ and $v' = \cos(x)$. Applying the product rule:

$$f'(x) = 2x \cdot sin(x) + x^2 \cdot cos(x)$$

Quotient Rule

If $u(x)$ and $v(x)$ are differentiable, then:

$$\left(\frac{u}{v}\right)' = \frac{u'v - uv'}{v^2}$$

Example 10.8: Differentiate $f(x) = \frac{x}{x+1}$.
Solution: Here, $u = x$ and $v = x + 1$. Therefore, $u' = 1$ and $v' = 1$. Applying the quotient rule:

$$f'(x) = \frac{1 \cdot (x+1) - x \cdot 1}{(x+1)^2} = \frac{x+1-x}{(x+1)^2} = \frac{1}{(x+1)^2}$$

10.2.3 Applications in Motion

In physics, the derivative is extensively used to analyze motion. If the position of an object is given by a function $s(t)$, then the velocity and acceleration can be expressed in terms of derivatives.

Velocity and Acceleration

Definition 10.2.2. *The velocity $v(t)$ of an object is the derivative of its position $s(t)$:*

$$v(t) = \frac{ds}{dt}$$

The acceleration $a(t)$ is the derivative of velocity:

$$a(t) = \frac{dv}{dt} = \frac{d^2s}{dt^2}$$

Example 10.9: Suppose an object moves along a line with position $s(t) = 4t^3 - 2t^2 + t$. Find the velocity and acceleration at time t.
Solution: First, find the velocity:

$$v(t) = \frac{ds}{dt} = \frac{d}{dt}(4t^3 - 2t^2 + t) = 12t^2 - 4t + 1$$

Next, find the acceleration:

$$a(t) = \frac{dv}{dt} = \frac{d}{dt}(12t^2 - 4t + 1) = 24t - 4$$

Therefore, the velocity is $v(t) = 12t^2 - 4t + 1$ and the acceleration is $a(t) = 24t - 4$.

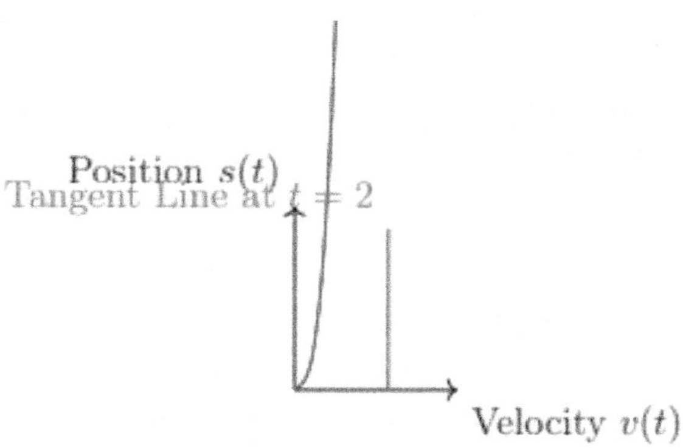

Figure 10.2: The tangent line shows the instantaneous rate of change of position, i.e., velocity.

Conclusion

Through exploring derivatives, power, product, and quotient rules, students can deepen their understanding of calculus's fundamental principles. The derivative captures changing quantities and has real-world applications in describing the nuances of motion amongst other dynamic systems.

Exercises

Exercise 10.4:

Consider the function $f(x) = 3x^2 + 5x - 7$.

4. Find $f(x)$, the derivative of $f(x)$.

5. Evaluate $f(2)$.

6. Interpret the meaning of the derivative at $x = 2$ in terms of the slope of the tangent line.

Exercise 10.5:

The position of a particle is given by the function $s(t) = t^3 - 6t^2 + 9t + 15$, where s is in meters and t is in seconds.

4. Find the velocity function $v(t)$.

5. Determine the acceleration function $a(t)$.

6. Calculate the velocity and acceleration at $t = 3$ seconds. Interpret your results.

Exercise 10.6:

Use implicit differentiation to find $\frac{dy}{dx}$ for the equation $x^2 + y^2 = 25$.

4. Solve for $\frac{dy}{dx}$ explicitly.

5. At the point (3,4), compute the slope of the tangent line.

6. Sketch the circle and the tangent line at the point (3,4) using TikZ.

Exercise 10.7:

Determine the critical points and intervals of increase and decrease for the function $f(x) = x^3 - 3x^2 - 9x + 27$.

4. Find the critical points by solving $f(x) = 0$.

5. Test intervals around the critical points to determine where the function is increasing or decreasing.

6. Illustrate the function graphically and indicate the points of increase and decrease on the graph using TikZ.

Answers with Explanations

Solution to 10.4:

4. The derivative of $f(x) = 3x^2 + 5x - 7$ is found using power rule:

$$f(x) = 6x + 5$$

5. Evaluating $f(2)$: $f(2) = 6(2) + 5 = 17$

6. The derivative at $x = 2$, $f(2) = 17$, indicates that the slope of the tangent line at the point where $x = 2$ is 17, meaning the rate of change of the function at this point is 17.

Solution to 10.5:

4. Velocity $v(t)$ is found by differentiating $s(t) = t^3 - 6t^2 + 9t + 15$:

$$v(t) = 3t^2 - 12t + 9$$

5. Acceleration $a(t)$ is found by differentiating $v(t)$:

$$a(t) = 6t - 12$$

6. At $t = 3$:

$$v(3) = 3(3)^2 - 12(3) + 9 = 0$$

$$a(3) = 6(3) - 12 = 6$$

The velocity is zero, indicating the particle is momentarily at rest, while the acceleration is 6 m/s^2 indicating a positive increase in velocity.

Solution to 10.6:

4. For $x^2 + y^2 = 25$, differentiate both sides with respect to x:

$$2x + 2y\frac{dy}{dx} = 0$$

$$\frac{dy}{dx} = -\frac{x}{y}$$

5. At the point (3, 4), the slope is:

$$\frac{dy}{dx} = -\frac{3}{4}$$

6. The sketch is below:
where the dotted line represents the tangent at the point.

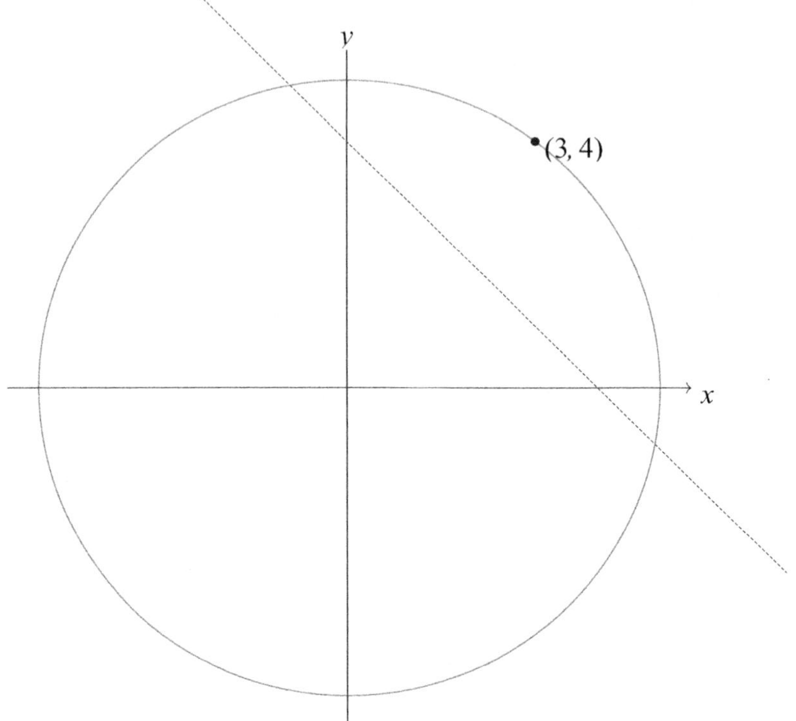

Solution to 10.7:

4. Finding the critical points by solving:

$$f(x) = 3x^2 - 6x - 9 = 0$$

Factor and solve:

$$3(x^2 - 2x - 3) = 0 \implies (x - 3)(x + 1) = 0$$

Critical points are $x = 3$ and $x = -1$.

5. Test intervals:
   a. Interval $(-\infty,-1)$, select $x = -2$, $f(-2) = 15$ (increasing).

   b. Interval $(-1,3)$, select $x = 0$, $f(0) = -9$ (decreasing).

   c. Interval $(3,\infty)$, select $x = 4$, $f(4) = 15$ (increasing).

6. Graph illustration with TikZ:

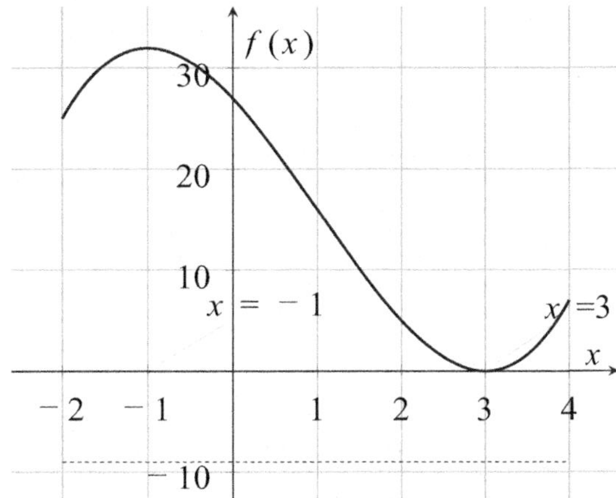

This graph shows increase and decrease with identified critical points.

10.3 Integrals

In calculus, integrals are a fundamental concept related to the idea of finding areas under curves, which correspond to the accumulation of quantities. This section will thoroughly explore integrals, starting with antiderivatives and progressing to the practical applications of integration, which are pivotal in various scientific and engineering disciplines.

10.3.1 Understanding Antiderivatives

An antiderivative of a function $f(x)$ is another function $F(x)$ such that the derivative of $F(x)$ is equal to $f(x)$, i.e., $F'(x) = f(x)$. The process of finding the antiderivative is called integration.

Definition 10.3.1. *An antiderivative of a function $f(x)$ on an interval I is a function $F(x)$ such that $F'(x) = f(x)$ for all x in I.*

Example 10.10: Find the antiderivative of $f(x) = 3x^2$.
Solution: We need a function $F(x)$ such that $F'(x) = 3x^2$. One possible function is $F(x) = x^3$, because

$$F'(x) = \frac{d}{dx}[x^3] = 3x^2.$$

Therefore, $F(x) = x^3$ is an antiderivative of $f(x) = 3x^2$.

It's important to note that the most general antiderivative includes a constant term C, because the derivative of a constant is zero. Hence, if $F(x)$ is an antiderivative of $f(x)$, then the most general antiderivative is $F(x) + C$.

10.3.2 Definite and Indefinite Integrals

The integral can be classified into two main types: definite and indefinite integrals.

Indefinite Integrals

The indefinite integral of a function $f(x)$, denoted by R $f(x)dx$, is the set of all antiderivatives of $f(x)$. The indefinite integral is expressed as:

$$\int f(x)\,dx = F(x) + C,$$

where $F(x)$ is an antiderivative of $f(x)$, and C is the constant of integration.

Example 10.11: Compute $\int (2x + 3)\,dx.$
Solution: Integrate each term separately:

$$\int (2x+3)\,dx = \int 2x\,dx + \int 3\,dx = x^2 + 3x + C.$$

Definite Integrals

The definite integral of a function $f(x)$ from a to b is denoted by

$$\int_a^b f(x)\,dx,$$

and represents the net area between the x-axis and the graph of $f(x)$ from $x = a$ to $x = b$.

The Fundamental Theorem of Calculus links the concept of differentiation with integration and asserts that the definite integral of a function can be computed using its antiderivative:

Theorem 10.3.1 (Fundamental Theorem of Calculus). *If F is an antiderivative of f on an interval* $[a,b]$, *then*

$$\int_a^b f(x)\,dx = F(b) - F(a)$$

Example 10.12: Evaluate $\int_1^4 (3x^2 + 2)\, dx$.
Solution: First, find the antiderivative: $F(x) = x^3 + 2x$. Then apply the Fundamental Theorem of Calculus:

$$\int_1^4 (3x^2 + 2)\, dx = \left[x^3 + 2x\right]_1^4 = (4^3 + 2 \times 4) - (1^3 + 2 \times 1) = (64 + 8) - (1 + 2) = 71.$$

10.3.3 Applications of Integration

Integration has wide-ranging applications across numerous fields, providing solutions to various practical problems.

Area Between Curves

To find the area between two curves $y = f(x)$ and $y = g(x)$ from $x = a$ to $x = b$, where $f(x) \geq g(x)$, the area A is given by:

$$A = \int_a^b [f(x) - g(x)]\, dx.$$

Example 10.13: Find the area between $y = x^2$ and $y = x + 2$ from $x = 0$ to $x = 2$.
Solution: Set up the integral:

$$A = \int_0^2 [(x + 2) - x^2]\, dx = \int_0^2 (-x^2 + x + 2)\, dx.$$

Find the antiderivative:

$$\int (-x^2 + x + 2)\, dx = -\frac{x^3}{3} + \frac{x^2}{2} + 2x + C.$$

Evaluate from 0 to 2:

$$A = \left[-\frac{(2)^3}{3} + \frac{(2)^2}{2} + 2(2)\right] - \left[-\frac{(0)^3}{3} + \frac{(0)^2}{2} + 2(0)\right].$$

This simplifies to:

$$A = \left[-\frac{8}{3} + 2 + 4\right] = \frac{8}{3}.$$

Volume of Solids of Revolution

A solid of revolution is generated by revolving a region around a line (axis of rotation). The volume V when rotating around the x-axis is given by the disk method:

$$V = \pi \int_a^b [f(x)]^2\, dx.$$

If using the shell method, for rotation about the y-axis, the volume is:

$$V = 2\pi \int_a^b x f(x)\, dx.$$

Example 10.14: Calculate the volume of the solid formed by revolving the region between $y = \sqrt{x}$ and the x-axis from $x = 0$ to $x = 4$ around the x-axis.
Solution: Using the disk method:

$$V = \pi \int_0^4 (\sqrt{x})^2\, dx = \pi \int_0^4 x\, dx.$$

Finding the antiderivative:

$$\int x\, dx = \frac{x^2}{2} + C.$$

Evaluate from 0 to 4:

$$V = \pi \left[\frac{4^2}{2} - \frac{0^2}{2}\right] = \pi\, [8] = 8\pi.$$

Conclusion

Integration is a powerful tool that not only supports solving complex mathematics but also offers practical solutions to real-world problems. In this manner, integrals become indispensable in the toolbox of mathematicians, scientists, and engineers alike.

Exercises

Exercise 10.8:

6. **Evaluate the indefinite integral:**

$$\int (3x^2 + 2x + 1)\, dx$$

7. **Calculate the definite integral of the function $f(x) = x^3 - 4x$ over the interval [1,3].**

8. **Find the area between the curves $y = x^2$ and $y = 4 - x^2$.**

9. A particle moves along a straight line such that its velocity at time t is given by $v(t) = 6t^2 - 2t$. Find the displacement of the particle from $t = 0$ to $t = 2$.

10. Solve the initial value problem:

$$\frac{dy}{dx} = 3x^2, \quad y(0) = 5$$

Answers with Explanations

Solution to 10.8:

6. To find the indefinite integral, integrate each term separately:

$$\int (3x^2 + 2x + 1)\, dx = \frac{3}{3}x^3 + \frac{2}{2}x^2 + x + C = x^3 + x^2 + x + C$$

where C is the constant of integration.

7. Evaluate the definite integral:

$$\int_1^3 (x^3 - 4x)\, dx$$

First, find the antiderivative:

$$F(x) = \frac{1}{4}x^4 - 2x^2$$

Now, calculate:

$$F(3) - F(1) = \left(\frac{1}{4}(3)^4 - 2(3)^2\right) - \left(\frac{1}{4}(1)^4 - 2(1)^2\right) = \frac{81}{4} - 18 - \left(\frac{1}{4} - 2\right)$$

Evaluate:

$$= \frac{81}{4} - \frac{72}{4} - \left(\frac{1}{4} + \frac{8}{4}\right) = \frac{81 - 72 - 1 - 8}{4} = 0$$

8. The area between the curves $y = x^2$ and $y = 4 - x^2$ is:

$$\int_{-2}^{2} [(4 - x^2) - x^2]\, dx = \int_{-2}^{2} (4 - 2x^2)\, dx$$

Solve:

$$= \left[4x - \frac{2}{3}x^3\right]_{-2}^{2} = \left(8 - \frac{16}{3}\right) - \left(-8 + \frac{16}{3}\right)$$

Evaluate:

$$= \left(\frac{24}{3} - \frac{16}{3}\right) - \left(-\frac{24}{3} + \frac{16}{3}\right) = \frac{8}{3} + \frac{8}{3} = \frac{16}{3}$$

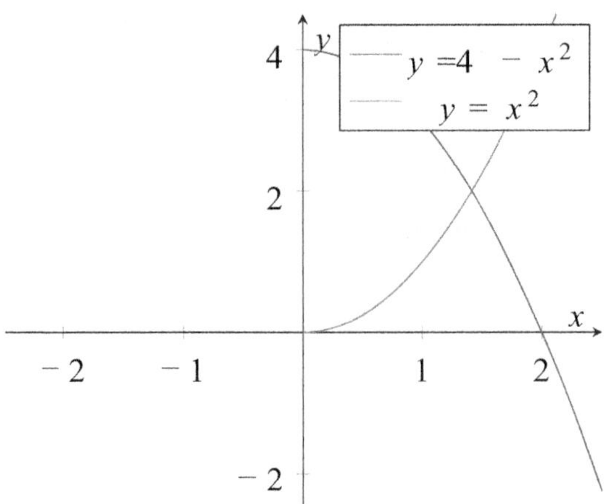

Figure 10.3: Area between $y = x^2$ and $y = 4 - x^2$.

9. For displacement, find the definite integral of velocity:

$$\int_0^2 (6t^2 - 2t)\,dt = \left[2t^3 - t^2\right]_0^2$$

Evaluate:

$$= (2 \cdot 8 - 4) - (0 - 0) = 16 - 4 = 12$$

The displacement is 12 units.

10. Solve the initial value problem:

$$\frac{dy}{dx} = 3x^2$$

Integrate both sides:

$$y = \int 3x^2\,dx = x^3 + C$$

Apply initial condition $y(0) = 5$:

$$5 = 0^3 + C \Rightarrow C = 5$$

Thus, the solution is $y = x^3 + 5$.

10.4 Applications of Calculus

Calculus is not only a beautiful subject within mathematics due to its theoretical elegance but also a highly practical tool with widespread applications in various fields. From optimization problems to understanding natural phenomena through physics, calculus plays an indispensable role in both academia and the industry. This section will explore some commonplace applications of calculus and showcase its utility in solving real-world problems.

10.4.1 Optimization Problems

Optimization refers to the process of making something as effective or functional as possible. In mathematics, we often seek to find the maximum or minimum values of a function given certain constraints. Calculus, with its powerful tools such as derivatives, provides a systematic approach to these problems.

Theorem 10.4.1 (First Derivative Test). *Let f be a continuous function on the interval* (a, b) *and differentiable on* (a, b) *except at a point c. If* $f(x)$ *changes sign from positive to negative at c, then f has a local maximum at c. Similarly, if* $f(x)$ *changes from negative to positive at c, then f has a local minimum there.*

Example 10.15: Consider the function $f(x) = -x^2 + 4x + 5$. Find the critical points and determine their nature.
Solution: First, find the derivative:

$$f(x) = -2x + 4$$

Setting $f(x) = 0$ gives:

$$-2x + 4 = 0 \Rightarrow x = 2$$

Evaluate the second derivative:

$$f'(x) = -2$$

Since $f'(x) < 0$, f is concave down at $x = 2$, indicating a local maximum. The maximum value is:

$$f(2) = -(2)^2 + 4 \times 2 + 5 = 9$$

Therefore, the function has a local maximum at $x = 2$ with a value of 9.

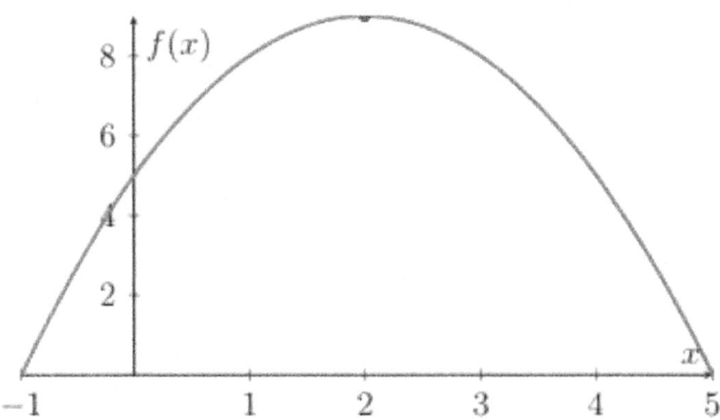

Figure 10.4: Graph of $f(x) = -x^2 + 4x + 5$, showing a local maximum at $x = 2$.

10.4.2 Area and Volume Calculations

Calculus provides a framework for calculating exact areas under curves and the volume of solids of revolution using integration. These calculations are crucial in fields like engineering, architecture, and manufacturing.

Proposition 10.4.2. *The area under a curve $y = f(x)$ from $x = a$ to $x = b$ is given by:*

$$\int_a^b f(x)\, dx$$

Example 10.16: Compute the area between the curve $y = \sqrt{x}$ and the x-axis from $x = 0$ to $x = 4$.
Solution: The area is given by the definite integral:

$$\int_0^4 \sqrt{x}\, dx$$

Calculating the integral, we obtain:

$$\int \sqrt{x}\, dx = \frac{2}{3}x^{3/2} + C$$

Evaluating from 0 to 4, we get:

$$\left[\frac{2}{3}x^{3/2}\right]_0^4 = \frac{2}{3} \times 8 - \frac{2}{3} \times 0 = \frac{16}{3}$$

Thus, the area is $\frac{16}{3}$ square units.

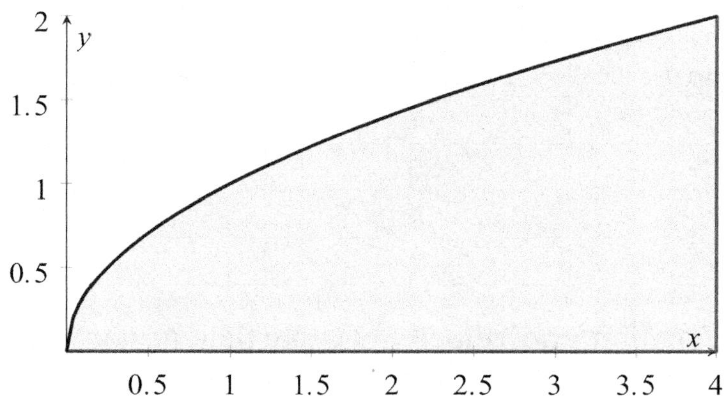

Figure 10.5: Area between the curve $y = \sqrt{x}$ and the x-axis from $x = 0$ to $x = 4$.

10.4.3 Physics and Engineering Applications

In physics and engineering, calculus is employed to understand systems' dynamic behaviors, analyze forces, and model physical phenomena.

Definition 10.4.1 (Velocity and Acceleration). *Velocity is the rate of change of position and is given by the first derivative of the position function with respect to time,* $v(t) = \frac{ds}{dt}$. *Acceleration is the rate of change of velocity and is given by the second derivative of the position function,* $a(t) = \frac{dv}{dt} = \frac{d^2v}{dt^2}$.

Example 10.17: A particle moves along a line such that its position at time t is given by $s(t) = t^3 - 6t^2 + 9t + 1$. Determine the velocity and acceleration at $t = 2$.
Solution: Calculate the velocity:

$$v(t) = \frac{ds}{dt} = 3t^2 - 12t + 9$$

$$v(2) = 3(2)^2 - 12(2) + 9 = 12 - 24 + 9 = -3$$

Calculate the acceleration:

$$a(t) = \frac{dv}{dt} = 6t - 12$$

$$a(2) = 6(2) - 12 = 0$$

At $t = 2$, the velocity is -3 and the acceleration is 0.

Time t	Position $s(t)$	Velocity $v(t)$
0	1	9
1	5	0
2	5	-3
3	1	0

Table 10.2: Position and velocity of a particle at various times.

This detailed exploration highlights calculus's profound role in solving sophisticated problems across various domains, underscoring its significance beyond academia.

Exercises

Exercise 10.9:

A company wants to create an open-top rectangular box with maximum volume from a piece of cardboard that measures 24 inches by 36 inches by cutting out equal squares from each corner and folding up the sides.

5. Write a function $V(x)$ to represent the volume in terms of the side length of the square cutouts.
6. Determine the derivative of the volume function.
7. Find the critical points of the volume function.
8. Use the second derivative test to determine which critical point gives the maximum volume.

Exercise 10.10:

Find the dimensions of a cylindrical can that will minimize the amount of material used for a fixed volume of 1000 cubic centimeters.

5. Set up the objective function for the surface area.
6. Determine the constraint related to the volume.
7. Use Lagrange multipliers to find the critical points of the function.
8. Interpret the results.

Exercise 10.11:

Calculate the work done in moving a particle along a straight line where the force acting on it varies according to the function $F(x) = 5x^3 - 3x^2 + 2x$ from $x = 0$ to $x = 4$ meters.

4. Set up the integral representing the work done.

5. Solve the integral to find the amount of work.

6. Interpret the physical meaning of the result.

Exercise 10.12:

A water trough is 10 meters long and has a cross-section in the shape of an isosceles trapezoid that is 3 meters wide at the bottom, 4 meters wide at the top, and 2 meters high. If the trough is filled with water to a depth of 1.5 meters, determine the volume of water in the trough.

4. Derive the function that represents the cross-sectional area of water as a function of depth.

5. Compute the integral to find the volume of water in the trough.

6. Confirm your result with a geometric calculation.

Answers with Explanations

Solution to 10.9:

For the first exercise, we set up the function for volume:

$$V(x) = (24 - 2x)(36 - 2x)x$$

Calculating $V'(x)$, we find

$$V'(x) = 4x^2 - 120x + 864$$

The critical points occur where $V'(x) = 0$. Solving gives critical points at $x \approx 2.86, 7.14$. Using the second derivative test, $V''(x) = 8x - 120$, we find $V''(2.86) < 0$, so the maximum volume occurs at $x \approx 2.86$.

Solution to 10.10:

For the second exercise: The objective function is the surface area $S = 2\pi rh + 2\pi r^2$, with the constraint $\pi r^2 h = 1000$. Using Lagrange multipliers, the critical points occur at $r \approx 5.42$ cm and $h \approx 10.92$ cm, minimizing material for the can.

Solution to 10.11:

For the third exercise: The work done $W = \int_0^4 (5x^3 - 3x^2 + 2x)\,dx$.

$$W = \left[\frac{5}{4}x^4 - x^3 + x^2\right]_0^4 = 640 - 64 + 16 = 592\,\text{Joules}$$

Hence, 592 Joules of work were done.

Solution to 10.12:

For the fourth exercise: The cross-sectional area of water:

$$A(h) = \frac{1}{2}(b_1 + b_2)h = \frac{1}{2}(3 + 3 + \frac{h}{2}) \times h = 3h + \frac{h^2}{4}$$

Integrate from 0 to 1.5 for the volume:

$$V = 10 \times \int_0^{1.5} (3h + \frac{h^2}{4})\,dh = 10\left[\frac{3}{2}h^2 + \frac{h^3}{12}\right]_0^{1.5} = 65.625\,\text{cubic meters}$$

The calculation confirms this volume.

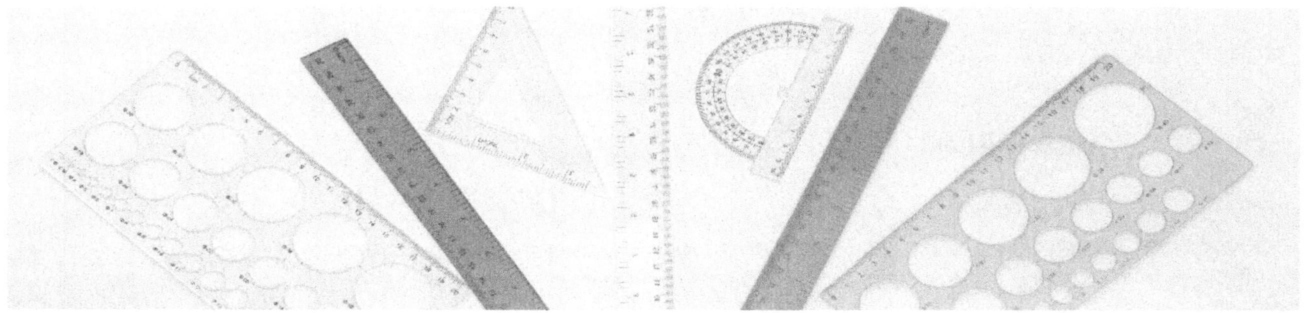

11. Practice Tests

11.1 TEST – I

Student Information:

- **Name:**____
- **Class/Section:**__________________________________
- **Date:**____

Instructions:

- Fill in the circle corresponding to your chosen answer for each question.
- Use a dark pen or pencil to mark your answers clearly.
- If you need to change an answer, erase or cross out your previous mark completely.

Scantron Answer Sheet

Answer Sheet

Q#	A	B	C	D
1	○	○	○	○
2	○	○	○	○
3	○	○	○	○
4	○	○	○	○
5	○	○	○	○
6	○	○	○	○
7	○	○	○	○
8	○	○	○	○
9	○	○	○	○
10	○	○	○	○

Q#	A	B	C	D
11	○	○	○	○
12	○	○	○	○
13	○	○	○	○
14	○	○	○	○
15	○	○	○	○
16	○	○	○	○
17	○	○	○	○
18	○	○	○	○
19	○	○	○	○
20	○	○	○	○

Note: Please ensure all selected answers are clearly marked. Review your answer sheet before submission to make sure you have answered all questions.

11.1.1 Contents of the Book

Multiple Choice Questions

1. **Which of the following is a solution to the equation $x^2 - 5x + 6 = 0$?**
   A. $x = 2$
   B. $x = 3$
   C. Both A and B
   D. None of the above

2. **The slope of the line passing through points (2, 3) and (5, 11) is:**
   A. 2
   B. 3
   C. $\frac{8}{3}$
   D. $\frac{3}{8}$

3. **The following expression is simplified to: $\frac{x^2-1}{x+1}$**
   A. $x - 1$
   B. $x + 1$
   C. $x^2 - x$
   D. None of the above

4. **Simplify the expression $5(x + 2) - 3(x - 1) + 7$:**
   A. $2x + 12$
   B. $2x + 14$
   C. $8x + 2$
   D. $8x - 2$

5. **Which is the hypotenuse in a right-angled triangle if the sides are 5, 12, and 13?**
   A. 5
   B. 12
   C. 13
   D. None of the above

6. The derivative of $f(x) = x^3$ is:

A. $3x^2$

B. x^2

C. $3x$

D. x^3

7. The sum of angles in a triangle is:

A. 90°

B. 180°

C. 360°

D. None of above

8. Convert $\frac{\pi}{6}$ radians to degrees.

A. 15°

B. 30°

C. 45°

D. 60°

9. Evaluate the limit: $\lim_{x \to 0} \frac{\sin x}{x}$

A. 0

B. 1

C. ∞

D. Undefined

10. Find the area of a circle with radius 7.

A. 49π

B. 14π

C. 28π

D. None of the above

11. Which statement is true about exponential functions?

A. They are linear

B. They have a constant rate of growth or decay

C. Their growth or decay rate is proportional to their current size

D. They can only represent growth

12. Which of the following is not a property of a parallelogram?

A. Opposite sides are parallel
B. Opposite angles are equal
C. The diagonals bisect each other
D. All sides are equal

13. What is the probability of rolling a 5 on a six-sided die?

A. 1/2
B. 1/6
C. 1/3
D. 5/6

14. If $f(x) = 2x + 3$, what is $f^{-1}(x)$?

A. $x - 3$
B. $\frac{x-3}{2}$
C. $\frac{x+3}{2}$
D. None of the above

15. Which of the following is an arithmetic sequence?

A. 2, 4, 8, 16
B. 3, 6, 9, 12
C. 5, 10, 20, 40
D. 1, 4, 9, 16

16. Which function is invertible?

A. $f(x) = x^2$
B. $f(x) = x^3$
C. $f(x) = |x|$
D. $f(x) = \sin x$

17. The determinant of the matrix $\begin{pmatrix} 1 & 2 \\ 3 & 4 \end{pmatrix}$ is:

A. -2
B. 10
C. 1
D. 0

18. Find the x-intercept of the line $3x + 4y = 12$:

A. (0, 4)
B. (4, 0)
C. (3, 0)
D. (0, 3)

19. Evaluate the integral $\int 3x^2\, dx$:

A. x^3
B. $x^3 + C$
C. $x^3 - C$
D. $3x^3 + C$

20. Calculate the future value of an investment of $1000 at 5% annual interest compounded yearly for 3 years:

A. 1157.63
B. 1157.62
C. 1157.84
D. 1158

11.1.2 Answer Keys

1.	**C**	11.	**C**
2.	**B**	12.	**D**
3.	**A**	13.	**B**
4.	**A**	14.	**B**
5.	**C**	15.	**B**
6.	**A**	16.	**B**
7.	**B**	17.	**A**
8.	**B**	18.	**B**
9.	**B**	19.	**B**
10.	**A**	20.	**C**

11.1.3 Detailed Solutions

1. **C.** Explanation: $x^2 - 5x + 6$ factors to $(x-2)(x-3)$, giving solutions $x = 2$ and $x = 3$.

2. **B.** Explanation: Slope $m = \frac{11-3}{5-2} = \frac{8}{3}$.

3. **A.** Explanation: The expression simplifies as $\frac{(x-1)(x+1)}{x+1}$ which reduces to $x - 1$.

4. **A.** Explanation: Distribute and simplify: $5x + 10 - 3x + 3 + 7 = 2x + 20$.

5. **C.** Explanation: In a right triangle with a hypotenuse, the longest side is 13.

6. **A.** Explanation: The derivative of x^3 is obtained using the power rule as $3x^2$.

7. **B.** Explanation: A fundamental property of triangles.

8. **B.** Explanation: Multiply $\frac{\pi}{6}$ radians by $\frac{180}{\pi} = 30$ degrees.

9. **A.** Explanation: A known result of the limit as $x \to 0$.

10. **A.** Explanation: Using the formula πr^2.

11. **C.** Explanation: This is the defining property of exponential functions.

12. **D.** Explanation: Only true for a rhombus.

13. **B.** Explanation: There is one favorable outcome out of six possibilities.

14. **B.** Explanation: Solving $y = 2x + 3$ for x gives the inverse function.

15. **B.** Explanation: The difference between consecutive terms is constant.

16. **B.** Explanation: It is monotonic, hence invertible.

17. **A.** Explanation: Calculation involves $ad - bc$ for a 2x2 matrix, $(1)(4) - (2)(3) = -2$.

18. **B.** Explanation: Set $y = 0$ in the equation $3x + 4 \cdot 0 = 12$.

19. **B.** Explanation: Integrate $3x^2$ to get $\frac{3x^3}{3} + C = x^3 + C$.

20. **C.** Explanation: $1000\left(1 + \frac{0.05}{1}\right)^{1.3} = 1157.63$.

11.2 TEST – II

Student Information:

- **Name:**____
- **Class/Section:**__________________________________
- **Date:**____

Instructions:

- Fill in the circle corresponding to your chosen answer for each question.
- Use a dark pen or pencil to mark your answers clearly.
- If you need to change an answer, erase or cross out your previous mark completely.

Scantron Answer Sheet

Answer Sheet

Q#	A	B	C	D	Q#	A	B	C	D
1	○	○	○	○	11	○	○	○	○
2	○	○	○	○	12	○	○	○	○
3	○	○	○	○	13	○	○	○	○
4	○	○	○	○	14	○	○	○	○
5	○	○	○	○	15	○	○	○	○
6	○	○	○	○	16	○	○	○	○
7	○	○	○	○	17	○	○	○	○
8	○	○	○	○	18	○	○	○	○
9	○	○	○	○	19	○	○	○	○
10	○	○	○	○	20	○	○	○	○

Note: Please ensure all selected answers are clearly marked. Review your answer sheet before submission to make sure you have answered all questions.

11.2.1 Contents of the Book

Multiple Choice Questions

1. **Calculate $\int \sin x dx$.**
   A. $-\cos x + C$
   B. $\cos x + C$
   C. $\sin x + C$
   D. $-\sin x + C$

2. **What is the probability of drawing a heart from a standard deck of cards?**
   A. 1/4
   B. 1/3
   C. 1/13
   D. 1/2

3. **Solve for x: $15x + 5 = 65$.**
   A. 4
   B. 5
   C. 3
   D. 6

4. **Determine the vertical asymptote of $f(x) = \frac{1}{x-4}$.**
   A. $x = 0$
   B. $x = 4$
   C. $x = -4$
   D. None

5. **What is $\log_{10} 100$?**
   A. 3
   B. 2
   C. 10
   D. 100

6. The polynomial $x^2 - 4$ can be factored as:

A. $(x - 2)^2$
B. $(x + 2)^2$
C. $(x - 4)^2$
D. $(x - 2)(x + 2)$

7. Compute the dot product of vectors $\vec{a} = \begin{bmatrix} 1 \\ 3 \end{bmatrix}$ and $\vec{b} = \begin{bmatrix} 4 \\ 2 \end{bmatrix}$.

A. 10
B. 8
C. 6
D. 11

8. Express $(x^2y^3)^2$ using the laws of exponents.

A. x^2y^5
B. x^4y^9
C. x^4y^6
D. None of the above

9. Determine if the function $f(x) = e^x$ is one-to-one.

A. Yes
B. No
C. Only for positive x
D. Only for negative x

10. Define the mean of the dataset: {2, 4, 6, 8, 10}.

A. 6
B. 5
C. 8
D. 7

11. Find the sum of an arithmetic series where $a_1 = 5$, the last term $a_n = 45$ with the number of terms being 9.

A. 180
B. 200
C. 225
D. 250

12. The range of the function $f(x) = 2x^2 - 3$ is:

A. All real numbers
B. $[-3, \infty)$
C. $(-\infty, -3]$
D. $(-\infty, \infty)$

13. Find the midpoint of the line segment connecting (1, 2) and (7, 8).

A. (2, 3)
B. (4, 5)
C. (3.5, 3.5)
D. (5, 6)

14. If an angle measures 145 degrees, what is its complementary angle?

A. 35 degrees
B. None, complementary angle doesn't exist.
C. 15 degrees
D. 45 degrees

15. Find the cube root of 64.

A. 4
B. 8
C. 16
D. 2

16. What is the inverse sine function of 0.5?

A. 30°
B. 45°
C. 60°
D. 90°

17. Simplify $\frac{4x^3}{2x}$:

A. $2x^2$
B. 2x
C. 2
D. $2x^4$

18. What is the logical opposite of the statement: "If it rains, then the ground is wet."

A. If it rains, the ground is not wet.
B. If the ground is not wet, then it does not rain.
C. If it does not rain, the ground is wet.
D. If the ground is wet, then it rains.

19. Calculate $\sqrt{144} - 8 \times 2$:

A. 0
B. 4
C. -8
D. 2

20. A regular hexagon has each central angle equal to:

A. 30°
B. 45°
C. 60°
D. 120°

11.2.2 Answer Keys

1.	**A**	11.	**C**
2.	**A**	12.	**B**
3.	**B**	13.	**B**
4.	**B**	14.	**B**
5.	**B**	15.	**A**
6.	**D**	16.	**A**
7.	**A**	17.	**A**
8.	**C**	18.	**B**
9.	**A**	19.	**C**
10.	**A**	20.	**C**

11.2.3 Detailed Solutions

1. **A.** Explanation: The integral of $\sin x$ is $-\cos x + C$.

2. **A.** Explanation: There are 13 hearts in a deck among 52 cards.

3. **B.** Explanation: Solve the equation: $15x + 5 = 65 \Rightarrow 15x = 60 \Rightarrow x = 4$.

4. **B.** Explanation: A value of x that makes the denominator zero is a vertical asymptote.

5. **B.** Explanation: $\log_{10} 100 = 2$.

6. **D.** Explanation: Recognized as a difference of squares.

7. **A.** Explanation: Dot product $(1)(4) + (3)(2) = 10$.

8. **C.** Explanation: Using $(x^a y^b)^c = x^{ac} y^{bc}$.

9. **A.** Explanation: The exponential function is one-to-one as it is strictly increasing.

10. **A.** Explanation: $(2 + 4 + 6 + 8 + 10)/5 = 6$.

11. **C.** Explanation: Sum $\frac{9}{2}(5 + 45) = 225$.

12. **B.** Explanation: Quadratic functions open upwards starting from vertex $y = -3$.

13. **B.** Explanation: Midpoint is: $\left(\frac{1+7}{2}, \frac{2+8}{2}\right) = (4, 5)$.

14. **B.** Explanation: Complementary angles add up to 90 degrees.

15. **A.** Explanation: $\sqrt[3]{64} = 4$.

16. **A.** Explanation: $\sin 30° = 0.5$.

17. **A.** Explanation: $\frac{4x^3}{2x} = 2x^2$.

18. **B.** Explanation: Logical negation involves both negating and swapping parts of the statement.

19. **C.** Explanation: Calculate $\sqrt{144} - 8 \times 2 = 12 - 16 = -4$.

20. **C.** (Central angle=360/6=60°)

Author's Final Note

"Adult Math Refresher Book" is crafted to empower students as they work through the essential math concepts. This book is designed with the belief that every learner deserves clear guidance and effective practice to build confidence in math and succeed on their journey.

"Adult Math Refresher Book" aims to offer a comprehensive resource that provides students with in-depth practice and strategies to master mathematical principles. This book prepares students for the exam and aims to strengthen their foundational math skills, setting them up for success in further studies and real-world applications.

As you begin your journey through math, the author, wishes you the best of luck. This book is intended to be a helpful companion through math challenges, filled with strategies to enhance your confidence and skills. The tips and exercises within these pages are crafted to help you become a capable and confident math learner.

Wishing you success in your studies and a strong foundation in math. Remember, the skills you gain here will be invaluable in your future educational and career pursuits.

For a complimentary PDF version of this book, contact jacob.Kohannim2056@gmail.com.

Jacob Kohannim

Printed in Dunstable, United Kingdom